Pete Lawrence is co-founder of The Big Chill festival, and he set up the ground-breaking roots and world music label Cooking Vinyl in the 1980s before starting The Big Chill as a monthly club in 1993 with Katrina Larkin. Two years later, they took the concept outdoors to the Black Mountains of Wales, a landmark event that led to the annual Big Chill festival.

Pete founded the highly respected *On magazine* in the early 1990s. He has also written for Tower Records' *Top*, *Jockey Slut* and *Update*.

Pete has DJ'd all over the world. He has produced nine Big Chill compilations – the most recent release, *Big Chill Classics*, marked The Big Chill's tenth birthday in spring 2004. He has also recently released two EPs under the name of Chilled By Nature. He lives in North London with his children, Ella and Joey.

Vicki Howard was born in 1975 in South London. After a fairly uneventful childhood, Vicki attended Oxford University. Having co-founded a theatre company, The OpiumEaters, and graduated with a BA Hons. in English, Vicki moved back to London. There, she worked in the City as a marketing executive, at Saatchi & Saatchi as a strategic planner and then at Interbrand as an account manager. Having moved into freelancing, she has been working for The Big Chill, for Mantra PR and as a book reviewer for *The Big Issue in the North*.

Vicki lives in North London, where she is working on her first novel.

D1036452

Crossfade

a big chill anthology

Edited by Pete Lawrence and Vicki Howard

Library of Congress Catalog Card Number: 2004103024

A complete catalogue record for this book can be
obtained from the British Library on request

The right of Pete Lawrence and Vicki Howard to be identified as the
editors of this work has been asserted by them in accordance with
the Copyright, Designs and Patents Act 1988

Collection copyright © 2004 by Pete Lawrence and Vicki Howard
Individual contributions copyright © the author 2004

First published in 2004 by Serpent's Tail,
4 Blackstock Mews, London N4 2BT
website: www.serpentstail.com

Designed and typeset at Neuad Bwll, Llanwrtyd Wells

Printed by Mackays of Chatham, plc

1 2 3 4 5 6 7 8 9 10

contents

acknowledgements

A big thank you to:
Katrina Larkin and all at Big Chill HQ
Pete Ayrton and all at Serpent's Tail
Iain Ross
Viv Andrews and Mark Brereton

And our thanks to Billy Bragg for permission to
quote 'Between the Wars' on page 65.

introduction: words in motion

Pete Lawrence and Vicki Howard

This is a book about passion.

This is also a book about music, about personality, about The Big Chill, about exploration and about society, but first and foremost, this is a book about passion. Passion suffuses this book on all levels, inspiring it, underpinning it, driving it. And passion transcends genres and pigeonholes. It does not adhere to convention and rules. It is about excitement and energy and freedom. It is about that moment when everything just falls into place on some intimate level and for sometimes inexplicable reasons, no matter what the rest of the world is doing. Passion is what music, what *Crossfade*, what The Big Chill is all about.

It was a little under a year ago that we first started distilling the idea of *Crossfade* as it stands today. We were absorbed in bouncing ideas around, driven by a love of music, a love of literature, a love of bringing people together, a love of The Big Chill, and a desire to find some way of capturing it all under one dust jacket. Book ideas that had been mulled over before, some that had been talked about on and off within The Big Chill for several years, were colliding softly with fresh ideas and new perspectives. Both coming from slightly different angles, we batted our interests around. Documentary met fiction. Music met food met cider met holidays met art. One element after another was thrown into the air to see what other element it could connect with, what final mix we could create. By the end of our exploratory adventure, we had several ideas scrawled down in a dog-eared red notebook. One idea stood out as the most obvious and one thread tied it all together: the thread that connected all the elements we had been speaking about was passion. So, then, we would let passion dominate this debut book. We would give ten Big Chillers – artists, friends, professional writers, non-professional writers – the chance to share their passion for music.

After all, passion is at the very core of The Big Chill multi-media event and festival. Ten years on from when Pete Lawrence and Katrina Larkin set up its inaugural event at London's Union Chapel – a Sunday afternoon and evening which in many ways may have turned the notion of clubbing on its head – The Big Chill is a thriving community where Big Chillers convene to share their passion for music, art, food, people, camping, the countryside… The list could go on and on. Much of this community meets annually at The Big Chill festival: a weekend at Eastnor Castle Deer Park in the Malvern Hills. Further one-off events through the year, both in the UK and abroad – along with the notorious Big Chill website forum – keep the community fuelled and connected.

As with all great passionate affairs, there is a sense of mischief and adventure that goes hand and hand with the artistic and production ethos of The Big Chill. Not only is the artistic programming and the event production expected year on year to be top-notch, it is also expected to be bold, different, progressive. It has been described as evolutionary entertainment, and in that respect The Big Chill tries to never stand still and to always sidestep pigeonholes. The Big Chill is never the same event or festival twice.

Which is where we come back to *Crossfade*. The Big Chill is continually looking for and experimenting with new and different forms of expression and creative enterprise. In their ten-year history, The Big Chill events and festivals have seen poetry working alongside circus performance, comedy working alongside visuals working alongside electronica, ice sculptures working alongside pyrotechnics working alongside acoustic folk singers. There is no set formula to The Big Chill. It is based year by year on the interests and dedication of its founders, the interests and dedication of its team and the interests and dedication of its community. The Big Chill is about letting those threads play in an arena together, creating a creative kaleidoscope of colour, vigour and love. And, in

part as a celebration of The Big Chill's tenth birthday, it was time to throw our passion for books into the mix.

This sense of kaleidoscopic motion and movement runs throughout *Crossfade*. It is almost ironic that we have chosen to theme the essays by genres of music, given The Big Chill's historical rejection of pigeonholing. However, each essay, when delved into, will reveal just how semi-permeable our contributors' notions of genres are. They are not hermetic, staunchly defined categories based on empirical evidence. No, the concept of genre in this book is fluid, metamorphic, inclusive. The absence of chronological sequencing of the essays in this book is also a reflection of our attempt not to play into the hands of the straighforwardly generic.

In fact, originally, we had played with the idea of this anthology being called *Musical Statues*. This was intended as a comment on the way in which musical genres only stand still if you stare at them. The minute you look away, they creep up behind you, change and grow, update and renew. Nonetheless, we opted for *Crossfade* as the more fluid and accessible name, and one which clearly outlines the way in which each essay in this anthology – each genre, if you like – slides into every other. There is no beginning and no end, only the still point of the turning world. And even that never stays still for long.

The written and spoken word has always been something that has been valued by The Big Chill. In its early years, we published *On magazine*, a free monthly A4 black and white, enthusiasts' fanzine, which in many ways brought together the early musical stands which formed the nucleus of The Big Chill's latest passions. In 1999, The Big Chill collaborated with The London Festival Of Literature to stage Words In Motion at Sadler's Wells. The event featured a new and previously untried symbiosis of modern art - music, specially commissioned DJ/VJ/spoken word mixes, dance performance, aerial gymnastics, and original lighting and environmental design, projections and graphics. And since becoming the first UK club event to go online in its inaugural year, The Big Chill's website has for some time provided an outlet for a range of essays, reviews and think-tank pieces, as well as its infamous and vibrant community forum, which has been attracting over a thousand postings on most days.

So given that some roots of a passion for words were already in place, it seemed a natural evolution to delve into the world of publishing. Once we had the theory in place, it became a case of joining the dots with the actual production. First, we decided on a publishing house. Serpent's Tail who, fortuitously, had grabbed our attention not only through putting us on its mailing list for its sales catalogue but also through its fascinating and varied list, seemed immediately to make a perfect partner for our plans. Subsequently, we approached our wishlist of contributors and were delighted when each and every one of them came back with a resounding 'yes'.

Our choice of contributors was, in fact, remarkably straightforward. We primarily wanted musicians, writers and/or journalists (in some cases, all three!) who were passionate about The Big Chill and about their chosen topic. We were lucky enough to have ten interesting and diverse individuals writing in this book.

As a brief synopsis, *Crossfade* contains essays by the following contributors. Susanna Glaser, child prodigy and author of her famous violinist father's biography, takes an autobiographical, vivid look at her topic, Bleep, placing it in the context of growing up in a classically trained musical family. 'Stripped Pine and Swedish Furniture: A Defence of Chill-Out' by once-was international trampolining champion Ally Fogg, approaches the notion of 'dinner-party music' in a humorous yet critically fortified manner, taking four albums and constructing a defence out of them. Pete Lawrence, co-founder of The Big Chill, takes a contemporary look at the roots and evolution of folk, attempting to debunk the myths of 'hey nonny nonnies' along the way. Writer and music journalist Tony Marcus tackles the slippery concept of nostalgia, outlining its anchors, its purpose and its props. The ambitious topic of jazz is dexterously handled by Mixmaster Morris, the maverick DJ and influential rave-scene figure, mixing autobiography with the vast jazz scene to vibrant effect. Hillegonda Rietveld, Senior Lecturer in Arts and Media at London's South Bank University, where she supervises postgraduate research towards PhDs on issues related to dance culture, takes us on a House journey from Chicago to Manchester's notorious Haçienda Club. 'Eclectic Electric: A Post-Punk Posting' sees Alan James, the Head of Contemporary Music at The Arts Council of England, illustrating and

interpreting the effects of the punk era. Stuart Borthwick, academic and co-author of eleven pop histories, offers a re-evaluation of the style-obsessed eighties – an era when he himself apparently sported a barnet akin to a mullet in reverse. Brighton-based Guy Morley, one half of Yam Yam (Big Chill Recordings), explores the impact of African music on British politics, providing a socio-economic musical panorama. And last but not least, the wholly idiosyncratic DJ Derek explains his passion for reggae and how one white middle-aged accountant made his way to the heart of the British Jamaican music scene, sensitively ghostwritten by Susanna Glaser.

So, ten contributors, ten areas of passion, ten idiomatic, personal and explorative essays. We are delighted to be able to bring you this literary stroll through The Big Chill and some of the characters that have made it such a fun journey these last ten years. And we are looking forward to bringing you further 'Words in Motion' literary excursions in the future, both at our events and festivals and beyond. Most of all, we hope you enjoy reading *Crossfade* as much as we have enjoyed compiling it.

Pete and Vicki x

bleep: a journey from classical to electronic music

Susanna Glaser

baa baa bleep sheep

> Experimental music generally is pretty unaccepted on the whole, but ironically it's completely necessary to the progress of all music. I mean, if people aren't pushing edges forward, then what's gonna happen?   Cristian Vogel

My love affair with what I call Bleep – and most others would more generally categorize as electronic music or IDM (intelligent dance music) – has been tricky to come to terms with. Take my family. My father was a famous violinist in Norway, my mother was also a violinist. My half-sister on my father's side is a famous pianist in Norway. My big brother is a pianist, my big sister is a violinist and my brother is a cellist. I'm the only one of four children who grew up together who didn't become a professional classical musician.

I still wrestle with my conscience. Somehow, within me, I feel I'm doing something wrong when I devour electronic music. That I'm delving beneath me, savouring the forbidden fruit and – even – in some way turning my back on my family. Recently, despite being heavily involved in (electronic) music through my work, my mother inadvertently introduced me to family friends as the 'non-musical' one.

Don't get me wrong. I had a happy, balanced childhood in Norway, where I was born. But as far as my family was concerned, there was only one kind of 'good music'. And that was classical music. Every other kind – pop, rock, dance, country, electronic, you name it – was somehow inferior. Of course. It's music made by anybody with the ability to play three chords on a cheap instrument or push buttons. That's any old moron, not intelligent people ('like us' it was implied) who had painstakingly learned their craft.

I remember my sister and I, guiltily sharing our love for Abba, which we weren't exactly encouraged ('Turn that noise off!') to listen to at home. Now, I'm not trying to say that Abba turned me on to electronic music. I'm sure one day I'll be telling my own kids that their listening habits leave just a little to be desired. But the overall feeling was that anything 'current' was out of currency, a pervasive influence which is with me to this day.

At first I had no conflict of interests. I was a natural classical musician. At the age of three I was picking out melodies on the pia-pia-piano to the delight of my parents. At five my parents thought (hoped) they had a prodigy on their hands and, as luck would have it, one of the finest Norwegian piano teachers lived next door. So there I tootled off, once a week, for half an hour's torture. Not mine, mind. The poor woman had to put up with a small girl whose innate ability to play like an angel was offset by her equally fantastic talent for temper tantrums and 'Damian'-child behaviour.

I love the piano. I'm not about to apologize for it anymore. All right, I didn't love it so much when I had to practise and the rest of the street's kids were out playing rounders. But I loved it. I could hate it too, when it wouldn't obey my fingers. Or my fingers, when they wouldn't obey my brain. When I got older I'd rage at them, bite them sometimes. Teeth marks punishing my lazy fingers. But mostly I loved it. When I was seven I would read my comics while I played it (multitasking even then). And when I was older, it became an escape, a place for myself for an hour (or two).

I got good, too. Really good. Becoming a professional musician, even a concert pianist, was in my blood and it was expected of me. I could have, maybe should have. I attended Junior Trinity College and later auditioned (and got into) some of the finest music schools

in the country (Purcell, Wells Cathedral). But something in me refused. Something was missing. Maybe I didn't like my peers who did classical music. They all seemed so smug, somehow. Maybe it was the feeling I was regurgitating not innovating. Maybe it was the constant struggle to tame an archaic instrument only for it all to fall apart through nerves in performance. Or maybe it was the 'Bleep'.

Bleep – deliberately synthetic music – is the complete opposite of the way I was brought up to think about music. Music was something that was 'live' and must be kept live. Never mind machine-made music, recorded music was bad enough. Like primitive peoples who believe their soul will be torn from them once photographed, I think my family felt that recordings were somehow dead, bereft, empty, soulless. Tape loops? Synth noises? Artificially created 'violins'? John Cage's prepared piano went far enough.

Quid quo pro – record-buying in my family was a no-no. We had a small selection of LPs with ballet music and concertos. And my brother nurtured an impressive selection of Elvis Presley tapes. Well, someone had to. But, in general, music was something you did, not bought. I still don't feel comfortable shopping for music. There's something reductive about sticking music on shelves. Here's this priceless wondrous entity humans have created where sounds and noises harmonize in infinite ways and trigger emotions outside our control. And it's there, clingwrapped like a frozen chicken, with a £15 sticker on it.

A refusal to commodify music goes hand in hand with a traditionalist approach to music. And a Bleep composer is the antithesis of a traditionalist, gleefully playing with the most up-to-date technology they can find. I, like my family and like many classically trained people, believed a computer would never compete with warm, acoustic instruments played by the human hand. The difference is that I have since discovered Bleep can be as warm, emotional and spontaneous as any classical.

This is not an attempt to denigrate classical music. It damn near *is* impossible for music today – which lives and breathes in a different context entirely – to compete with the purity of a Bach prelude and fugue, the rich beauty of Beethoven's Quartets or the sheer cliff-top rush of Mahler. It's difficult for electronica to make your heart ache just like it does during Shostakovich's epic Fifth Symphony, make you smile at the innocence of Tchaikovksy's familiar ballets or make you feel as if you're breathing in the fresh air of a Dvorak's *New World*.

And there's the physical aspect. Try to play the piano and make it sing rather than sound like a bunch of strings hit by a small hammer. It isn't easy – and takes time and tears (and bitten hands) to achieve. You can't 'bleep' a piano. And you wouldn't want to. Feeling the music when you're a violinist, for instance, is as much to do with feeling the warmth of the wood under your chin, feeling the strings vibrate, or – if you're a pianist – the piano keys moving back atcha, the pedals squeaking stiffly. It's about the instrument becoming part of you.

There's the team aspect of being in an orchestra. You and ninety-nine others have been rehearsing for weeks, going over and over the same bars until they seem meaningless. You've been engaged in making written music, two-dimensional and colourless, come alive. And at the concert there you are, all moving, rising, sinking, sweating and simultanously creating, re-creating and riding the waves of the music with you.

But classical music requires a committment our twenty-first-century lives haven't got time for. The listening public may enjoy a bit of Classic FM and sales of certain MOR classical artists may be hitting the high notes with record-busting sales, but just how many new recordings of well-known works are needed by the world?

It's ironic, really. Our increasingly sophisticated recording technology is what makes Bleep so pliable, yet the very same technology has fossilized classical music. Additionally, contemporary classical is often too weird, too formalized and too self-consciously experimental for even an increasingly rarefied classical-music community to warm to. Where new classical music does get an airing these days, it's at least in part due to the Bleep entering the classical music arena, with composers like Massive Attack collaborator Craig Armstrong premiering pieces with The Royal Scottish National Orchestra, for instance.

Since the sixties so-called 'pop' music has rushed to fill this ever-increasing gap between the lowbrow of traditional pop and the highbrow of classical, feeding the need for a music which stimulates and yet entertains. A music which is fashionable, innovative and

fresh yet doesn't patronize its listeners. Oh, and which isn't over in two minutes thirty seconds. Since The Beatles opened Pandora's Box with *Sgt Pepper* pop music has cross-fertilized and spawned ever new forms. Music which once consisted of three chords and an easily recognizable chorus was permitted, encouraged, to be infinitely more complex.

Now, in the early part of the twenty-first century, we can take our pick from a plethora of sounds. Pop, europop, dance, techno, gabba, house, drill'n'bass, rock, jazz, free-improv, country, soul, funk, hip hop and more. And Bleep, or electronic listening music, which, for me at this point in time, most embodies the spirit of adventure, the warmth of the spirit and the infinite potential of the complex human imagination through sound. For a family who shunned technology (we had a black and white TV until we moved to the UK when I was nine), that's pretty radical.

a brief history of bleep

> [I] can feel what's going on in a piece of electronic equipment…
> it's something between discovering and witnessing.
>
> (Bob Moog)

Bleep is obviously a modern phenomenon but it's not new. Bleep has also been pulsating for more than a hundred years at the edges of classical music. A mechanical way of expressing the soul had begun back in the mid 1800s. Back in 1860 the deliciously named mathematician Hermann Ludwig Ferdinand von Helmholtz studied sound using an electronically controlled instrument. Once he'd broken the mould, others followed, with Thaddeus Cahill's tone wheel and Elisha Grey's self-vibrating electromagnetic circuit.

The next development was vacuum-tube technology – adopted by early radio-engineer pioneers – which led to more familiar instruments such as the theremin, which we still love to play around with. Tape recordings and tape experiments were pioneered by composers such as Edgard Varèse with his *Poème electronique*, created especially for the 1958 Brussels Exhibition and which used multiple speakers in a building designed by Le Corbusier: surround sound is older than you think. Frenchmen Pierre Schaeffer and Pierre Henry collaborated and *musique concrète* (music made from altered or rearranged natural sounds) was born. Stockhausen, the granddaddy of Bleep, took things a step further – no 'natural' noise for him, it was all to be purely electronically created.

The 1950s and 1960s were a time of joyful experimentation with the new electronic ways of creating sound. The composer was freed from the orchestra and the physical aspect of the performer and was instead able to get his or her hands dirty, working directly with his or her material like a painter or sculptor. Sci-fi movie *Forbidden Planet* was released in 1956 – the first film to have a totally electronic music score (interestingly, Louis and Bebe Barron's soundtrack wasn't credited as 'music' but as 'electronic tonalities'). The BBC's Radiophonic Workshop kicked into being and their experiments ended up producing everybody's favourite spooky alien (and bleepy) soundtrack – Delia Derbyshire's *Dr Who*.

Integrated circuits began to be introduced in the 1960s and synthesized sound pioneers such as Robert 'Bob' Moog revolutionized and democratized access to electronic music with his ready-made off-the-shelf synth. And it was perhaps here that electronic music divided itself into 'serious' avant-garde music, pushed by the likes of Terry Riley, Philip Glass and Steve Reich, and the more 'pop' end of electronic music. Simon & Garfunkel, The Byrds, The Beatles and even The Rolling Stones all bought Moogs.

Then the seventies arrived. And in strode Kraftwerk. Four classically trained Germans creating alien addictive 'pop' music using room-sized Moog synthesizers. Bleep was born. I remember when I first heard Kraftwerk. It must have been 1991, nearly twenty years after their heyday, and I was sitting in my university boyfriend's scruffy room. Firstly, I couldn't believe I'd missed out on this music, how had it happened? When? Secondly, I absolutely loved it. I couldn't get enough of it. After he'd put on *Autobahn*, he played me *Trans-Europe Express*.

I'd never 'got' indie. I hated pop. I detested rock. I liked hip hop, funk and soul – especially on a night out – but had never immersed myself in its culture. But this, this I could feel, understand, recognize! I can understand the instant impact Kraftwerk must have had on the black-music community in the States. As Afrika Bambaataa once

said of *Trans-Europe Express*, 'I thought that was one of the best and weirdest records I ever heard in my life. It was funky.'

Equipment got smaller, cheaper and ever more accessible. When Roland introduced the TB303, little would they know their analogue bass unit would be warped into something rather more squealy and squidgy. Then, somewhere during the early eighties, kick-started by Afrika Bambaataa's 'Planet Rock', electro happened. Taken up by kids obsessed with boing-y computer-game noises, deliberately artificial cyborg-funk and pitch-shifting vocodered lyrics, Bleep now had a home.

It even became a genre in its own right (although to me Bleep, as I'll explain, is now a broader phenomenon, more than simply a genre). Sheffield's Warp label – home of the back-to-the-future sounds of LFO, Aphex Twin and Autechre – nurtured its home-grown mash of Detroit Techno, electro and 'silly little blobs of synthetic noise' and almost set up a label called 'Bleep'. Twenty years later they've made it an online download shop instead, bleep.com.

into the bleep

> In the years since Sputnik, electronic music has developed and become about as complex and confusing as the rest of this 'future' we all find ourselves living in.   Michael Heumann

As Bleep has evolved, so has the music made possible by it. But some music will always stand out for me. Schneider TM's debut album *Moist* (City Slang) led me to exclaim in *i-D Magazine* in 1998: 'You're a kid, looking up at the sky, getting your head around infinity, space, stars, life. *Moist* has the same spiralling sensation. Through squabbling synths and wrestling rhythms, Dirk Dresselhaus has harnessed the infinity of electronic sound. Awesome.' And he had. Humorous off-rhythms, bubbly melodies, coruscating noises, fluttering beats, crunchy, farting bass stabs, staccato synths, white-noise fuzz. And that's just the title track.

Super_Collider were another band who rammed my ears against the wall, grabbed my soul by the throat and then left me flailing helplessly back in the real world. I didn't know whether to laugh, cry or go mad when I heard their debut album *Head On*. Taking Prince's futuristic soul, James Brown's crazed funk and stretching it over what I then called 'distended, distorted basslines and uncompromising techno-electro-experimentalist noiseniks', they'd managed to take the extremes of the human vocal and meld them seamlessly with extremes of technological sound. You didn't think 'computers' when you heard it, yet you knew that apart from Jamie Lidell's voice, it most certainly was.

It can delight with off-kilter beauty like the gently two-step-influenced Four Tet track 'I'm On Fire' (Domino). It can terrify like Autechre's apocalyptic 'Gantz Graf'. And it can inject a dance-bomb up yer bum, like LFO's 'Freak' or Les Rhythmes Digitales' 'From Disco To Disco'. It's the delicate, dusty melancholy crackles of Russian electronica artists EU. It's the fluttering butterfly beauty of Japanese artists Asa Chang & Junray. It's ambient and it's hyper. It's beautiful and ugly. It's fizzy like The Micronauts and fuzzy like Boards of Canada. It's mellow distilled beauty like Manitoba's *People Eating Fruit* (Leaf). It's rampant, dirty and irresistible like Sir Drew's *She Woman Cat Type Thing* (Kingsize).

It appears warped to extremes on harsh two-step found on white labels and called odd things like 'International Rudebwoy' and 'Nasty Knickers'. It hugs you like Mocky's 'Sweet Music' and it endears itself to you like the elf-like childishness of the Icelandic band Múm. It can make you sob against expectation, like Metamatics' 'Byeway(Clan)' or it can make you grin with sunshine like Roy Vedas, whose vocoder-bleeping 'Fragments Of Life' inspired even Cher to twist her voice into something rather bleepily wonderful on 'Believe'. Labels like Tigerbeat6, Lo Recordings and Rephlex help disseminate the 'have fun with it' message of Bleep while other labels like Ninja Tune, Leaf, City Centre Offices and Warp encourage its experimental beauty.

There's extreme Bleep, making sure electronic music enters new frontiers. You can hear the future of music in noise terrorist Venetian Snares (just check the madness of 'A Giant Alien Force More Violent & Sick Than Anything You Can Imagine' (Hymen)) the hard-edged riddims of Knifehand Chop and the ribald cut-up clowning around of Donna Summer (a bloke called Jason who knackers his laptop in the way old rock stars used to smash up their guitars). And as the equipment becomes more pliant and the audience more

demanding, so the music has ripened with soul, melancholy, density, textures and richness.

It doesn't have to be so-called 'intelligent dance music' either. The dance-orientated beats of Chemical Brothers, The Prodigy, Basement Jaxx, Daft Punk, Dem 2 and more have all Bleeped their way into my heart. And Bleep has now entered the mainstream, while it has yet (cross fingers) not lost its touch in the process. Mr Oizo's farting 'Flat Beat' became a worldwide hit after Levi's used it on their adverts. The otherworldy staccato of Missy Elliott's 'Get Ur Freak On' didn't hold her back. And Madonna's latest single 'Die Another Day' is another major-artist track hitting the charts these days, full of vocodered swooping bleepy magic.

feel the bleep

> [Music] takes us out of the actual and whispers to us dim secrets that startle our wonder as to who we are, and for what, whence, and whereto.   Ralph Waldo Emerson

Sometimes I'm just overwhelmed by the amount of amazing music out there. And I'm so happy I found it. Because I was pretty oblivious to any kind of popular music when I was growing up. I know that as new forms of electronic music started to seep through the nation, I'd felt a part of me wake up. I remember going bonkers to 'We Call It Acieed' by D Mob at my sixth-form Christmas party. At university I'd found myself in a dark basement, strobe lights where a sinister, alien, banging sound filled the space which was unashamedly electronic and terrifyingly so. But it was only after I heard Kraftwerk I started to take more notice.

Soon after, I discovered the intricately programmed rhythms of drum'n'bass (Wow! Music that tickled the brain as well as the hips!) and I was introduced to exclusively computer-produced electronic music in general. Suddenly non-classical music wasn't something that whizzed by as I travelled life, it was something I could grab hold of, sniff, poke and enjoy too. In fact, if I didn't, I was seriously missing out! It was a completely new feeling for me. I was introduced to music I'd never considered, nay, come across before. Here – check out Aphex Twin! Or what about some My Bloody Valentine?

This was the mid nineties and I was listening to everything from LFO to Way Out West, with Super Furry Animals, Wagon Christ and Squarepusher in between. Björk made experimental music approachable. A world opened. A world I'd not noticed because deep down I wasn't really supposed to, wasn't allowed to. But – look! – more and more classically trained people were admitting they were into electronic music *and* what's more, the music being made was so freakin' brain-intense I couldn't consider it inferior anymore.

Bit by bit, I honed my taste for electronic music. Some of my friends started up a small Sunday afternoon club in our local Cardiff caff – TWAT (The Warm As Toast Café, if you must know!) – and I wanted to get my fingers stuck in. So there I was, the Modipop Girl, with scant music knowledge and a non-existent record collection (I borrowed records from the others to play out), playing random shit to punters, Goldie one minute, Stereolab the next, Aphex Twin sandpaper rabble next to Coldcut followed by Björk's 'Every Morning' remixed by LFO followed by Catatonia's 'Sweet Cat'. Lucky I had the early slot, really, as bemused punters would skulk at the bar terrified of what I'd play next. Not much has changed, to be honest.

Modipop Girl didn't practise her technique – maybe all that work on the piano for a non-existent career made her wary of getting in too deep – but she garnered music knowledge and her own records. Big beat broke through and she embraced its grinning abandon and wobbly bleeps. Meantime Portishead, Fridge, Gus Gus, Lamb and Moloko filled the backroom space where I often played, the precursors of the kind of Bleep The Legendary Jesse Belle would play poolside at The Big Chill in Naxos five years later. And all the time I was soaking up electronic music like a sponge, whether it was trip hop or jungle or IDM. And I was getting hungry for more.

I moved to London. From having known absolutely nothing about this kind of music in 1994, it was now 1997 and I knew more about underground electronica than any of my immediate friends. My life revolved around computers and music. How more removed from my roots could I get? The Legendary Jesse Belle was born – a purveyor of hip-jigging Bleep and electro-infused breakbeat. But she was less interested in perfecting floor-filling crowd-pummelling sets or noodling at home

perfecting her mixing than she was in just playing the music out for its own sake.

I'm no trainspotter and never will be. The gaps in my musical knowledge are like ravines – people occasionally stumble across them and stare down the deep holes of popular music knowledge in despair. And, crucially, Jesse Belle never settled on one genre. She is, in effect, unmarketable as a 'DJ'. Unsurprisingly, she hasn't been accepted by any of the DJing cliques in London. Then. She was invited to play at a Raya-promoted ICA night and caught the attention of The Big Chill's Pete Lawrence. At Enchanted Garden (1998) Jesse Belle made her Big Chill debut. She, I, had finally found a home.

Maybe it's my background, maybe it's the way I came into electronic music. But here, for the first time, was a crowd open-minded enough to soak up music the way I did. A crowd uninterested in labels, searching for quality not quantity, wanting to be stimulated and surprised, not pummelled into dance submission. The Big Chill didn't show me the Bleep, but it allowed me to offer what I had discovered for myself in my own unique way. I could even begin to celebrate my classical upbringing – not apologize for it. I could bring it into sets – playing my brother's piano-solo recordings alongside Digitonal and Margo. It was a defining moment.

beeps byte

All cultures develop through ways of listening

Pauline Oliveros

For the introduction of a new kind of music must be shunned as imperilling the whole state; since styles of music are never disturbed without affecting the most important political institutions.   Plato

Bleep isn't just about music. File-sharing is only one aspect of a generation brought up on digital music, mp3s and wavs. It's also a community and a lifestyle. In fact, I'd say Bleep is an era, a chapter of musical history which encompasses and reflects a huge cultural shift in our society. Bleep, after all, is at the root of the Internet revolution which is forcing today's monolithic music industry to rethink its strategy, or, more accurately, to panic.

Bleep could not have happened without the Internet and the technology created to transfer music and discussion about music across the ether. It could not have developed with the speed it did without bypassing traditional media via the Web. Pauline Oliveros, one of the earliest electronic-music pioneers, put her Deep Listening catalogue online in 1990 (before the Web) because traditional shops such as Tower Records constantly sold out of (and didn't reorder) her studio's records. state51, one of the first Internet companies in Britain (hence the ironic name), also spotted the potential of the Web and its ability to spread niche music around the world, pioneering the UK's first music and record-label websites.

Meantime micro-communities throughout the 'global village' have sprung up, including hundreds of music-focused Internet discussion groups devoted to their take on the electronic music phenomenon – the microsound-list, the 313-list, the IDM-list, the ambient-list, take your pick. One of the first of these groups was UK-Dance (www.uk-dance.org) – an eleven-year-old online community obsessed with dance music (funnily enough) – which I joined in 1997. Through these groups, music and information about music is shared across continents in seconds. Music crosses the borders once hindered by culture and distance. Mixes put online by a DJ in São Paulo can be heard simultaneously in Rejkjavik, Moscow and London. And as the members share their music, they share their cultures too.

Ironically, I was terrified of computers when I first came across them. The underfunded (back then, at least) computer room at Fitzwilliam College, Cambridge, was a dreary small cupboard-like space where the skinny, antisocial geeks hung out. I was forced to venture in there when my third-year dissertation was due – but the place scared me. The Bleeps I heard there seemed ominous – signalling 'errors', the kinds of errors which bleach your work out of existence…Best not touch any strange buttons. But, like many others, I found the advent of the World Wide Web made computers fun to use.

Through UK-Dance and others I discovered that the underground electronic-music community is fiercely loyal. Bleep is not only about

music, it's about politics too. It's about joining against the hijacking of the Web by corporates in general – and especially major music labels with their misguided approach to the file-sharing phenomenon. Download protest day 'Grey Tuesday' on 24 February 2004 was dominated by the online electronica community, outraged at EMI's decision to sue Dangermouse's clever mix of Jay-Z's *The Black Album* and The Beatles's *The White Album*. According to the organizers 100,000 copies of *The Grey Album* were downloaded for free that day. It's the Bleep that did it, Mum.

Technology has enabled music to be transferred between musicians across continents, collaborating on music bit by bit, sometimes with somebody they'd never have met had it not been for the Net. Like online gaming, software can be placed on the Net and manipulated by many users at one time – like New York-based artists Jennifer and Kevin McCoys' Live Internet Multiuser Mixer (LIMM). Log on and you too can play with the sounds and visuals – remix, add, manipulate or just sit back and watch as others do it for you. Tim Bran, formerly of Dreadzone, pioneered the online 'studio' Res Rocket in the mid nineties, where musicians can log on wherever they are in the world and jam in real time.

Makers of Bleep have embraced that – and as such Bleep isn't bound by geography the way some other music genres are. US duo 310, for instance, created entire albums by sending mp3s and CDs with digital music data on them to each other, Tim Donovan based in New York City, Joseph Dierker in Seattle. Electronic music festivals, like the 'headphone' festival Placard, are organized via mailing lists with musicians living on different continents. The electronic nature of the event means that Placard, when held (sometimes simultaneously) in its various homes of Paris, London, Tokyo and New York, can share its audiences across events. Whether you're in Japan, Russia, Britain or Sweden, you'll find creators, collaborators and fans of Bleep.

Bleep is also about an entire generation who have grown up to fuse visuals with music with electronics without question. We grew up watching *The Chart Show* – an entirely presenter-free Top Ten video show. Meanwhile Coldcut invented VJing – a way of mixing, cutting up and scratching visuals on the fly, to enhance the way electronic music was illustrated. This cut-up visual technique has now filtered into conventional TV production and film, while visuals are now an expected part of a night out, sometimes the focus (as with London-based VJing club night The Audiovisual Lounge) whether the music is electronic or not. Some composers create both simultaneously, like Riz Maslen, aka Neotropic, whose *La Prochaine Fois* cut up Super-8 footage of her travels with a seguing music soundtrack.

Music, now that it holds hands with computer geeks, has become an interesting hybrid. In many ways, it could be in danger of becoming more rarefied than the classical-music world. To create new interesting sounds, it helps if you know computers and, if you're a programmer, the world is your oyster. Some programmers have become musicians – by adapting programming to create music. Slub, a London-based duo, have taken the essence of generative Perl programming and reinvented it for their music needs, creating one-off pieces of live techno-based music. It helps if you're interested in electronics too. Musicians like Autechre have constructed their whole music output by deconstructing shop-bought instruments, gleefully taking them apart and putting them together like ten-year-old boys with transistor radios.

Although I'm immersed in Bleep culture, making it is one aspect which I think will remain forever alien. Take my first encounter of a close kind with a real life 303. DJ Lindsey, a Swansea personality, had me back to his after one of his Swansea bashes. Now, don't get the wrong idea. He was going to let me see his baby! His Roland TB303, that is. I was so hyped up. And then. Whump! Back to earth. I just thought, this is so crappy looking, this little mini-piano-like thing, and grinned lamely. It was like a toy. How could anyone take that seriously? I knew I loved the sound it made. But I didn't want to accept its 'electronic' banality. A box with wires. I felt cheated.

Music-making is about being able to use, talk and understand software. But much as I try, when people discuss music-making software I find myself drifting. There seems to be such a big gulf between the music I appreciate and the way it is made. Whereas the end result can be magical, the making part's about arguing whether Protools is better than Cubase, whether an Absynth is better than a Muon Electron (no, I *don't* know!) and how you should loop that sample. Music doesn't use technology any more, it *is* technology.

I've tried to get closer to it, I really have. I paid good money for a music-making course. I've tackled sampling and Cubase. I have Reason on my computer at home and a midi keyboard (all right, it's a Yamaha Clavinova). I could get started whenever I like. And yet I'm nowhere near making my first track. I opened Reason once and couldn't make head nor tail of it. And it's not as if I'm brain-dead. It just doesn't seem natural to me. Maybe I will never be able to bridge that particular gap. Maybe I'll always have a kind of Bleep addiction but without being able to do much about it myself.

Electronic music is still male-dominated (although this is changing). Here I am, yet another female who is enthusing on the sidelines. Maybe it's because girls just aren't encouraged to get out their screwdrivers and flip open the backs of their toys, never mind expensive pieces of audio equipment. You need to break stuff to see what's inside, right? – and that can get you in trouble, not something a good girl does. Plus, the lonely world of the bedroom boffin, hunched over the solitary whirr of his computer, doesn't really hold that much appeal for me, to be honest.

But as the cultural aspect of Bleep sweeps outwards, so the mystery and the outcast geekiness of it is dissolving. Bleep is more than ever about social activity now, whether online or offline. UK-Dance is just one example and The Big Chill Forum is even closer to home. An online arena for The Big Chill's festival goers, it's a place where music discussion (often about electronic music, I might add) is intermingled with cuppa-tea-style chats about life, the universe and everything. Bleep's audience is widening to include people simply interested in the music itself, not its methods. And Bleep's not solely confined to computers either, with the best music produced as a blend between both acoustic and electronic. The possibilities of the Bleep music age are only just opening out.

into the bleep

The way now seems to me completely open for a futher development of instrumental music, since its irreplaceable qualitites – above all its constant versatility, its 'living' quality – can now be combined with the acquisitions of electronic music to make up a new unity.   Karlheinz Stockhausen

I can run but I cannot hide. Even in the womb I'd been surrounded by classical music. Bleep is me. But so is my classical side. While I jump up and down in the living room and sing along to the speeded-up street sounds of 'Days Like This' by DJ Pale Face featuring Charlie Grace, I also find I only truly find peace when I'm playing Bach preludes and fugues on my own at home. I used to worry – I thought I'd never feel comfortable with my childhood background and my very different adult self. And as Bleep in all senses of the word – including my work, my world, my life – became bigger and bigger, it became more important to me than ever to make peace with my past.

It was an unexpected discovery which has led me to be able to do just that. For the past five years or so, I've been researching the life of my father, who was a well-known violinist in Norway. He died when I was seven and I'm only now 'getting to know him' through my interviews with the friends of his who are still alive and his family. And for the first time in my life, I realized something had been holding me back, musically speaking – and which had been completely rustled up by my imagination. I realized that were he still alive he would feel proud of me and not, as I had started to believe within me, feel let down by my love affair with Bleep.

On closer inspection, it turns out my father was no old fogey with a closed ear to new music. Far from it, he positively encouraged new contemporary music, performing world premieres of new compositions by various Norwegians. All right, the music was string-based – not computerized – but he wasn't the staunch traditionalist figure I'd made him out to be. I've spent a lot of time trying to find what part of my father I inherited. It might be rose-tinted idealism. But I like to think that his concern for encouraging and pushing contemporary music during his time corresponds with my involvement in the world of Bleep.

'It's just a bloke with a laptop,' my friends will moan. Yes, and no. A 'laptop' musician like Leafcutter John could indeed present a dull figure to somebody fed on a diet of guitars, drums and rock'n'roll pizazz. But laptop musicians aren't all the same. The way Leafcutter interlaces the acoustic with the electronic, his ability to create a kind of 'folk' intimacy coupled with his friendly yet often hilariously acerbic comments to his audience mean there's no 'just' about this laptop

composer. Oh – and his 'synth bra' complete with nipple attachments which he manipulates is pretty fun too.

There are others who understand that while the laptop's portability extends the reach of the electronic composer, it can also alienate its audience. So Chicks On Speed dress up and vogue in paper dresses. Super Collider look like nothing you've ever seen. The aforementioned Donna Summer chucks his laptop around like it's a rawk guitar (last time I saw him, he was trying to keep the near-broken thing working by slapping on gaffa tape while on stage). Alexis O'Hara, a sound artist from Canada, literally plugs herself into the machine, her voice layered and manipulated by electronics. In today's wireless world technology can be twisted into anything you want it to be. Whatever it is, it's not stark, robotic or soulless.

The growing feeling that I'm perhaps not turning my back on my family or my 'roots', if you will, is compounded by the way the traditional music world really is beginnning to sit up and take notice of what was once spotty-adolescent-bedroom-produced laptop music. In the past, most attempts at incorporating pop or dance music with classical have been tragic. You either got lumpen laughable classics-goes-pop trite or, maybe worse, electronic music swooshing about with pretensions. Instead of narrowing the gap between the music types, they only served to wrench them violently further apart.

But things have changed. Yes, the horrendous crimes towards music committed by Vanessa Mae, Charlotte Church and Myleen Klass still grind away on Top of the Pops. But on the other side a new breed of musician and music consumer is appearing. When the Royal Festival Hall invited the London Sinfonietta and Warp Records to collaborate in 2003, initial impressions were doom-ridden. For one thing, would the slick, skater-cool followers of Warp fork out for the chance to see Aphex Twin's 'afx237 v.7' reinvented for orchestra or the chance to hear John Cage's *Prepared Piano Sonatas* performed live in a sit-down environment? Plus musically it'd never work – you can't combine Mira Calix's skittering, rustling 'Nunu' – complete with live insects in a glass cage on stage – with a bunch of string instruments, can you?

I had good reasons for my doubts. I had witnessed Jeremy Deller's Acid Brass at first hand in 1997. It was an interesting but musically embarrassing attempt at translating dance-music classics, like A Guy

Called Gerald's 'Voodoo Ray', to brass band. They even released a CD – *Acid Brass: A Collection of 10 Acid House Anthems played by The Williams Fairey Brass Band* (Mute). It's a novelty, little else. But astonishingly Warp and the Sinfonietta made the leap required – and repeated the feat a year later.

The Bleep has entered our common consciousness, whether we recognize it or not. Most of us would have been bleeped at in the hospitals we were born in. We take lifts which ping with floor-counting bleeps. Supermarkets zing with a chorus of bleeps. Travel on the Tube and you're inundated with bleeping doors closing. In the past our phones dialled tick-tick-tick as our fingers got stuck in the holes. Now they say beep-bop-boop-beep-beep – making a melody all of their own.

The music of Bleep is now infused in our daily life. Adverts and TV programmes thrive on electronica. Whole films like *Morvern Callar* are soundtracked by underground electronic music. From *Speak&Spell* to *Simon Says* and from R2D2 in *Star Wars* to early fun with the Sinclair Spectrum 64, my generation grew up with electronic beeps and bleeps. Now, with the advent of Bluetooth we've entered the age of the ubiquitous computer – and the ubiquitous bleep. It's our language. At the same time as we detest the constant bleep of modern life – we love it too. It's us.

I'm a person who never did drugs – and never 'got' house music. That is, unless the Bleep was there, fizzing into my synapses, its squelches like sodium bicarbonate in my blood. The rush I got dancing to Josh Wink's 'Higher States Of Consciousness' had nothing to do with drugs and everything to do with the Bleep, squeezed and squashed into ever-changing shapes, its high-pitched squelch reaching parts of me nothing has ever done since.

Bleep is electronic music which, as well as being able to revel in its characteristic squirty, squidgy, sweet'n'sour noises, also manages to create Music with a capital 'M'. It has soul, intricacy, delicacy and warmth. Bleep has matured, Bleep has become 'real music', Bleep has become something I can embrace as my own. Bleep is my pin-up. Bleep is my pop star. It took me more than twenty-five years, but I've finally found a sound I can say, yeah, that's 'my sound', that is.

recommended listening

Schneider TM – *Moist* (City Slang)

Four Tet – *Pause* (Domino)

Super_Collider – *Head On* (Loaded)

Kraftwerk – *Autobahn* (EMI)

Moloko – *Do You Like My Tight Sweater* (Echo)

Daft Punk – *Homework* (Virgin)

Basement Jaxx – *Remedy* (XL)

Cristian Vogel – *Rescate 137* (NovaMute)

Cursor Miner – *Explosive Piece Of Mind* (Lo Recordings)

Various Artists – *Tigerbeat6 INC* (Tigerbeat6)

Luke Vibert – *Yoseph* (Warp)

Various – *Breaks, Bass And Bleeps* (Rumour Records)

EU – *Reframing* (Pause_2)

Pilote – *Antenna* (Certificate 18)

Various Artists – *RND_0.34873349921* (Pause_2)

Mocky – *Mocky In Mesopotamia* (Mocky Recordings)

Manitoba – *People Eating Fruit* (Leaf)

Múm – *Yesterday Was Dramatic – Today Is OK* (Tugboat)

Aphex Twin – *Selected Ambient Works Vol. 2* (Warp)

Digitonal – *23 Things Fall Apart* (Toytronic)

Pauline Oliveros – *No Mo* (Pogus)

Various Artists – *We Are Ten* (3x2CD package) (Warp)

To Rococo Rot – *The Amateur View* (City Slang)

Mouse On Mars – *Idiology* (Domino)

Hans Appelqvist – *Tonefilm* (Komplott)

stripped pine and swedish furniture: a defence of chill-out

Ally Fogg

Chill-out is a genre made by no one, played by no one and appreciated by no one.

This might come as a surprise. After all, every record shop has a chill-out section, the music press regularly carries reviews of chill-out albums, and an entire sub-genus of the music industry has gorged upon the profits of chill-out compilations. And yet you'll look long and hard to find a musician or DJ who plays chill-out music. Instead:

'Actually I make melodic electronica…'

'It's sort of upbeat ambient…'

'It's downtempo dance really…'

'You could say what we do is instrumental cinematic soundtrack soul with a bit of jazzy breakbeat, a touch of hip hop and some gentle funk.'

'Chill-out? Piss off.'

It wouldn't matter much if contemporary chill-out music's image problem stopped there. It doesn't. Although many of the individual acts are regularly hailed by the taste and style gurus as the hippest kids on the block, the genre itself is routinely maligned. No favourable review of a chill-out album would be complete without a jibe about stripped pine, Swedish furniture or dinner parties and the standard disclaimer: 'Not just another chill-out album.' The artists regularly seek to dissociate themselves from each other too, adding to the impression that this is not a genre to be proud of.

There are reasons for this, of course, most of which boil down to 'chill-out' being, frankly, a rubbish name. More on that later. But a Roland by any other name sounds just as sweet. It's the music that matters, and this genre is unleashing some of the most enthralling, emotive and inspiring music of the late twentieth and early twenty-first centuries.

I believe that since the late nineties, bands like Air, Bonobo, Zero 7, Röyksopp, Lemon Jelly and many, many others have taken chill-out music in a new and distinctive direction. Taken individually, these acts are brilliant, innovative producer/musicians. Together they comprise something more. They are, according to the rock-journalism cliché, a 'new wave'. Unfortunately, 'new wave of chill-out' is an even more rubbish name for a genre than the one we started with, so let's cut our losses and stick with what we have: chill-out music.

I'm here to tell you that chill-out music is bloody marvellous. Anyone who is involved in it as a musician, a producer, a DJ or as a paying customer should be damn proud to be a part of it. We shouldn't attempt to deny it or dissociate ourselves from it. We should stand up tall and say, yes, I make, play and like chill-out music. Dare I say it? I'm chill-out and I'm proud?

Before I go any further, I'd like to get a statement of the obvious out of the way. Chill-out music has always been around. It was invented the first time our ancestors drank some fermented fruit juice and then found themselves dancing the night away under the stars. As the sun rose and history's first hangover started to kick in, the guy hitting the log with the mammoth bone doubtless lowered the tempo and softened the beat. And hanging behind his shoulder was a younger, keener, more energetic wannabe-log-beater urging him to play some more 'ardcore. Music has always been used as an aid to relaxation, contemplation and tranquillity, as commonly as it has been used as an aid to dancing, fun and socializing.

The origins of chill-out as a self-contained genre, however, are inextricably linked to post-acid-house dance culture: it is the music for chill-out rooms, and the music to neutralize the chemical excesses at the end of a frantic night out. The phrase and the music have now been so effectively co-opted by mainstream consumer society that it is easy to forget these radical origins. The next time you watch Alan Titchmarsh creating the 'chill-out corner' of a garden to a soundtrack by Lemon Jelly, remember this: it probably wouldn't be happening if the likes of Mixmaster Morris hadn't been soothing the hearts and bending the brains of drug-addled ravers at Brixton squat parties, circa 1990.

So, when I talk about chill-out music over the following pages, I don't just mean 'music you can chill out to'. That could be anything from opera to heavy metal depending on your tastes. Nor do I mean 'anything you might find on a chill-out compilation', which will often include, classical, pop, R&B and the quiet songs from popular dance albums. I'm not even talking about chill-out's closest musical relatives: ambient, electronica, IDM, dub, nu-jazz and trip hop, much of which crosses over significantly with chill-out, but each luxuriating happily in a category of its own.

Although chill-out rooms, with a typical soundtrack of ambient or dub, had been around since the earliest days of acid-house parties, the musical genre really came into its own in the early nineties, as the huge success of a number of chill-out albums inspired other artists and labels. The KLF's extraordinary 1990 ambient sonic collage *Chill Out* was the landmark: a forty-five-minute, distinctly tongue-in-cheek odyssey through sound effects and environmental noise, from chugging trains and crashing waves, through snatched samples of TV, radio and recorded music, while delicate instruments fluttered in the background. The KLF's Jimmy Cauty also participated alongside Alex Patterson in making The Orb's 1991 debut *Adventures Beyond the Ultraworld*, another monumental, genre-defining masterpiece.

William Orbit's brilliant *Strange Cargo* series had actually begun back in 1987, although it was the release of *SCII* and *III* in 1991 and 1993 respectively that caught the public's attention, setting Orbit on a path to becoming either one of the world's most successful and sought-after producers, or the world's biggest sell-out, depending on your perspective. 1992 saw the release of the world's first compilation with the words 'chill out' in the title, volume one in the gruesomely titled and packaged *Chill Out Or Die* series. The development of a distinct sub-genre of Ibiza chill-out was confirmed with Jose Padilla's original

Café del Mar compilation in 1993, which would go on to spawn the most commercially successful and critically acclaimed chill-out series of them all.

Throughout the nineties, the chill-out genre continued to turn up regular classic albums. Future Sound of London, Global Communication, Nightmares on Wax, Thievery Corporation, The Gentle People, Fila Brazillia and Biosphere all put their own unique takes on the genre. Although these acts were releasing brilliant, timeless albums, their sales and profile were markedly lower than those achieved by the Orb and KLF in chill-out's early years. By the end of 1997, chill-out's balloon looked to be well and truly deflated – the salad days of 1992, when the Orb had performed their ambient classic 'Blue Room' on *Top of the Pops* and headlined the Saturday night at Glastonbury, seemed to be consigned to history. Nobody could have guessed that chill-out was about to enter its most artistically and commercially successful period of all.

The KLF's *Chill Out* album was the first landmark album for the genre. Although environmental sound recordings and experimental ambient music had been around for decades, never before had it been marketed to such a mass – and appreciative – audience, and the possibilities for the genre were suddenly different. The second landmark was on 27 January 1998, the release of *Moon Safari*, by the French duo Air.

The significance of *Moon Safari* is not entirely musical. It was an exceptionally good album, but hardly revolutionary. Their sweet, soundtrack-influenced electronic pop was unusual but not unprecedented, and some chill-out purists were unconvinced by the electro-populism of the hit singles 'Sexy Boy' and 'Kelly Watch the Stars'. Its significance was instead in the audience it reached. Unlike previous chill-out albums, the people who bought and loved *Moon Safari* were mostly not just frazzled clubbers, potheads and dedicated musical explorers, but the population at large. It was bought not only from specialist record shops but from supermarkets and high-street chains. It was the music industry's golden egg: a crossover hit.

What was good news for the Virgin Records group, however, was a mixed blessing for other chill-out acts. *Moon Safari* became not just the benchmark by which to measure the worth of other bands, but the stick with which to beat them. The reality of the situation was that a number of musicians of similar ages and backgrounds, and with access to similar technology, began making similar music at a similar point in time. Blue States released their debut album *Nothing Changes Under the Sun* only a couple of months after *Moon Safari*. In 1999 Nightmares On Wax released *Car Boot Soul*, an album which took the veteran band's lazy smoker's dub much closer to the soundtrack-influenced sound of their arriviste contemporaries.

Any doubts that a new wave of chill-out was evolving were surely swept away in 2000 with brilliant debuts from Bonobo, Kinobe and Lemon Jelly. Quantic's *5th Exotic* and Zero 7's *Simple Things* arrived in 2001. Debuts from Slovo, Fragile State, Röyksopp and Bent, plus Lemon Jelly's hugely successful sophomore LP *Lost Horizons* followed in 2002, then excellent debuts from Hint, Jon Kennedy, Chungking and TM Juke in 2003 take us up to the time of writing.

Is it fair to group these acts and others similar into a single movement or, as I'd argue, a new wave? From a musical perspective, I believe so. There were many shared influences, most noticeably the soundtracks of Ennio Morricone, Lalo Schiffrin, Jack Nitzsche and especially John Barry. The production echoed soul legends Quincy Jones and Charles Stepney. There were significant nods to funk, jazz and the retro sounds of vintage synths and electric pianos. There was also the introduction of 'songs' as opposed to 'tunes', complete with meaningful lyrics and a verse/chorus structure – this may sound a trite observation, until one ponders the near-total absence of such fripperies within the chill-out scene circa 1988–1998.

Ironically, by the time this current chill-out boom began, the music had moved out of its family home – the backrooms of clubs. It became increasingly difficult to find clubs which supplied a genuine chill-out room. Instead they offered 'Room 2', where the style of music in the main room would be replicated at a slightly slower tempo. The reasons for this are partly musical fashion, and largely a slow shift in the intoxicants of choice in clubs throughout the nineties. Chill-out music had relocated to the living rooms of the land, and there it thrived.

The other noteworthy detail about these acts is that only one, Air, was on a major record label. The others were all signed to independents, which by the usual standards makes chill-out an underground phenomenon, amusingly, more punk than punk. However, the music industry is seldom slow to spot a gap in the market. In the wake of *Moon Safari*'s success, and in the early instances taking a clear lead from the *Café del Mar* series, chill-out compilations and sloppily compiled mixes began to arrive on the shelves of high streets and supermarkets by the fistful. The phenomenon reached its peak in the summer of 2001, when no late-night TV commercial break was complete without at least one variation on *Now That's What I Call The Greatest Ministry of Ibiza Chill Out Album in the World Ever.*

Most were predictable to the point of hilarity. A twenty-four-track double CD would invariably begin with FSOL's 'Papua New Guinea', include one track each from Bonobo, Bent, Lemon Jelly, Kinobe, Zero 7 and other similar acts; the slow songs by successful dance acts like Underworld, Leftfield, Groove Armada, Moby, Basement Jaxx and Moloko. There would be a token soul song, a token film theme (usually *Blade Runner*) and then it would all be rounded off by William Orbit's *Adagio for* (Bloody) *Strings*. Get a few of these chill-out compilations, pass them round your friends, and it is actually possible to play chill-out bingo. 'I just need "At the River" and "Les Nuits" for a house…' As I was researching this chapter, I found myself looking at the Amazon entry for an EMI compilation entitled *Totally Chill Out*, and discovered that 'customers who shopped for this item also bought *This Is Chill Out; Essential Chill Out Six Pack; Chill Out 2000 Vol.3; Global Psychedelic Chill Out Vol.1* and *First Impressions: A Mix of Classic Drum & Bass to Chill Out To.*'

You might have guessed from my tone that I am not a huge fan of these compilations. For a number of reasons I'd say they are the worst thing ever to happen to the genre. I believe a good chill-out album should take the listener on a journey. The tempo, pace and purpose of the genre lends itself brilliantly to an extended musical narrative, and the best chill-out albums or DJ mixes will traverse many moods, from the melancholic to the joyous, from the dramatic to the humorous, from the challenging to the romantic. One analogy I like to draw is with a gourmet banquet. It should have an aperitif, a starter and a succession of flavours: some savoury, some bitter, some unusual, some sour and some sweet. By sequencing a couple of dozen of chill-out's greatest hits in succession, the typical mass-

market compilation resembles a banquet consisting of nothing but the petit fours. Each one delicious and desirable in its own right perhaps, but consume too many in succession and you're liable to start feeling nauseous.

Of course, you or I don't have to listen to these compilations if we don't want to. And in their defence it could be argued that they offer mass-market exposure to acts from small, independent labels who struggle to attain airplay and press coverage. There are royalties paid for the tracks, which provide much-needed income for these labels and artists. That's the theory at least. In practice, no artist ever became rich by licensing tracks to compilations. Someone has made a lot of money from these albums, but it isn't the musicians. It may even be possible that their prominence and numerousness put them into direct competition with the original artists' albums. Why should a customer travel to a specialist music shop in the seedy creative quarter of the city to seek out a Blue States album on Memphis Industries Records, when he or she can buy *Chilled Ibiza 3* (Warners) in the local supermarket? Of course this is also true in the worlds of uptempo dance music, where mixes massively outsell and outnumber original-artist albums. The difference, I would argue, is that techno, house and other forms of contemporary dance music primarily thrive upon the interaction between the DJs and their boxes of 12″ singles. Chill-out music thrives upon the album format, and if the market is so flooded with commercially minded compilations that the original albums are drowned, both the listener and the music are done a grave injustice.

My other principal objection to these compilations is perhaps slightly irrational, and I'm prepared to open myself up to accusations of snobbery. They're simply vulgar. The cheap predictability of the marketing and advertising of these products (and I use that word with care) puts them, in my mind at least, into a cultural basket alongside fast food, 0898 chat lines and George Foreman's *Lean Mean Grilling Machine*. It is hardly surprising that so many artists wish to dissociate themselves from a 'chill-out scene' if this is what it represents.

Now these same artists could easily avoid any such associations by simply declining offers to license their tracks. Some acts, notably Zero 7, made a conscious decision to stop giving permission for their tracks to be used. Many others are less fussy. It's hard to condemn any one act or label as they have bills to pay, and although the remuneration involved may be small, it is still effectively an offer of money for nothing – at least in the short term. Few of us would readily turn down such an offer. A similar defence could be put up against chill-out music's other great image problem: its popularity as the soundtrack for TV advertising and as the incidental music on documentaries and lifestyle programmes. Personally I don't have a problem with the latter. There's been many an occasion when I've found myself contentedly watching a gardening programme for no other reason than I'm enjoying the music. Griff Rhys Jones's affected shuffle through the BBC's recent hit series *Restoration* would have been considerably more irritating had it not been for the soothing beauty of Lemon Jelly's soundtrack. Air's third album *Talkie Walkie* was released on 26 January 2004. I heard it on a TV news item on 27 January 2004.

Like many music obsessives, I am less comfortable about music I love being used in commercials. Unlike the use of tunes as incidental and background music, which is normally administered by the Performing Right Society without the artists' involvement, music can only be used for advertising with the active consent of the performer. Many people, myself included, feel that a piece of music loses something of its magic when it becomes little more than a jingle. Very few pieces of music have risen in my affections through appearing on an advert.

But in reality chill-out music's reputation as 'music to sell mobile phones by' is largely unfair. The most extreme example of a band who are defined by a commercial is probably Kinobe, forever tagged as 'that band who did the Kronenburg ad'. The fact that their music has been used less frequently in commercials than a supposedly radical, politicized rock band like the Manic Street Preachers, for example, goes unmentioned. There's an illuminating website at www.commercialbreaksandbeats.co.uk, which logs the music used on nearly 2,000 different British TV commercials since 1996. A quick browse will confirm that chill-out acts are no more guilty of selling their souls to the ad-man's dollar than any other genre. I eagerly await the day I see a music critic describe David Bowie as making 'music to sell cars by' or The Rolling Stones as 'music to sell computers by'. Only Moby, whose polished, anodyne downtempo could conceivably be described as chill-out music, would appear to be guilty as charged, with a somewhat shameful nine commercials, mostly for cars, to his eco-friendly vegan name.

So what is it about contemporary chill-out that makes me love it so much? To answer that question I'd like to look closely at four albums which are among my own particular favourites of recent years. Each is a classic in its own right, but more importantly for my purposes, each marks a cornerstone of contemporary chill-out music's beauty and worth. Together I think they could form the four points of a twenty-first-century chill-out compass. Throw a string around them, and you could lasso the entire genre.

The first point of our compass is an album full of spirituality, romance and warmth: Zero 7's debut masterpiece *Simple Things*. At the opposite, (Northern) pole is Röyksopp's *Melody A.M.*, a work of technological supremacy, icy cool and eclectic range. Pointing to the right is one of the most fun-filled, joyous and childishly mischievous albums ever recorded, *Lost Horizons* by Lemon Jelly. And to the left, *Nommo* by Slovo, a cerebral, passionate LP, the beauty of which is only matched by its political urgency.

Zero 7's ascent to the pinnacle of the downtempo scene was as unlikely as it was sudden. Unlike most of the artists on the scene, their route in was not from the DJ booth or the live stage, but from the other side of the mixing desk. The story goes that Sam Hardaker and Henry Binns met at school in North London, and discovered a shared love of hip hop, soul and soundtracks over a spliff while bunking physics. They nevertheless progressed to the same engineering college and then served a studio apprenticeship together in Mickie Most's RAK studio alongside rising production star Nigel Godrich. In 1997, seemingly stuck in the junior role of assistant sound engineers, they cajoled Godrich into giving them access to the mastertapes of *Climbing Up the Walls*, from Radiohead's as then unreleased album *OK, Computer*. The remix they created was a masterpiece, deconstructing the original moody rock song, then reassembling it as a sort of acid-lounge vignette. It was received with adulation, and led to further remix offers including Terry Callier's *Love Theme From*

Spartacus, and more bizarrely, a Lenny Kravitz single, *If You Can't Say No*. As if to underline what unlikely superstars they made, Sam and Henry were invited to Kravitz's birthday party, but turned away at the door for not looking sufficiently rock'n'roll.

The buzz surrounding Zero 7 as a remix duo was substantial, but the release of two EPs of their own music in the year 2000 confirmed the arrival of truly special talents. Although limited to 1,000 copies per release, they generated extensive press coverage and ensured that the excitement surrounding the band, who were being described as 'the British Air' – much to their annoyance, delight or puzzlement, depending which interviews you read – was reaching unprecedented levels for a downtempo act by the date of release, 23 April 2001.

The high expectations were to prove more than justified. *Simple Things* was, and is, a magnificent album. The production is, of course, sensational; in a manner pioneered on the early remixes, Zero 7 show an uncanny gift for layering sounds, mostly high, bright and beautiful. They create a sound that seems as familiar as a child's favourite blanket and yet, simultaneously, utterly their own. The core of the sound is the relationship between the luscious strings provided by session-music megastars The Brilliant Strings, the gorgeously melodic, slippery bass work of Pete Trotman and the myriad synth pads, samples, Rhodes piano lines, harmonic sweeps and subtle flourishes laid down by Binns and Hardaker themselves.

Years spent trawling the dustiest corners of record shops paid dividends. Although few realized it at the time of release, the opening track 'I Have Seen' is a cover of a long (and unfairly) forgotten psychedelic pop song by early Seventies Manchester band The Peddlers, playing with the London Philharmonic Orchestra, no less. Zero 7 were remarkably faithful to the original arrangement, but listen to the two versions in turn and the brilliance of Binns and Hardaker begins to emerge. The addition of a gentle hip-hop rhythm gives a gentle bounce, and the emphases of the beats are stretched, giving a languid calm to the song. The staccato break which ends the chorus is already a startlingly clever piece of composition by The Peddlers' Roy Philips, but in Zero 7's hands it is given the tiniest rhythmic tweak and becomes heart-stopping. The strings which draw you back in

Crossfade
stripped pine and swedish furniture:
a defence of chill-out

37

to the music, seemingly a fraction of a beat after you'd expect them, offer almost indecent relief.

Similarly, the instrumental 'Out of Town' is based around a long sample from, of all places, the *Hawaii Five-O* soundtrack. Zero 7 pick it up like a baton (or perhaps a paddle), add the soft hip-hop rhythms again, gently fold in extra layers of strings, before Simon Elms's sweet trumpet arrives to take the song off on a sun-splashed melodic adventure. It's done with a gentle ease that typifies the album. Each component, each instrument, is eminently catchy and tuneful – there are few albums with such easily whistlable bass lines, for instance. And yet each part complements the whole, rather than fighting for attention.

But the real secret ingredient to Zero 7 is not the musicianship, however good that might be, or even the marvellous production. What turns *Simple Things* from a great album into a masterpiece are the contributions from three singers, Mozez, Sia Furler and Sophie Barker. All three turn in performances of quite audacious achievement, spilling over with passion, soul and spirituality. Each is very different, yet each seems to belong perfectly with the Zero 7 sound. First up is Mozez, with his smooth, soulful, honey-tinged voice, which swells to every note in a near-perfect mirror of the strings which so define the band's sound. On 'I Have Seen' he is low and insistent, almost menacingly intense. On the album's title track, the album's most melancholy, downbeat tune, there is a touch of sadness, almost despair, as his voice stretches towards a falsetto and threatens to crack with emotion. His finest moment, however, is the magnificent 'This World'. Pete Lawrence has called this 'the greatest soul ballad ever written' and I'd only argue with one thing – I'm not convinced it's a ballad. To me it is a twenty-first-century spiritual. It urges love and hope as a route from suffering and despair, with lyrics which are unashamedly sentimental: *We've only lost the vision of the stars we're meant to be.* In lesser hands this could have become mawkish, been easily dismissed as regurgitated hippie-speak. The beauty of the melody and the arrangement, the subtlety with which samples and musical details tickle your attention, the brilliant cascading bass, and above all Mozez's passionate delivery means it never even approaches this. People will marvel at this song for as long as recorded music is heard.

Sophie Barker's voice couldn't be much more different. Clean, pure and pitch-perfect, it's a voice that chimes with clarity. It shines on 'In the Waiting Line', one of several songs on the album to address themes of time and motion, *Nine to five, living lies. Every day stealing time – Everyone's taking everything they can.* Sophie's voice is relaxed, soft and gentle, making a plea for a slower way of life. The lyric fits impeccably with the lazy tone of the whole album.

The third singer is the quite remarkable Sia Furler. The young Australian is an acclaimed solo artist who had a UK top-ten hit ('Taken for Granted') to her name even before hooking up with Zero 7. Although she has recorded some beautiful music of her own, on *Simple Things* something quite magical happens. Duetting with Sophie Barker on lovely pop ballad 'Destiny', her husky, slightly rasping voice perfectly off-sets Sophie's purer tones. Like most of the album, 'Destiny' is notable for its subtlety, an understated gentleness to the music and vocals. That quiet sensitivity is blown apart by Sia's second vocal: 'Distractions'. This is essentially a slightly cynical, witty love song, written in a country-blues vein. But Sia's multi-tracked voice lifts it into a different realm. It howls with an almost agonized passion, Sia twisting her vowels around the lyrics and giving a new and different strength to the words. It's difficult to believe that the three words *I love you*, the root of so many songwriting clichés, could be so forthrightly reclaimed. Here they are repeated with such fire and belief that they arrive like a punch. Then she hits you again. And again. It is no exaggeration to say that 'Distractions' ranks among the greatest vocal performances ever recorded. I saw them perform the song at the Big Chill's Enchanted Garden in 2001, Zero 7's first headline performance. Their initial reception had been cooled by a frustratingly extended setting-up period, but when Sia sang that song, hearts melted. The usual 'electric' clichés do not begin to describe the palpable shiver which rippled through the crowd at that moment.

In the early years of this decade, only one British chill-out act has even begun to approach the critical and commercial success of Zero 7, and that is Lemon Jelly. Although they are both duos from North London, with a shared a love of old vinyl, sweeping strings, downtempo beats and broad polyphonic sonic canvasses, in other respects the two bands could not be more different. Whereas Zero

7's songs are mostly structured in the traditions of soul, pop and jazz songwriting, with melodic narratives and identifiable verses and choruses, Lemon Jelly's music is structured as dance music, repeated patterns of notes or beats, layered upon each other, arriving regularly every four bars. Whereas Zero 7 are resolutely anti-image, a band defined by their sound not their marketing, Lemon Jelly are enveloped by design, image and style. And whereas Zero 7's ascent to success was rapid and highly publicized, Lemon Jelly crawled into public consciousness largely by word of mouth.

Nick Franglen and Fred Deakin first met as teenagers, although it would be around fifteen years before they began making music together. With hindsight, their respective early careers pointed toward the gentle lunacy of Lemon Jelly. Franglen became a landscape gardener to the stars, creating natural environments for the likes of Phil Collins and Trevor Horn. After nearly causing a mischief to Freddie Mercury with a collapsing ornamental bridge, Franglen realized his calling was elsewhere. He turned to sound engineering and production and would soon be creating sonic environments for everyone from Björk and Blur to the Spice Girls. Deakin, meanwhile, was establishing himself as probably the world's most eccentric DJ and club promoter. His many innovations included a club called Misery, the antidote to Ministry, where clubbers would be made to do some ironing or chopped onions would be thrown on the dance floor. At Impotent Fury, Deakin would use a spinning 'wheel of fortune' to determine the style of music, from drum'n'bass to country'n'western. His clubland adventures also led him into graphic design, his gift for making flyers eventually spawning the successful design company Airside, and a sideline as lecturer in communications design at Central St Martin's College.

All of these elements would be brought to bear in creating the conceptual entity that is Lemon Jelly. Their musical output was initially restricted to one EP a year, released between 1998 and 2000. Each was of only a thousand copies and exquisitely packaged in a style best described as kindergarten psychedelia, all lurid colours and cartoon swirling patterns – a perfect match for the music, in fact. These records quickly became prized possessions, changing hands for vast sums – ironically, much more than Deakin and Franglen ever made from them. Lemon Jelly continue to issue occasional limited-edition singles, which are probably better considered as objets d'art than pieces of vinyl. Eschewing the traditional music-industry demands for photoshoots and Rankin portraits, Lemon Jelly only use graphic cartoons of themselves for publicity purposes. They insist that this is not because of any great desire to be private, secretive or mysterious, but simply because band photos are really rather boring.

The spirit of Deakin's club adventures still shines through at the band's live gigs. At their debut performance at London's Astoria they issued T-shirts instead of tickets – no shirt, no entry. On tour they spurned a support act in favour of a game of bingo, with the Grim Reaper as bingo caller, and issued party bags with balloons, badges and sweets. It's hardly surprising that Lemon Jelly prove popular with young children. Franglen once joked (?) that they see their key market as the over-70s and the under-5s. They once took this to a natural conclusion by playing a matinée gig for children only, leading to the unseemly spectacle of 20-something Lemon Jelly fans desperately trying to borrow nieces and nephews for an afternoon.

It's hard to think of another band that could pull so many stunts and gimmicks, carve themselves such a kitsch image, while still retaining even a shred of musical credibility. Lemon Jelly have done this and more. It seems the closer they skirt to comedy, the more seriously they are taken. Part of the reason is doubtless the skill, wit and intelligence they bring to their project: everything from the design to the live decor is created with the utmost style and class. But I would like to think the reason their reputation has survived all their mischief is because however brilliant their design and image making may be, their music is even better.

The three early EPs would later be collated to become the debut album, *lemonjelly.ky*. The songs were excellent, of course, but *.ky* never quite held together as a fully balanced album – it was never written to be such. It wasn't until October 2002 that Lemon Jelly released what they themselves described as their first 'proper' album, and the one which would bring them belated public and commercial recognition, *Lost Horizons*.

Listening to Lemon Jelly is an entirely escapist experience. *Lost Horizons* begins with a faint wink to the theme tune from Roald Dahl's

Tales of the Unexpected, setting the tone for an experience somewhere between *Charlie and the Chocolate Factory* and *James and the Giant Peach*. In this magical world, there are sweets and pretty things all around, but darker, scarier thoughts are never so far away. When you scratch the childish veneer, there is a very sharp, adult intelligence at work. It is also full of laughs.

Lost Horizons uses those laughs, however, in a very clever way. The almost-legendary 'Nice Weather For Ducks' centres around a nursery rhyme, performed with stuffy, pompous genius by the comic actor Enn Reitel. It brought the band a major radio hit and instantly divided the world into love it and hate it camps. Needless to say, I love it.

Listen beyond the vocal break, and you will hear an astounding piece of music. From two superb complimentary acoustic guitar loops, underscored by fast, fluttering breakbeats, it takes you on a joyride of wild sudden corners and hilarious rhythmic changes. The horn part which suddenly lifts the tune after the first chorus is extraordinary, and as all the pieces slot together, the tune rises to a magnificent climax and then suddenly…it stops: *All the ducks are swimming in the water – faldoraldoraldo, faldoraldoraldo.*

The sheer infantilism of the vocal line is more than just a gimmick or cheap laugh, I think. It actually serves to disguise or distract your attention from the complexity and technical excellence of the music – an endearingly modest move for talented musicians. There is no bragging, no spotlight on technical skills. When you think about Lemon Jelly songs in the abstract, what you remember are mostly the vocal samples: the astronaut on 'Space Walk,' looking at the Earth and saying *It's beautiful, just beautiful.* Or the 'Rambling Man', proudly listing all the places he has visited, from the North Pole to Naxos. Or if not a vocal sample, then a musical gag – a quirk like the Russian choir which brings home the breakbeat workout 'Return to Patagonia'. But while these grab your attention, the subtleties of the music are allowed to do their work in peace. Heavily based around 4, 8 or 16-bar loops, they have a hypnotic effect: each melodic loop as simple and pretty as a flower in its own right, but then arranged into a perfect floral display.

These simple structures offer a relaxed accessibility, but that could quickly become boring. Lemon Jelly avoid this fate thanks to the staggering complexities of their arrangements and their rhythms. Listen to 'Elements', with its offbeat broken beat; 'Return to Patagonia', with its insistent layers of Art Blakey-style jazz loops; and more subtly perhaps, the irresistible swing groove of 'The Curse of Ka'Zar'.

If Lemon Jelly's biggest fans are truly the under-5s, we must conclude the future is in safe hands.

For all their charm, there is something slightly affected about Lemon Jelly's peculiarly English eccentricities – rather quaint and fey. That is not something that could be said of Röyksopp. This is the band who worried that live electronica was boring, so they once constructed a metal machine weighing over 100 kilos, five metres wide and two metres high, containing all their musical equipment. The duo would climb inside, stick their hands through holes to reach equipment, and see by sticking their heads through a glass ball. The machine also incorporated a chimney, complete with belching smoke.

Torbjorn Brundtland and Svein Berge, another pair of childhood friends, grew up in Tromso, just outside the Arctic circle, a town where it is dark for nearly six months of the year. Fans of electronica from an early age, they grew up under the shadow, then latterly under the wing, of local hero Geir Jenssen, of ambient legends Biosphere and Bel Canto.

In the late nineties the duo dabbled in a number of projects, one, other or both of them recording, producing and remixing with a number of acts including Kings of Convenience, Drum Island and the rather special (if unimaginatively monikered) jazz-house act Those Norwegians. When they finally settled as the duo Röyksopp, something remarkable happened. It was called *Melody A.M.*

Released in the autumn of 2002, it marked the arrival of a major talent. *Melody A.M* is a superb mass of contradictions. It fuses the clean, friendly electronica of Biosphere with downtempo rhythms and breaks; it utilizes broad planes of cinematic strings alongside delicate ambient electronica; it brings together the panoramic aural sculpture of Brian Eno with the mechanical leanings of Kraftwerk; and it offers some of the most sublime home-headphone listening alongside a couple of genuine club hits.

Those two tunes, 'Eple' and 'Poor Leno', are so memorable and so integral to *Melody A.M.* that one has to ask whether this should really qualify as a chill-out album at all. 'Eple', with its spiralling, chiming melody could almost be an Orbital remix; 'Poor Leno' could be the work of Underworld. Yet there is something rather polite about the pitched-up hip-hop beat which carries 'Eple' – played late at night or on a hungover early morning, it offers reassurance rather than an assault. And 'Poor Leno', which rattles along on a 4/4 beat and piles up a series of stuttering electro synths, remains a gentle song. If Underworld really had recorded this tune, it would probably have picked up a jaggedness, just a hint of the dark violence which techno music thrives upon. Röyksopp instead add luscious strings and the gentle voice of Erlend Oye, comfort blankets which prevent the song ever becoming aggressive or intrusive. To these tracks you could add the fabulous 'Röyksopp's Night Out', with its frantic opening, like an action sequence by David Holmes. But that too pulls back, towards a softer, lazier jazz-funk sound with a touch of Lalo Schiffrin about it, before exploding into action once more.

Beyond those three uptempo celebrations, *Melody A.M.* is a marvel of eclecticism. 'Remind Me' is a sweet electro-pop song, and is so reminiscent of Air that I've always thought it almost unfair that Röyksopp are virtually the only contemporary chill-out act to have escaped the accusations of copying the French duo. 'So Easy', which opens the album, is an unbearably catchy instrumental based around a sample of an old Burt Bacharach record. It's also a tune which was used on a particularly memorable mobile-phone commercial, sadly ruining it for many of us through over-exposure and the inescapable retinal imprint of that giant-screen baby. 'Sparks' was saved that fate, and remains sublime. A beautiful synthetic ballad which owes a notable debt to nineties trip hop, it is made special by the deeply affecting vocal melody, casually performed by Anneli Drecker. Even the gossamer-light 'Come', which almost imperceptibly carries the final seconds of the album, is a luxurious snap of ambient electronica, like a lost work by Boards of Canada.

It's impossible to escape the geographical origins of this album. It is an album to keep you warm in the long nights. There are icicles hanging from the sharp piano lines of 'Eple', 'In Space' and 'She's So', and yet they are never chilling – it's rather like watching through triple-glazing as the icebergs melt under the central heating provided by the warmth of the arrangements.

A criticism often made of the chill-out genre, and I think it is a fair one, is that it is broadly introspective. By its very nature it seeks to comfort, to soothe and caress. It shies away from conflict and confrontation, offers a refuge from the stresses of modern life. But music, like all art, thrives on engagement with human experience and the world at large. There is something ultimately distasteful about an art form which seeks to generate a Panglossian sense that all is right with the world, when the world is, in reality, far from all right. If the ultimate goal of chill-out music is to generate a feeling of peace and tranquillity, it needs to address the causes of our stress and tension. I believe the world becomes a less frightening place when one begins to understand it, and one role of any art is to help us do exactly that. Chill-out music should not be exempt from this. Any doubts that this is achievable should be firmly dispelled by the magnificent album *Nommo*, by Slovo.

Unlike the three other albums I've been discussing, *Nommo* has not been a commercial success. It has not been laden with Brit, Mercury, Shortlist or MTV award nominations. It has never charted and at the time of writing it appears beset by distribution problems and is only available through the band's website (www.slovo.co.uk). Yet those who hear it quickly become evangelical about it. Rock star turned BBC radio DJ Tom Robinson recently named it as the one album he would grab were his house on fire. It is an album of ragged beauty, raw passion, sadness, anger and hope. Where most contemporary chill-out is digitally polished, clean and pure, *Nommo* is organic and earthy. And while most are led by production techniques and technology, *Nommo* is built around the astonishing virtuoso gifts of guitarist Dave Randall.

Randall is a successful session musician with credits including Dido, Doudou Cissoko, Emiliana Torrini and One Giant Leap, although he is best known as one-time resident guitarist with clubland superstars Faithless. As a teenager he showed a voracious enthusiasm for musical knowledge and technique, and claims his influences as a guitarist range from the raw sparse rhythms of hip hop to the intricate frills of heavy metal. His sound and songwriting is heavily influenced by a North American folk tradition that spans Robert Johnson, Woody Guthrie and Ani di Franco, but also by contemporary dance music, the sounds of Africa and Asia and the languages and voices of the whole world. His music is universal and pancultural, an achievement he largely credits to living in Brixton.

Musical and cultural mix'n'match fusions are ten-a-penny these days. The unique brilliance of *Nommo* is that Randall perceives this communion of cultural influences through a very urgent and contemporary political lens. His songs are steeped in his active participation in global struggles for peace, human rights and social justice.

Although mostly written and recorded before September 11 2001, *Nommo* wasn't released until late 2002, during that brief lull in the 'war on terror' before the campaigns in Afghanistan and Iraq. It forms an astute and intelligent critique of the New American Century, but also spills with hope and positivity, the celebration of human potential.

Tellingly, it begins with the street sounds of Gaza City, a gentle acoustic guitar line accompanying the pained Arabic voice of a Palestinian woman describing *Saaba*: life's hardship. It is suddenly interrupted by the voices of 'Frank and Harry', two American broadcasters merrily swapping banter about consumerism, marketing and *how can we help your product look better?* before a deeply funky bassline and thumping kick drum demand you join a party. The juxtaposition is subtle. As with most of the album, the intellectual kick is not spelled out, but tucked between the lines. It is a stunning start to an album, a perfect example of how music can make a statement without shouting slogans.

Something similar happens in the short but breathtaking musical sketch '21 Today'. Over hypnotic synth pads and increasingly edgy guitar and percussion, voices from twenty-one different countries name their homeland and a date: *China 1945–46, '50–'53. Korea '50–'53. Guatemala '54, '60, '67–'69* and so on through a list of twenty-one countries. With a little background knowledge (or a quick glance at the album's sleeve notes) you will know these are the twenty-one countries bombed by the United States of America since the end of World War II. The track ends with the chime of a cash register. There is no proselytising, no ranting, just bare facts which make a point far more forcefully than any number of clichéd 'Give Peace A Chance' anti-war platitudes.

Even when *Nommo* wears its political heart most openly on its sleeve, there is more to it than meets the eye. Towards the end of 'Di Wengi Sane', after a riotous salad of sitar, hip hop and a spectacular drum track borrowed from jazz legend Max Roach, there is a sample of a political speech, which concludes *In this world there is room for everyone. The earth is rich and can provide for everyone. Our way of life can be free and beautiful.* The sample is not the voice of Martin Luther King or Noam Chomsky, but that of Charlie Chaplin. The words are spoken by the Jewish barber and Hitler lookalike Hynkel at the end of *The Great Dictator*, Chaplin's satirical attack on fascism. Looking for political wisdom? Don't ask a politician, ask a barber.

Good politics don't always make good music, as anyone who ever heard a Flux of Pink Indians album will testify. And it would be unfair to categorize *Nommo* as 'just' a political album. Musically it is brilliant. Your attention might be caught by Randall's breathtaking fretwork, such as the ragtime guitar solo that is picked up and moulded into an urban dance groove on 'Sertao Blues', or the simple but effective licks that echo through 'Hound Dog'. You may find yourself enthralled by the range of the instrumentation, vocal samples, spoken-word sections and the raps of Anthony DeMore. But I'd lay heavy odds that you will be drawn first to the deceptively simple, acoustic songs which provide focus to the album, anchoring it to the familiar.

Kirsty Hawkshaw, veteran of the chill-out scene since her days as the blissed-out acid-queen voice of Opus 3, excels on 'Killing Me', 'Come Down' and the beautiful, haunting 'Whisper'. Each one is gorgeous; but the most striking voice to be found on *Nommo* is that of Icelandic star Emiliana Torrini on the sublime 'Weebles Fall'. This is a wonderful song; I must have played it a thousand times in the past eighteen months and it still has my goosebumps rising every time. The metronomic guitar part is perfect in its simplicity; the cello and bass impeccable as the counterpoints. But it is Torrini's amazing vocals that set it apart. A sweet, almost childish lightness to its tone, it seems to float in the air on its way to your ears. Lyrically, it is perhaps not the album's sophisticated moment; the verses comprise a series of blatant lies – weebles fall; the sun spins round

the earth, concluding each verse with...*and the way we're living is the only way.* But when the chorus arrives, *we close our eyes, recite our daily lies. Get high, so high, we self-lobotomize,* Torrini's delivery is so sensitive, so impassioned, it's impossible not to be shaken by her gentle remonstrations.

As a footnote to the story of Slovo's debut album, it's worth knowing it was largely recorded in an ageing warehouse, then home to an alternative news service, a variety of independent musicians and venue for some legendary free parties. Since the recordings, the building has been bought and renovated. Slovo's little room is now part of an apartment owned by Kylie Minogue. The ground floor is now a branch of Starbucks.

Kerching.

The differences between these four albums are pronounced. Had I picked another four and then another four after, the differences would have become ever more expansive and pronounced. The ignorant refrain that chill-out music 'all sounds the same' should have been firmly laid to rest. Within the genre there are of course similarities in their influences and their sound, but I believe the most notable common feature of these artists is their eclecticism. Modern chill-out music is a wondrous sonic soup of genres, styles, techniques and instrumentation. Perhaps this is one of the reasons for its success.

Chill-out is accessible to fans of dance, pop, soul, folk, classical, electronica or jazz. It is a fulcrum and, one would hope, a crossroads. Techno fans who develop a taste for Röyksopp may use this as a starting point to explore the world of jazz. House fans who discover Lemon Jelly may begin to develop an appreciation for the repetitive melodic structures in the classical music of Satie or Debussy. Or if they prefer, they can slip an album on in the background, lose themselves in a crossword puzzle and simply chill.

There is a tendency for writings about music to encourage deep, perhaps excessive analysis. It's probably fair to say that without extensive background knowledge and close study, a listener is likely to be largely unmoved by Edgard Varèse's *Hyperprism* or even John Coltrane's *A Love Supreme,* and needless to say, the same is not true of any chill-out album. But does that make it any less satisfying, involving or worthwhile? Of course not. A piece of music like Zero 7's

'This World' should be celebrated as a musical pinnacle on its own terms, as surely as the *Choral Symphony* and 'Ace of Spades'.

Yes, chill-out music is the perfect accompaniment to a romantic meal or a quiet evening's socializing. Yes, chill-out music sounds great at the end of a long evening's indulgences, when the only other appropriate entertainment would be early morning children's TV. So does that mean the music has all the depth of a *Teletubbies* triple-bill? Of course not.

Fetch a pair of headphones, slip on a great chill-out album, and it can take you scuba diving into the depths of a coral reef, or orbiting in the far frontiers of space. It can offer a masterclass of musicianship and production, it can offer laughs and tears and inspiration and joy.

Or if you want to, play it on your Bang and Olufsen while eating balsamic-soaked rocket salad and panini off your Swedish-pine coffee table.

I'm not going to stop you.

recommended listening

Air – *Moon Safari* (Source)
Blue States – *Nothing Changes under the Sun* (Memphis Industries)
Nightmares On Wax – *Car Boot Soul* (Warp)
Aim – *Cold Water Music* (Grand Central)
Kinobe – *Soundphiles* (Pepper)
Thievery Corporation – *Mirror Conspiracy* (18th Street Lounge)
Zero 7 – *Simple Things* (Ultimate Dilemma)
Fila Brazillia – *Maim That Tune* (Pork)
Röyksopp – *Melody A.M.* (Wall of Sound)
Lemon Jelly – *Lost Horizons* (Impotent Fury/XL)
Quantic – *Apricot Morning* (Tru Thoughts)
Slovo – *Nommo* (Rufflife)
Bent – *Programmed to Love* (Sport)
Chris Coco – *Next Wave* (Distinctive)
Jimpster – *Domestic Science* (Kudos)
Lol Hammond – *All This Is Bliss* (Big Chill)
Bonobo – *Dial M for Monkey* (Ninja Tune)
Fragile State – *The Facts and the Dreams* (Bar de Lune)
Hint – *Portakabin Fever* (Ninja Tune)

Chungking – *We Travel Fast* (TummyTouch)

TM Juke – *Maps from the Wilderness* (Tru Thoughts)

Jon Kennedy – *Take My Drum to England* (Grand Central)

If you must buy compilations or mixes, please buy good ones!

Kruder and Dorfmeister – *The K&D Sessions* (Studio K7)

Big Chill Presents…*Glisten* (Big Chill Recordings)

Tom Middleton – *The Sound of the Cosmos* (Hooj Choons)

recommended reading

David Toop – *Ocean of Sound* (Serpent's Tail)

Mark Prendergast - *The Ambient Century* (Bloomsbury)

folk : the tide flows in, the tide flows out

Pete Lawrence

early one morning

'Imagine a stocky man in a chunky sweater, finger in his ear and a big fuzzy beard flecked with the froth from a pint of real ale. Imagine him recounting a tale of Cornish smugglers, or running through The Spinners' greatest hits. This is the image of the "folkie", an anachronistic figure oblivious to the rest of the world.' So said the *NME* in September 1987, a time of excitement and change for the folk scene. The rock weekly – despite its regular reliance on 'Hey nonny no' stereotypes and lazy clichés – went on to debunk the 'myth' in the same article, describing it as 'the most complex family tree in the forest. It encompasses everything that is worthy in music and spits on the synthesized, simulated efforts of the heartless, the music makers without guts…it does not have its finger in its ear, it has its finger on the pulse.' Curiously, preconceptions over the last decade or more have clearly shifted and boundaries blurred to the extent that, were one to disregard the comments about anachronism and oblivion, replace real ale with a cognac and substitute The Spinners with The Wurzels, they could easily have been referring not to a sixties anachronism, but to one of the most versatile and iconic electronic music producers of today – sometime Big-Chill regular Tom Middleton.

The scene at that time was so broad that it was pretty much impossible to encapsulate or pin down, unless you were Radio One

DJ and television presenter Andy Kershaw, the WOMAD festival or the influential *Folk Roots* magazine, who were each pioneers in the celebration of musical and cultural eclecticism at the time. Aside from Texan singer-songwriter Michelle Shocked at the top of the independent album charts, and big successes for Zimbabwe's Bhundu Boys, the busking blues of Mississippi's Ted Hawkins and the trashcan punk-trad of the The Pogues, we were witnessing the dawn of the 'world music' phenomenon, with artists such as Salif Keita, Ali Farka Toure and Youssou Ndour assuming almost godlike status amongst the cognoscenti. That wasn't all. Paul Simon released the South African-influenced *Graceland* to widespread commercial success even if he was breaking the ANC embargo; Fairport Convention guitarist and founder member Richard Thompson was reviving a career with renewed vigour and a brace of strong compositions; and artists such as The Proclaimers, Tanita Tikaram, and 10,000 Maniacs were all making an impression. Kate Bush, Peter Gabriel and David Byrne were all discovering the joys of delving into their ethnic muses, but in their cases, it was the music of Bulgaria, South Africa and Latin America, and not Shropshire or Northumberland, that was the inspiration. England remained the last outpost of discovery for the new world-music aficionados.

In the years immediately preceding this boom, there had also been a short-lived, pub-based movement known as 'cowpunk', which had taken the belts and braces rusticity of Dexy's Midnight Runners' *Too Rye Ay* phase and combined it with an urban-street-punk attitude, with cowboy hats and check shirts replacing the zips and safety pins. Fronting it were Camden's Boothill Foot-Tappers, and bands such as the Electric Bluebirds, the Skiff-Skats and the Balham Alligators were all mixing accomplished alt.country-inspired musicianship with a love of rural Americana. As a parallel, and almost coincidentally, the underbelly of the American college sound was also flirting with what was comically referred to as 'new authenticity', with guitar bands such as The Long Ryders, Green On Red, Rainer and Das Combo, and the soon-to-be-acclaimed REM calling the shots. Anything that seemed over-produced or synthetic was out (or in the charts). Down-home rural authenticity, along with its guitars, accordions, fiddles and banjos, was in, at least in a short-term-anti-fashion sense.

come write me down

Folk's appeal was a curious one. Its distance from – and disregard for – the pop world brought with it a fascination. Rather than any notions of it being the flipside of cool or post-cool, it was so obviously not even entering any such arena on any level, and the scant media attention it received seemed to be achieved by genuine appreciation or raw enthusiasm.

At the time folk music didn't really have PR people. Its innocence and raw honesty was exciting, slightly illicit and in many ways as subversive as anything punk ever achieved, but with more underground credentials, even if it lacked the risk element of likelihood of getting hit by flying glasses or spat on at live gigs. It even had a sexiness. At least some of it did. It indulged a sense of lineage and history that was at the time the antidote to synth pop overload and a surfeit of new, shiny boys' toys. One had to hunt for the gems, discover the stuff that artists rated through word-of-mouth, in the days before newsgroups and e-mail digests. For some it was the search for the grail of 'authenticity', though I've always been suspicious of the word and its associations. Above all, it was and always will be effortlessly hipper than anything more self-conscious. It wasn't the word on the street, it was the chinwag on the bridle path. If the post-acid-jazz *Straight No Chaser* shades and berets hung out in its adopted spiritual home in Hoxton, east London, then folk music's rustic homestead was probably in an old Welsh Borders pub somewhere near Clun in West Shropshire.

the lost and found

Rewinding further back to the days when I was an impressionable lad hooked on chart music and moving into double digits, 1969 – which, to this day, may still have a valid claim to being in pop music's most golden era – was probably the year when I first got into folk music on any level. It was August that year, and a strange, rough and ready, slightly-out-of-tune acoustic singalong tune called 'Si Tu Dois Partir'. At the time I had no idea who Fairport Convention were or how they would later take their place in the annals of folk history, but the Cajun-influenced tune caught my imagination at the time. Four months later, my childhood partner-in-crime, Martin Corbett, and myself were about to launch headlong into a new and untried musical excursion – deep into the murky waters known as progressive rock (also known as 'heavy' and 'underground' music). Blame an *NME* supplement that came out that Christmas for whetting our appetite, for it was that esteemed journal that suddenly brought the underground into the lives of two impressionable lads of the ages of twelve and fourteen. Curiously, the Island Records budget sampler *Nice Enough To Eat* (cost 14/6d) was the first purchase and though it opened with a Fairports'track, it also featured the likes of Jethro Tull, Nick Drake, Sandy Denny, Quintessence and Dr Strangely Strange. Island were to prove a formative influence on British folk music, and even today, many new fans are discovering Drake, Richard and Linda Thompson, John Martyn and Cat Stevens for the first time. Alongside Island, there were labels like Transatlantic (Pentangle, Robin and Barry Dransfield, Humblebums) and Harvest (Shirley and Dolly Collins, Tea and Symphony, Third Ear Band, Pink Floyd and Syd Barrett) and the newly formed Chrysalis (who signed Jethro Tull from Island).

A year or two on and the occasional gem was coming through, whether it was Richard Thompson, the Fairport guitarist's first solo album *Henry The Human Fly* or Ukranian Melanie Safka's 'Brand New Key' single, later covered and rewritten as 'Combine Harvester' by West Country cider jokers The Wurzels, who had a massive hit with the song in 1976. At the more serious end of the spectrum, Richard and Linda Thompson's *I Want To See The Bright Lights Tonight* (Island, 1974) and subsequently *Pour Down Like Silver* (Island, 1975), after their joint conversion to Islam were both classic records highlighting the power of folk song as confessional, or as a potent vehicle for revenge, disillusionment and decay, as in Richard Thompson's 'Withered and Died' in which 'dreams have withered and died'.

No wonder a semi-official Thompson release was subsequently entitled – only semi-humorously – *Songs Of Doom and Gloom From The Tomb*. Soon the couple would be very publicly bickering and fighting during their live shows, which made for riveting and compulsively charged live sets. After what seemed like an acrimonious split, Richard still continues to write some strong songs. Linda has recently made a second comeback.

The folk sound had probably transposed itself on to my widening tastes around the early eighties, after graduating from pop to 'prog', and then Americana (Ry Cooder was the catalyst here, opening up a whole spectrum, from the country blues of Leadbelly and Blind Willie Johnson, through to a global folkloric consciousness via the likes of Bahamian oddball Joseph Spence, Hawaiian pedal-steel guitarist Gabby Pahinui and gospel singer Washington Phillips, via the rural Americana of Woody Guthrie and The Carter Family).

It was 1983 and I'd just been to Glastonbury for the first time. King Sunny Ade, The Beat, Melanie, Incantation, Curtis Mayfield and Moving Hearts and wall-to-wall sunshine, and I was championing the eclectic cause. Irish folksters Moving Hearts in particular had made an impression on me whenever I'd seen them in the early eighties – Donal Lunny's dextrous stringed instruments, Davy Spillane's extraordinary emotive uillean pipes and the political vocals from Christy Moore and Mick Hanly. From the Hearts' music, I'd gone on to check Planxty, De Danann and early Clannad, almost a decade after the Chieftains had been introduced to me via a favourite track called the 'The Timpan Reel' (*Chieftains 5*, CBS) via an Irish friend, Chris Gordon, who had swapped me the odd Irish record or anecdote in return for a session listening to Little Feat or Canterbury prog-folksters Caravan.

Radio One DJ and world-famous Englishman of renown, John Peel was also, at the time, featuring a whole host of folk records (he had launched his own folk-based label, Dandelion, in the late sixties with artists such as Principal Edwards Magic Theatre, Medicine Head, Clifford T. Ward and Stackwaddy). He was also inviting the likes of Chieftains' front man Paddy Moloney on to his nightly Radio One show. This era of Peel was probably, given the way that musical tastes have panned out, the most vital, although perhaps not as compulsive as his imminent total conversion to punk. If there were any signs of a folk movement at the time, it may have been purely based around entrepreneurs such as Peel, as much as Mike Oldfield's *Hergest Ridge* and *Ommadawn*, Steeleye Span's early albums and the odd Gryphon track heard on Bob Harris's Radio One show. But then the charts were no stranger to folk at the time. Especially at Christmas. Steeleye Span's a capella 'Gaudete', Oldfield's 'Portsmouth', and even at the height of punk it was still happening – step forward Fiddlers Dram and their (ahem) much loved No. 1 'Day Trip to Bangor'. Also having hits at various points in the seventies were The Strawbs with 'Part of the Union' at the height of workers' unions' unrest during the Tories' three-day-week heyday, Stealers Wheels' catchy 'Stuck in the Middle With You', Gerry Rafferty's anthemic 'Baker St' and Ralph McTell's reflective 'Streets of London', a natural progression from Donovan and The Seekers in the late sixties, at very least.

a brave ploughboy

Along the way, it seemed that no one was really doing the folk thing properly at the time, apart from Topic Records, my near neighbours in Stroud Green, north London, who had the most awesome catalogue, built up since 1939, but weren't exactly marketing it to new audiences back in those days. So the idea for the Cooking Vinyl label was born in May 1986, after my friends Stuart and Celia Todd had approached me about working together on a project of my choosing, as long as I could enthuse them with whatever idea I came up with, using the proceeds from the sale of their corner shop in Hampshire. Presuming that little could be as unfashionable as folk, I presented myself with something of an uphill task – how to present and energetically market a new label dedicated in its entirety to folk and roots music from around the world. I'd just completed three years' apprenticeship with a record distributor called Making Waves, and in the process discovered that I was fast developing a taste for music that I had to dig a little deeper to find – for South African Mbaqanga, for deep soul and the original rhythm-and-blues sound, for some of the gospel music that I had heard on Alexis Korner's inspirational Radio One show, and even for that other four-letter word – folk. There were times when I convinced myself that the only way we'd get by in the face of an increasingly homogeneous retail stocking policy and the mysterious dismissal or demotion of anyone seen to be a 'music person' (rather than an accountant) in the major national retail chains at the time, was through copious amounts of Messianic zeal.

What Cooking Vinyl was probably best noted for, during my time there in the late eighties, was a somewhat risky A&R policy, several unlikely hybrid fusions and a zeal for self-publicity which attracted an interesting and loyal bunch of diehards, as it gradually crossed over into more mainstream consciousness whilst remaining steadfastly left-field and true to its roots. Edward II were a landmark group in the development of English roots music, and central to the label's ethos. Their earliest recordings, a series of limited-edition cassettes (*Ethos, Demos, Promos*) mainly sold at gigs, eschewed the idea of drums and instead grouped around married couple Rod and Danny Stradling, on melodeon and percussion respectively, underpinned by deep dubby basslines from part-time Mekon and folk theorist John Gill, and completed by another melodeon and a banjo. They soon added two more members of The Mekons on guitar and drums – the latter, Steve Golding, cut his teeth on some classic new-wave tracks, most notably Elvis Costello's 'Watching The Detectives'. Their choice of set was steeped in Welsh Border dance, with medleys of tunes from local villages – 'Brimfield Polka', 'The Bromsberrow Heath Three-Handed Reel' and 'Clee Hill'. If not quite England's version of its own 'Route 66' regional song culture (Billy Bragg's 'A13' spoof of the Chuck Berry song excepted), it was at least an unselfconscious rural equivalent. It made me want to go to those places at least once. As Ell evolved, their musical influences delved deeper into black reggae culture and the rapidly growing acid-house scene, with remix collaborations in 1989 involving both London-based dub maverick Mad Professor on *Two Step To Heaven* (Cooking Vinyl) and acid-house sampledelica of Mixmaster Morris and Des De Moor's Irresistible Force on *The Swedish Polka/Mixes* (Cooking Vinyl), before adding vocals to make their most successful album in 1991, *Wicked Men* (Pure Bliss).

The Barely Works – who modelled their sound on the classic English country-dance bands – were a glorious mishmash of trad energy and dextrous musicianship, peaking as the eighties made way for the nineties. Featuring a line-up of hammered dulcimer, banjo, fiddle, accordion and drums, rounded off with a tuba playing the bass parts, they were as English as bangers and mash, though simultaneously sticking two fingers up to any notions of constraint and purity. Original conceptualizer, Matt Fox, was realistic: 'The whole thing needs a bit more imagination. I think that the classic distinctive ceilidh sound is boring. People associate it with childhood, kids' programmes and music and movement at school.' Fox wanted to inspire people to dance because of the music, not to start from dance as an end in itself. 'There must be a way of getting around the stop/start nature of ceilidhs. When we used to dance to Motown records, we'd work our movements out ourselves but still do it in the context of a group or line of dancers.'

Paul James had for some years been at the helm of Blowzabella – one of the most exciting dance bands in the country, a totally acoustic (bass excepted) outfit who made a hell of a racket and came up with tune titles such as 'Spaghetti Panic' and 'Pingha Frenzy'. Since 1978 their music had evolved from relatively simple performances of traditional dance tunes to complex arrangements involving adventurous harmonic and rhythmic changes, many of which were based on material composed by themselves. While combing the archives in the library at Cecil Sharp House for English bagpipe tunes, the band came across a seventeenth-century tune called 'Blowzabella', the Italianate name being a reference to Italian music which was popular in London at that time. The name and the tune stuck. They came up with the amusingly titled *Blowzabella Wall Of Sound* (Plant Life, 1986) and also covered US band Violent Femmes' 'Higher Ground'. Their instrumentation included a variety of European bagpipes, hurdy-gurdy, saxes and woodwinds and the obligatory fiddle and melodeon. Their annual Blowzabella Workshop Festivals were the stuff of legends. I attended two – one in Bath and another in Ickworth Park in Suffolk. Both were notable for the fanaticism and extraordinary passion of their fans.

Ancient Beatbox was Paul James's spin-off project with hurdy-gurdy player Nigel Eaton. It was in many ways the midi-based offspring of Blowzabella, and the opening track from *Ancient Beatbox* (Cooking Vinyl), 'My Eyes are Filled With Clouds', also featured the vocals of Sheila Chandra, to which the band shot an evocative video filmed for indie-based television programme *Snub TV*, filmed at the Devil's Punchbowl, near Guildford. Paul James's influence extended well beyond the folk circuit, but was still steeped in English – and European – tradition:

> I first became aware of sampling from the usual sort of records – MC5's *Kick Out The Jams*, samples of bagpipes and hurdy-gurdies retuned, manipulated and fired back off keyboards. Some Tears for Fears, a Stock Aitken and Waterman kick drum. What we do is English but tempered by a European outlook. We tend to look

south and east rather than west. The drones sound eastern but are actually Mediterranean, extending towards Greece and the Balkans. A lot of the rhythms are from traditional native European dance music – jig time, 2/4, 6/8, 9/8 and so on.

In retrospect, the English folk bands on Cooking Vinyl who were pushing the envelope most interestingly at the time – The Oyster Band (who grew out of The Oyster Ceilidh Band), Edward II, Ancient Beatbox, The Barely Works and God's Little Monkeys – were the ones that really defined my original ethos for the label most succinctly. My Cooking Vinyl years, as I call them (the label still exists, although without my involvement and with a very different musical policy), were notable for mixing up unlikely musical influences like never before, whilst still relating them back to their formative cultural influences. On a wider global perspective, Rykodisc and Hannibal Records chief Joe Boyd was another such proponent, mixing up jazz, flamenco and Malian kora sounds on the ground-breaking *Songhai* (Hannibal) album:

> There seems to be a pattern in the relationship of a country to its traditional music. An infatuation with Afro-American music comes to dominate the tastes, particularly of the young. Eventually the culture rediscovers its own folk music and begins to incorporate traditional elements and a respect for traditional cultural values into the mainstream of its popular culture. The pattern can be observed from Spain to India, from Zaire to Bulgaria. Unfortunately, it seems to have skipped over England.

speed the plough

Folk dance and club dance, paradoxically, have a surprising number of factors in common. They both form very insular clique-ridden scenes. Whilst the folk scene seems to be cautiously venturing away from the tried and trusted, the club scene morphs and mutates at ever-increasing speed, breeding new hybrids, formulas and mixes. Both work on the notion of 'handing down' from one to another, reinterpreting and then claiming as its own. In folk music, it was songs and dances through the generations; for the dance scene, the remix or 'borrowed' break might surface just hours after its introduction on a dance floor or via a 'white label' test pressing, thanks to the effects of sampling technology. Beats and rhythms were being handed down from DJ to DJ, borrowed, adapted and sampled using simple computer software which can be bought or blagged for next to nothing and operated in anyone's bedroom studio. New sounds and ideas developed at an alarmingly quick rate and the notion of 'performance' or passive entertainment was largely superseded by the heightened collective consciousness of the environment – if there was anyone on stage, they were usually no more important a part of the show than, say, the dancers. Rappers and toasters got up and did their bit on the mic, while all manner of mayhem was let loose via the myriad tambourines, whistles, air horns and assorted percussion instruments that were all part of the primal spirit of rave culture at its peak as the eighties turned into the nineties.

Whilst the techno sound of Ilford or Sheffield was in every way as local as the Rye fisherman's lament about 'Herrings' Heads', the predictably futile search for any vestiges of musical pub 'tradition' in the expected outposts of Suffolk or Sussex was far more likely to be met with televised football on a big screen. Although the rave generation were still aware of folk, it was in a largely different context, more often for the ironic appeal rather than a genuine love of the roots. In 1991, while the Ashbrook All Stars scored an unlikely hit with a record that sampled Steeleye's 'Gaudete', one still got the distinct impression that it may well have been the only folk record that they owned.

The parallels and paradoxes were never more evident than during the Cooking Vinyl years. At an Oyster Band gig at Newcastle Riverside in 1989, the band were in full flight, ripping through 'Tin Cans' – a predominantly instrumental dance tune – when a circle of teenagers gathered at the back of the club, with individuals or couples taking turns to express themselves in the middle of the circle. The first two couples were skilled and confident, obviously being familiar with some folk-dance steps. Then a young lad in a shell suit entered the circle, got down on his back and curled up in a ball and twirled around, break-dance-style, at once gaining generous applause from bemused onlookers.

Folk music, despite lacking a McLaren-style Svengali figure and any of the fashion accoutrements of the dance or punk scenes, finally made the front cover of *NME*. Michelle Shocked was profiled along with the headline 'Folk Gets Its Finger Out'. This issue was plotted and planned several weeks before by myself and the news editor at the time, Terry Staunton, sitting in a pub just off New Oxford Street. It was all about exploding a few myths. Their assertion that folk was 'fresh as tomorrow's French bread' still rings true to these ears now.

over the hills to glory

I'd been aware of the clichés – the Arran sweaters, the fingers in ears, the milkmaids and ploughboys, the 'fol-de-rols' in the hay – and I was bemused as to how a nation was so keen to take the piss out of its own heritage. Warm beer, bubble and squeak and garden gnomes were one thing, but with a musical heritage encompassing The Copper Family from Rottingdean, Sussex, Fred Jordan, a Shrophire farm-worker, Norfolk carpenter Walter Pardon, and not least The Watersons from Yorkshire, arguably described as the first family of folk, there was much to shout home about too. It appeared to me as fascinating and faintly untouchable at the same time, like entering some inner sanctum, a land where notions of tradition assumed totally new and often surreal qualities, where the past merged with the present and the future all at once.

For Jonny Trunk, founder of Trunk Records, folk music is an ongoing voyage of discovery even though he might often be looking to the past: 'The folk list seems to be growing as I find more obscure people who made superb but unsuccessful music in the sixties. I love the way they could turn something so harshly traditional into something so beautiful. And to me that music just improves with age.' Trunk had been releasing unusual left-field soundtrack music through his highly respected label and had also started London's only alternative folk gathering, Folkey Dokey, because 'it gave us an opportunity to get the shove ha'penny board out in public'. His earliest influences had encompassed children's TV music such as *Fingermouse* and *Play School* – 'simple, melodic, appealing music that you could always sing along with'. Throughout his early teens Trunk hated such music, but soon came his epiphany. 'I saw *The Wicker Man*, which has superb British folk music made by a gay American, which changed everything for me. I'd never heard such raw passion or such sex and simplicity before. Weird adult nursery rhymes, breathtaking instrumental music. I was hooked.' For Trunk, the essence of folk music is 'English people singing brutal songs about love, life, death, sex and items of food in a simple, melodic style'.

American folk music had only made a marginal impact on me at this point. I'd been aware of Peter, Paul and Mary, The Sandpipers, The Mamas and Papas, Buffy St Marie and The Kingston Trio, and the legacy the music had created in the early sixties. But traditional and country-based music in general remained central to the emergence of much North American pop and rock, reinvented by the likes of Bob Dylan, Joni Mitchell, The Band, Simon and Garfunkel, Kate and Anna McGarrigle and Gram Parsons, not to mention the phenomenon which swept through hippy culture, known as The Grateful Dead – and popularized country and bluegrass singers such as Dolly Parton, The Louvin Brothers, Emmylou Harris and Linda Ronstadt. The late eighties saw a mini-revival from the younger elements of 'new wave' US folk, led by The Horseflies from New York State and Boiled In Lead from Minneapolis.

Today, the roots are still feeding branches. The soundtrack to *O Brother, Where Art Thou?* has introduced roots-based artists such as Ralph Stanley, Alison Krauss and Gillian Welch to eager new ears. And now the Spinal Tap crew have turned their attentions to folk, US-style, with the film and DVD release of *A Mighty Wind*, a benign debunking of the benevolent, right-on leftish earnestness that still characterizes the folk world just as much today as it did back in the days of the sixties' folk revival. The title song alone, 'A Mighty Wind', somehow sums up the mood that still exists in folk clubs or primary schools across the country today.

> *A mighty wind's a-blowing, across the land, across the sea.*
> *It's blowin' peace and freedom, it's blowin' equality.*

Unlike America, Britain had pretty much lost its rural culture as early as the eighteenth century, with the effects of the Industrial Revolution being felt; folk song survived in the music halls, but scarcely at all elsewhere. Collectors like Cecil Sharp and Australian classical composer Percy Grainger luckily had their notebooks in hand, but there was a generation looming who knew little of the 'handed down' heritage of their parents and grandparents.

By the sixties and seventies, the revivalists had to construct an entire British folk tradition from whatever they could gather from the past. British talents such as Davy Graham, Martin Carthy, June Tabor, The Watersons and Dick Gaughan were making strong records.

Up-and-coming American folkies from Dylan to Paul Simon also came over here to play. Then a whole sub-genre known as folk rock emerged in the seventies led by artists such as Fairport Convention, The Albion Band, East of Eden, Gryphon and The JSD Band. Amazing Blondel were a very unusual band who played music that sounded very old. Like a bunch of wandering minstrels with lutes, they sang of noble ladies and castles, with a slightly wacky humour. These artists tapped into the college circuit, and the fringes of the burgeoning progressive-rock bandwagon, though the more public face of folk in Britain had descended into TV humour and parody with cod-folk stand-up comedy from the likes of Mike Harding, Jasper Carrott, Richard Digance and Fred Wedlock. As Charlotte Grieg noted in the *Independent* in January 2004, 'It seemed that there was little place in the clubs any longer for the strange, dark music at the heart of the British folk tradition. There were a few exceptions, of course – notably the club at Cecil Sharp House in north-west London, where people still liked to sing folk ballads – but, on the whole, people who wanted that kind of perverted stuff had to look elsewhere.'

Shirley and Dolly Collins, from Hastings in Sussex, have long been regarded as central to the English folk-song revival of the 1960s and 1970s. Their mother's family kept alive a great love of traditional song, but they were known best for their innovation. In 1964, Shirley recorded the landmark jazz-folk fusion of *Folk Roots, New Routes*, with Davy Graham. *Anthems In Eden* (BGO) featured a suite of songs centred around the changes in rural England brought about by the First World War, and is still seen as influential with its ensemble of early-music instruments – rebecs, sackbuts and crumhorns, offering a fresh-sounding alternative to the predominance of the guitar. The album was followed by the starkly beautiful *Love, Death & The Lady* (Fledg'lin), and *No Roses* (Mooncrest), recorded in 1971 with the twenty-five musicians of the Albion Country Band, was a further experiment that grew into a triumph – a benchmark of British folk rock.

the world turned upside down

The folk-club environment itself wasn't one that I took to naturally. It seemed so overbearingly formal, with its neat rows of seats, its hushed reverence, its protocols and its own haughty anti-fashion presentation with the stiff use of certain words and formalities – 'and now, Ladies and Gentlemen…the raffle'. Its interval and floor-singer spots seemed equally archaic, even in the more go-ahead clubs such as The Chestnuts in Walthamstow, east London. At the time, I only just resisted the temptation to acquire a job lot of brown acid to slip into a few frothing real ales, if only to glimpse the possibilities of a world beyond the humdrum.

Nevertheless, I tiptoed in, and was quite awestruck with what I found, in places such as the oddly V-shaped upstairs room of a shabby, smoky Islington pub called the Empress Of Russia in December 1985. I still have a dodgy bootleg cassette recording of the night. It was an astounding gig, not just for the informal nature of the artists The Watersons, but for its sheer and honest vocal power, the shrill and nasal unaccompanied Yorkshire voices, as upfront and in my face as anything would ever be, as can be heard on collections such as *For Pence and Spicy Ale* and their debut *The Watersons* (both Topic), which includes the classic roving travellers' song '30 Foot Trailer'. They did also make albums with backing musicians, most notably one called *Bright Phoebus* by Mike and Lal Waterson (Trailer), which I've played to death since I got it. It's apparently as rare as hens' teeth.

Billy Bragg was a protagonist of 'urban folk', trying to bring together two quite political strands. The dynamic Essex-born travelling one-man band had clearly been inspired by punk music. But in 1984, there was the now infamous industrial strike by the Miners' Union in Britain, during which he went to play gigs in the minefields to show support. He discovered 'old men and women there, singing old songs, but they were more political and more focused than The Clash'. Tradition and political polemic came together, not for the first time, though for Bragg it was clearly a revelation:

> Because I also was aware of the folk traditions, I felt that these two traditions could come together. And it wasn't just me. The Pogues were very forceful also at the same time. It kind of represents a return to basic ideas: about communication, about community. That there was a community of people who feel strongly.

Struggle, politics and war in particular seem to bring out the very best in terms of folk song. Leon Rosselson has been an active and noted member of the British folk scene for almost forty years. His early songs were topical-satirical (some of them were featured on TV's satire show *That Was The Week That Was*), and he broadened out from there, absorbing different influences and experimenting with different song forms. His song 'The World Turned Upside Down' has been recorded and popularized by, among others, Dick Gaughan and Billy Bragg (who took it into the pop charts in 1985) and has been sung on numerous demonstrations in Britain and the US. His 'Ballad of a Spycatcher', ridiculing the UK ban on Peter Wright's book, went into the independent singles charts in 1987 in a version backed by Billy Bragg and The Oyster Band.

Elvis Costello's 'Shipbuilding', a minor chart hit when covered by Robert Wyatt, is arguably one of the greatest ever folk songs. One of the few to match it is Billy Bragg's 'Between The Wars'.

> *I was a miner, I was a docker*
> *I was a railwayman between the wars*
> *I raised a family in time of austerity*
> *With sweat at the foundry, between the wars*
> *I paid the union and as times got harder*
> *I looked to the government to help the working man*
> *They brought prosperity, down at the armoury*
> *We're arming for peace, me boys, between the wars*
>
> *I kept the faith and I kept voting,*
> *Not for the iron fist, but for the helping hand*
> *Theirs is a land with a wall around it*
> *And mine is a faith in my fellow man*
> *Theirs is a land of hope and glory*
> *Mine is the green field and the factory floor*
> *Theirs are the skies all dark with bombers*
> *Mine is the peace we knew between the wars*
>
> *Call up the craftsmen, bring me a draughtsman*
> *Build me a path from cradle to grave*
> *And I'll give my consent to any government*
> *That does not deny a man a living wage*
> *Go find the young men, never to fight again*

Crossfade

Call up the banners from the days gone by
Sweet moderation, the heart of this nation,
Desert us not, we are between the wars

Without doubt, politics and folk song are inextricably connected, with folk song often giving voice to political expression and dissent. For Bragg, it can be traced back to Woody Guthrie, the father of the tradition: 'He's the first political songwriter. I have been inspired by The Clash and by Bob Dylan and by that generation of American singer-songwriters of the 1960s, but it goes back to Woody.'

As well as politics, community has always been a central strand to the ongoing folk tradition, whether through family heritage and connections, or through folk club and festival. John Gill: 'People's lives no longer have such a static base. These communities now have to be constructed whether it be through marketing, record sales, festivals or media coverage.'

Where did the clans gather? I visited the Cambridge Folk Festival for several years in the mid-to-late eighties, often accompanied by Cooking Vinyl label artists and once as stand-in drummer with Edward II. Many great highlights were to be had – most notably rousing sets from Louisiana band Beausoleil, Irish singer-songwriter Christy Moore, The Kipper Family (a spoof Copper Family 'tribute' from Trunch, Norfolk), and top-notch US singer-songwriters such as Loudon Wainwright, Butch Hancock, John Prine, Jimmie Dale Gilmore and Guy Clark.

Cambridge somehow wasn't enough. As well as folkies and a few beards, and even a fair few pewter tankards strapped to belts, it had rock fans and way too many youngsters to be really authentic. I needed a full dose of the hardcore. A friend whom I'd known well since school days, Dave Roberts, had been talking about the week-long Sidmouth Festival for some time, probably because his parents lived there at the time so he had an escape route. We finally decided to take the plunge in 1989. Aside from being a very hot week, it was to prove musically and culturally groundbreaking, as it confirmed to me that folk most definitely had a whole second side – called 'dance'.

I was totally oblivious at the time to the rivalry, perhaps even animosity, that existed between the song and dance elements

– each claiming that their own was the lifeblood of the scene and subsequently pouring scorn on the other as a lesser entity.

the star above the garter

I was familiar with the 'Floral Dance' most famously recorded by Brighouse and Rastrick Brass Band, who shot it up the English pop charts. I'd been to a couple of ceilidhs too, as I reached puberty. The first one was at a local school in my home town Leamington Spa at the age of fourteen, and it had almost succeeded in putting me off for life as girls aggressively stepped in and literally swept me off my feet to obscure dances which made no logical sense to me at the time and were also way too fast for my panicking adolescent brain to assimilate. But with the music now beginning to make some sort of sense, it all somehow began to fit into place, especially by listening to seminal seventies albums such as *Morris On* (Island) and The Albion Country Band's *Kicking Up The Sawdust* (BGO).

It all slotted into place for me at an Oyster Band Christmas ceilidh in Canterbury some time in the late eighties. That in itself was as fun as it gets, but it was at another occasion in Barham, a nearby village hall, that I had another landmark experience. Morris dancers ('sides' I believe they are called) had never really floated my boat – and the prospect of a side called the Shropshire Bedlams displaying their wares in a small village hall in Kent didn't really fill me with excitement. It was only when they started to put on their American-style football helmets that the surreal factor was upped somewhat, never mind the sticks, which were somehow being clapped together with more than the usual amount of gusto. To see them sliding around the floor of the hall in football helmets was an unexpected revelation as well as being deliciously at odds with expectations.

At Sidmouth Festival, I fully realized what a sensual and sexual experience country dancing could be. After the initial disappointment of walking into the Sidmouth festival-arena area and confronting a Zimmer-frame sales stand as the first stall, things could only get vibier. Thankfully, they did once we set foot in the late-night-extra marquee on the outskirts of the town, curiously still alive and kicking well after midnight – not what folk festivals were normally known for. The sexual tension in the air was palpable. Spirits were high, alcohol had lubricated the wheels to the extent that the likes of myself could go and make total fools of ourselves on the dance floor and not be totally self-conscious about it. But in terms of rootsy raunchiness, never mind speed dating, barn dancing delivered the physical body language and the ideal forum for flirtation. A most enjoyable way to get to know everyone in the room extremely fast. In terms of social interaction and community, the barn dance knocked me sideways as well as – temporarily at least – knocking the concept of the rave into a cocked hat in terms of unbridled fun and sheer passion. It was a good old-fashioned 'knees up' at its most unadulterated.

But all was not as it seemed. Where were the delineations between Morris dancing, barn dancing and English country dancing? Certainly, I wasn't aware of such a rich rural dance heritage, centred largely around players born in the nineteenth century such as Scan Tester, Walter and Daisy Bulwer, and Billy Cooper, later to be enshrined in compilations and reissues on labels such as Topic and East Anglia's Veteran imprint. Their music was largely for country dances, quadrilles and the round dance derived from the waltz and the polka, once popular at harvest frolics and servants' balls. There are indeed direct links with the church string bands described in Hardy's *Under The Greenwood Tree* and the old village bands associated with friendly societies, flower walks and fair days, all a world away from the skateboard park or youth club of today. Today's teenagers are far more likely to be at least more familiar with Irish dancing via *Riverdance* than they are to be aware of the more leaden and formal humpty-dumpty English tunes and steps. Musically you can hear it in the notes and the straighter way the tunes are played, contrasted with the sexier slides of Irish or even Scottish traditional music.

According to Cecil Sharp's *The Country Dance Book*:

The Morris is a ceremonial, spectacular and professional dance. Performed by men only, it has no sex characteristics. It is remarkable for the absence of the love motive from all its movements…there is scarcely a single dance in which the performers so much as touch each other. Finally, it must be understood that the Morris is not, primarily, a pleasure dance.

So, clearly, given the number of Cheshire-cat grins on faces, it had not been a Morris dance that I was at. By contrast, Sharp notes that 'The country dance still is the ordinary, everyday dance of the country-folk', for the pleasure that it afforded the performers, and the social intercourse that it provided. In *The Art of Wooing and Complimenting*, Edward Phillips says, 'Ladies, you will be pleased to dance a country dance or two, for 'tis that which makes you truly sociable, and us truly happy; being like the chorus of a song where all the parts sing together.'

But despite its steadfast Englishness at the time, the sound of an English country-dance band in full flight – as on the *English Country Music* collection on Topic – is still an intense experience to savour. Billy Cooper (1883), Walter Bulwer (1888) and Daisy Bulwer (c.1892) were active musicians in rural Norfolk for over half a century. These recordings, made together with visiting friends in the Bulwers' cottage in the village of Shipdham, capture the essential vitality and robustness of the music they played for dancing in pubs and at Saturday-night hops and wedding parties. Curiously, though the sound is as 'garden shed' as it gets, the ensemble sound has a strange element of the exotic, no doubt due to the instrumentation used: hammered dulcimer, melodeon, mandolin-banjo, pipe and tabor, concertina, all of which were now far from commonplace in popular music. As John Gill noted on a BBC *Rhythms Of The World* documentary on English traditional music in 1989: 'The sound is probably more alien than rai or bhangra records which use more familiar synth and drum sounds.'

Somehow England – and Englishness – for so many people had its boots stuck firmly in the mud. It represented a not-in-my-backyard, mind-yer-own-business separatism that was phlegmatic to the point of being austere. With the advent of quick and inexpensive air travel and the dawn of the 'jet-set' in the sixties, the suggestion of travel, the exotic was suddenly on offer. And best of all, any possibility of escapism from humdrum England. The image of multicultural London and to a lesser extent other cities such as Bristol, Manchester and Birmingham and their hip urban-street culture also captured the imagination, not least that of a turn-of-millennium Labour government determined to up its credentials with the cool and the young. But being English still wasn't something to shout about, particularly given the antipathy towards its own (and the closely allied US) foreign policy. And celebrating the traditions of a largely agrarian and very conservative sector of old England was probably the height of non-fashion. It made more sense, given the times, to broaden one's perspective away from purer notions of Englishness. John Gill noted that 'reggae is a good example of a contemporary English folk music that is alive and absorbing a variety of urban influences'.

The biggest blow of all to English country-dance music has probably been the ruthless facelift given to country pubs by the large breweries since the 1970s in particular. By substituting steaks for skittles and passive satellite football for step dancing, they've ensured increasing profits at the expense of an active continuing tradition – in the pubs at any rate. But despite all this, its legacy lives on, although in mutated form. Though you will still see Morris men playing spontaneously in the corner of a pub in Ledbury, Ashbourne or Bungay, you are also likely to see bands such as Blowzabella or The Oyster Ceilidh Band at many UK festivals. And country dancing looks set for a revival, through interest from people outside the folk world, who are generally curious for something new and community-based, even if they are lacking in their knowledge of the history and heritage of set dancing.

bringing in the luck

Talking to Joe Boyd at the time, the personification of English folk culture, for him, was the pool of songs and chants that dominated the football terraces during the weekly match and the not-always-friendly interaction between rival supporters. Although we English cherish our history and traditions – ancient churches and universities, Tudor buildings, ancient manuscripts and Shakespearean heritage – when it comes to songs and dances, for some reason people start to shuffle about and feel embarrassed. The tweeness of Morris dancing in particular invites cynicism. Like maypole dancing, it was banned by Cromwell, which certainly lends it an air of pagan temptation. But those who get out to see the one or more of the 350 or so folk song and dance festivals each year usually love it. With Sidmouth International Festival reaching its fiftieth anniversary this year, and Cambridge its fortieth as I write, the traditions still have a strong focus as larger events.

It is the smaller, more informal gatherings – many on the streets of our market towns – that are the real jewel in the crown. On May Day itself, celebrations take place all over the country. In Rochester, Kent at 5.32 am on 1 May, the Jack-in-the-Green, a leafy creature about the size of a telephone box, symbolizing spring, is aroused at the top of Bluebell Hill. A circle of twelve Beltane fires, one for each month of the year, is lit and the Jack is greeted by a May Day song, followed by revelry and dancing. The Furry Dance takes place in Helston, a quaint old coinage town in West Cornwall, emblazoned with the first greenery of spring, particularly bluebells and hazel. It takes the form of a dignified procession, with the men wearing top hats, the women their finest dresses, and the children all in white. The Mayday Floral Dance follows a traditional route, even passing through people's homes, shops and gardens.

The Abbots Bromley Horn Dance, first performed at the Barthelmy Fair in Staffordshire in August 1226, is another of the few ritual rural customs to survive the passage of time. Every September, antlered figures, standing in two lines facing each other, begin a dance punctuated by the click of antlers meeting. The horn dancers, comprising six deer-men, a fool, hobby horse, bowman and Maid Marian, perform their dance to music provided by a melodeon player at locations throughout the village and its surrounding farms and pubs, involving a walk of about ten miles.

For Jonny Trunk and many others, the battle for preserving British tradition goes much deeper than boycotting the nearest Harvester Inn or donning antler horns once a year:

Many traditions have been lost or at least have disappeared from the mainstream. If you think about it, much of the ceremony and custom was based on events we all depended on so very much – the beginning of spring, the celebration of harvest. These days we have what we all want when we want, whatever the season, so those celebrations are lost. But when you look for and find traditional events going on in this country, they really are wonderful and often quite moving, but you have to go out of your way to find them. I stumbled across a traditional village May Day Fayre this last year and the dancing was not around a maypole. No, it was the local line-dancing troop in cowboy boots strutting to Shania Twain. Lord help us all.

we won't go home till morning

In a thread about folk on The Big Chill Web forum, The King Of The Delta Blues (not the Blues player) saw folk culture as:

> a liberating experience that touches deep inside, and also relates to the essence of ancestry and lineage that the best folk song and dance achieve. It kind of makes me think about Jung and the collective unconscious thing. Like ancestral knowledge being passed down through generations. I tried to read up more on this but got a bit swamped down and then got me book nicked.

For Sketchy, 'it fires up a torch inside of you, particularly in combination with fungalstars and the sort of equinox air that steals your breath away, s'roots'n'culture innit'.

So, in the interim, how have things moved on in folk circles? Well, the answer is not that much in many respects. At least, not in the anticipated areas. Whilst in the late nineties, The Watersons and Martin Carthy were receiving nominations and MBEs, and daughter Eliza Carthy was being featured in broadsheet supplements, the dance aspect of the scene appeared to have stalled after the early promise shown by the likes of Cock and Bull, The Ran Tan Band, Gas Mark V, Tiger Moth, Tickled Pink and Geckoes. Although, hearing Whapweazel from Northumberland at last year's Towersey Festival in rural Oxfordshire, there is evidence of stirrings in the undergrowth, despite their clinging to more folk-rock style musicianship patterns.

Whilst the younger fraternity of the last twenty years – Kathryn Tickell, Eliza Carthy, Kate Rusby, Jim Moray – continue to lead from the front, one of the most significant developments has been via the more experimental end of the electronic music scene, a distance away from any folk-rock notions of 'rogue folk' and agit-punk style favoured by The Oyster Band, Blythe Power, Chumbawamba in the mid-to-late eighties, or from the more Celtic powerhouse dance-floor hybrid offered by Afro-Celts, Martyn Bennett or Shooglenifty. Four Tet's *Rounds* (Domino) set the agenda for a new style of folktronica, a more introverted and reflective contemporary style born out of the aftermath of the dance and electronica era of the nineties, where producers were initially conceiving the music in their bedroom on a computer, before taking it out live. Adem's *Homesongs* (Domino) and James Yorkston and The Athletes' *Moving Up Country* (Domino) come from the same direction, fusing a computer-savvy freshness with a purity born of the acoustic approach.

The Memory Band released probably the most important album to date of this new wave in May 2004, entitled simply *The Memory Band* (TMB, 2004). Conceived by founder Stephen Cracknell, responsible for several Gorodisch recordings on the Leaf label and a member of the legendary Trunk Records, it started as an imaginary band, built inside a computer and inspired by a live soundtrack that he worked on as an accompaniment to *The Wicker Man* at The Big Chill, Eastnor Castle, 2002. The Memory Band immediately showed a predilection for confronting the darker side of English song on tracks such as 'Fanny Adams', which alluded to a brutal child murder in Alton, Hampshire in 1867, as well as visiting the ancient rites of wassailing on 'Calling On'. The line-up was made real by the gradual involvement of musicians, playing violins, harmoniums, guitars and 'whatever else is available', with a view to 'exploring new musical languages, with plenty of singing and dancing on a Sunday', whether derived from Kraut-rock, hip hop, northern soul or the folk tradition. For Cracknell, 'The entire body of music, from ancient to modern is regarded as fair game for plundering'. In the words of the *Guardian*'s Peter Paphides, 'The history of folk music is being bastardized by urbanites…and long may they continue if this exercise in agrarian spookiness is anything to go by.'

Just as Friday-night 'knees-up' ceilidhs in the seventies at Camden's home of folk music, Cecil Sharp House, put the boot into the sedate establishment which was the English Folk Dance and Song Society, as well as bringing a distinctly urban grittiness to what had been seen by many as an essentially rural, time-warped curio, today sees the updated idea of the ceilidh or country dance set to become popular once more as a new social forum. Meanwhile, The Memory Band, Four Tet, James Yorkston, Adem, the Fife-based Fence Collective and Alice McLaughlin from the London-based Soul Folk collective are praised by fans and critics alike for their fresh take on folk composition.

Hey Nonny Yes!

recommended listening

Various – *English Country Music* (Topic)
The Watersons – *The Watersons* (Topic)
The High Level Ranters – *Northumberland For Ever* (Topic)
Shirley Collins – *No Roses* (Pegasus)
Fairport Convention – *Liege and Lief* (Island)
Steeleye Span – *Please to See The King* (Charisma)
Richard and Linda Thompson – *Pour Down Like Silver* (Island)
The Albion Country Dance Band – *Kicking Up The Sawdust* (BGO)
Andrew Cronshaw – *Wade In The Flood* (Transatlantic)
Dick Gaughan – *Handful Of Earth* (Topic)
Richard Thompson – *Strict Tempo* (Hannibal)
Martin Carthy – *Out of the Cut* (Topic)
The Oyster Band – *Twenty Golden Tie Slackeners* (Running Man/
      Pukka)
Billy Bragg – *Back To Basics* (Go Discs)
The King's Singers – *Watching The White Wheat* (EMI)
Blowzabella – *The Blowzabella Wall Of Sound* (Plant Life)
Edward II – *Let's Polkasteady* (Cooking Vinyl)
The Waterboys – *Fisherman's Blues* (Ensign)
Sandy Denny – *Who Knows Where The Time Goes* (Island Box Set)
The Barely Works – *The Big Beat* (Cooking Vinyl)
James Yorkston and The Athletes – *Moving Up Country* (Domino)
Four Tet – *Rounds* (Domino)
Adem – *Homesongs* (Domino)
Various – *Stepping Up* (Topic)
The Memory Band – *The Memory Band* (TMB)

recommended reading

FRoots magazine
Cecil J Sharp – *The Country Dance Book Parts 1 and 2* (Stiles)
Dave Jones – *The Roots of Welsh Border Morris* (pamphlet)
Douglas Kennedy – *English Folk Dancing* (Bell)
Charles Kightly – *The Customs and Ceremonies Of Britain* (Thames
      and Hudson)
The *Independent*
www.jazzdimensions.de

nostalgia for an acid state of mind

Tony Marcus

In July 1990 *The Face* ran an interview with Marshall Jefferson. Marshall made what is probably the fourth house record (1986's *Move Your Body*) and his *Open Your Eyes* (from 1988 but possibly 1987) might well have been the first ambient house record. Marshall is a place for beginnings. In that 1990 interview he told *The Face* his secret was he had never stopped loving disco and never gotten over hearing Frankie Knuckles play at Chicago's Warehouse Club. It might only be 1990 and the beginning of the 'dance-music decade' but Marshall had already been earning his living DJing, travelling and producing for some time – moving at the speed of drugs and beats. He spoke like a character from a James Jones novel (*The Thin Red Line*) – a grunt that spent too long at the front line. 'I'm old, man. I'm 30 now. I just want to sleep.'

The Face journalist (John McReady) lays on a treat for Marshall. He slides a tape into the stereo of the car. McReady writes:

> It's made up of disco classics by MFSB, Barry White, Carl Bean and Jean Carne. Marshall remembers them all from the Warehouse. In a multi-storey car park in the city, he is hypnotized by Carl Bean's seminal gay anthem 'Born This Way'. Photographer Mike Kerry can't get him out of the car to take pictures of him. He smiles and turns the volume up again. 'Oh…Oh…man.

Marshall's reverie is for a lost gay black American dance floor – a secret world – as Jon Savage later theorized, where gay black men who in many cases were ostracized by their communities, families and church formed a new church, new family and community. And enjoyed nights of drugs, sex and (disco) thunder. None of the most famous of these clubs – The Loft, Sanctuary, Warehouse, Muzik Box, Paradise Garage – was still running by 1990. Perhaps Marshall was experiencing that power of memory to conjure a place that no longer exists in the physical world. Perhaps he was right back in a hot human forest, blasted by noise, amyl, dope, acid, MDMA, cocaine, PCP, youth, love, lust, skin, noise, vanity, ego and wonderful promise. Or he could have been remembering what it was like to be young.

Dance or rave culture is the most nostalgic of all contemporary youth and music cultures. Perhaps because it was built upon a vanished and poorly documented foundation – it is only recently that writers have started to tell the lost history of disco, Paradise Garage et al. And the story is always about irrecoverable loss – the only good recent movie, Whit Stillman's *The Last Days of Disco*, sensed the subject was somehow about passing, the story of a culture about to end. Disco isn't the only root of house and rave and dance but it's the most vanished road that leads to the present – if you look back the way behind disappears. And if you look back in Ecstasy then the journey is misty, glittering and sentimental. Dance music is also the most nostalgic of all youth cultures because of its drug of choice. Before it was a party drug, MDMA was a drug favoured by therapists – it brought people together, they said. It helped patients confront trauma. It induced empathy. It made people feel soft and open and special and vulnerable. It made them romantic and given over to reflection.

The therapists liked to call the drug ADAM. The killing joke played on the rave generation was the LA drug dealer who gave MDMA the name 'Ecstasy'. The story is told in Bruce Eisner's *Ecstasy: The MDMA Story*. According to Eisner the dealer called the drug Ecstasy because he thought the name would 'sell'. Ecstasy has got more of a ring to it than 3,4-methylenedioxymethamphetamine – first synthesized by scientists working for Merck in 1912 who couldn't figure out a commercial use for the drug. There's some evidence the US military tried it as a 'truth drug' in the 1950s and there are references to MDA (MDMA-lite) as the 'love drug' in the late sixties. The current MDMA scene began in 1976 when Alexander Shulgin resynthsized MDMA. He passed it around the US therapy community, who found it useful, and there was an attempt to keep the drug off the street. The therapists and researchers didn't want a repeat of what happened with LSD – when the research and therapeutic community lost control of what they felt was a useful, revelatory drug. Speaking to *WIRED* last year, Shulgin remains unhappy that MDMA got 'out'. Shulgin said:

> Outside of the therapeutic community there was, as there almost always is in these cases, a person or a few people who figured out that they could sell MDMA and make a lot of money. They were the ones who gave it the name, 'Ecstasy'. The drug should have been called 'empathy' for what it did, but I believe they felt that 'empathy' didn't have the same sensational ring to it. So they called it 'Ecstasy', which is a strange name but it stuck. And it was sold more and more at bars, parties, what have you.

There's an interesting chill-out or dinner-party game you can play... what would the rave or dance scene have been like if Ecstasy had been marketed as Empathy? Because Ecstasy suggests Paradise and Paradise is always Lost or Remembered. The story of Paradise on Earth is always the same. Paradise is always lost and man (and also woman) is forever haunted by the glimpse or taste of what they know is their real and lasting or everlasting home. Ecstasy is the mother of all nostalgias. Like all potent brand names and magic words Ecstasy brought its own history into the drug and possibly also the drug experience. The word is religious or spiritual in origin but Ecstasy doesn't feature in the Bible – either the New or Old Testament. The word is first popularized in the writings of Christian mystics from about 1200 onwards – people like St Teresa of Avila, Augustine, Thomas Aquinas, St John of The Cross, Catherine of Siena, Hildegard von Bingen and William Blake. This Christian ecstasy is about union with the divine soul, says Evelyn Underhill in her book *Mysticism*. Ecstasy was seeing Heaven or touching God. Underhill writes: 'It represents the greatest possible extension of the spiritual consciousness in the direction of Pure Being: a profound experience of Eternal Life.' She adds, 'The word has became a synonym for joyous exaltation, for the inebriation of the Infinite.' The experience is also, notes Underhill, 'temporary'.

Religious ecstasy, like MDMA, is always receding – the renaming of MDMA was peculiarly prescient. There have only been a handful of funded studies that examine Ecstasy. In 1987 Dr Jerome Bell and Marsha Rosenbaum received a grant from the US National Institute of Drug Abuse for a 'sociological exploration of MDMA users'. Their findings suggest that Ecstasy, out of all drugs, lends itself to a nostalgic vision. 'An oft-repeated sentiment was that the first time was the best. This perception tended to change for some users as time went on, but others continued to feel that there was special magic to the initial MDMA experience(s).' And that: 'Some respondents believed that one could only have a certain number of good MDMA experiences before the drug "lost its magic"'.

The distance between the 'magic' of the first pill and the diminished returns that followed became more poignant and almost operatic when it happened on a grand scale – when the drug was mainstreamed. Writing in *The Face* in November 1991 around the beginning of the 'Great British Ecstasy Boom', Mandi James records that: 'As tolerance levels develop and people still crave and chase that initial buzz, greater quantities are being consumed and a short-list of ailments have appeared. Regular users complain regularly of insomnia, involuntary twitching, hot flushes, backache, tooth problems, cramps and susceptibility to minor ailments such as flu and sore throats.' Of course the cramps and flushes may be caused by Ecstasy over-use – and there is a caveat here about what exactly is in the various pills – and also the raver's 'lifestyle' – staying up late, smoking, being in close proximity to other smokers, exposure to cold night air, poor diet and junk food – if the greatly mythologized 'Ribena' carton is typical of the Ecstasy user's diet circa 1991.

The very resonant agony of Ecstasy is that MDMA is purportedly so very nice. The very niceness of the experience was documented in the research of US psychiatrist Dr George Greer who from 1980 to 1985, along with his wife, conducted over 100 therapy sessions with MDMA for eighty individuals. Their work remains the largest published study of the therapeutic use of the drug. Greer's research data includes the experiences of a married couple in their early thirties who were initially given 75mg of MDMA, then three doses of 50mg at intervals of forty-five minutes, ninety minutes and four hours after the initial dose (UK Customs reckon 80mg is the MDMA content of the 'average pill'). Greer quotes a letter from the woman, writing two weeks after the MDMA experience. 'I wish I could be writing to tell you that the exhilaration both (my husband) and I felt two weeks ago is still alive… but with a return to the daily world of responsibilities, the feeling has diminished. Not that it's left completely: what has remained is the memory of that (day) and the clarity of thought and emotion it left me with. And that is very precious to me.' She adds that on the drug, 'I fell in love with (my husband) all over again.'

Greer comes to a startling conclusion: Ecstasy offers a 'homecoming', a restoration of the natural state of man – or woman. 'Some of our patients said that under the influence of MDMA, and for days to years afterwards, they "feel more loving", "can easily forgive pain of the past" or "let go of grudges and misunderstandings". We believe these results were not caused by MDMA, but were achieved by the patients making decisions based on what they learned during the MDMA sessions, and by their remembering and applying those decisions for as long as they were able to and willing to after the session was over. We believe this occurred because taking MDMA with an intention to learn, with an attitude of acceptance…enabled people to experience their true nature, which is essentially loving and forgiving.'

When I used to take a lot of MDMA I used to feel, for as long the drug was at its most intense, that I'd fallen out of time. And sometimes, especially when I looked at other people on Ecstasy who were standing or moving near me, and also far 'gone', I sensed none of us wanted to come back. The worst thing about being really into Ecstasy is when the drug starts to fade. That's when you go looking for another pill. The mysterious thing about Ecstasy is where the drug takes you – it might feel like paradise or ecstasy or 'home'. I think most users, even if it was years since they last took a pill, harbour a strange, secret nostalgia for that memory, that drug-place, that experience.

The word 'nostalgia' itself means a kind of sickness or longing for 'home'. The word was 'invented' in 1688 by Johannes Hofer, at the time a Swiss medical student describing symptoms he observed in people working and living far from the countries of their birth. Nostalgia comes from the Greek *nostos*, meaning to return home, and the Latin *algia* or pain. Hofer's nostalgia is about the pain of longing to return home.

Nostalgia was a real disease, he declared, something that started in the heart or imagination and led to physical symptoms that could result in death. Symptoms included insomnia, anxiety, anorexia, palpitations, melancholy and thoughts of suicide. Military doctors throughout the seventeenth century diagnosed numberless cases of nostalgia – mainly in the ranks of soldiers, often press-ganged into service and forced to serve in appalling conditions.

The history of nostalgia is the story of a word that moves from the medical to the cultural sphere. In her theory/history text *The Future of Nostalgia*, Svetlana Boym says that by the twentieth century nostalgia is no longer a disease of the body but a 'historical emotion'. It is nothing to be ashamed of, she argues, nostalgia isn't necessarily about sentiment or weakness or even fear. Boym writes that nostalgias may be strong and even visionary – they can represent a clearly felt idealism. 'Creative nostalgia reveals the fantasies of the age, and it is in those fantasies and potentialities that the future is born. One is nostalgic not for the past the way it was, but for the past the way it could have been. It is this past perfect that one strives to realize in the future.'

There was a moment in the late eighties when it looked like acid house was going to finish the business of the sixties – or revive the best myths in the book of pop. The first description of 'acid house' club Shoom in the *NME* from October 1988 presents an unbelievable recreation of a decades-old fantasy. 'At the end of each night, the crowd hold hands and the DJ plays The Plastic Ono Band's "Give Peace a Chance". It sounds more sixties than the sixties.' Shoom DJ and founder Danny Rampling later told Matthew Collin: 'The way I was feeling at that point was the golden age was dawning. Aquarius was on us.' Collin, writing in his book *Altered State*, noted the Shoom crowd had (almost) no terms of reference with which to describe the experience. 'Because of their very nature, the Shoomers weren't about to write a manifesto, so all they had were reconstructed hippie myths – "peace and love".'

The late eighties and nineties weren't the sixties but acid house and rave culture adopted the trappings of flower power. Rainbows, clouds, birds and videos of Woodstock and Pink Floyd would be projected on the walls of his new club The Trip, Nicky Holloway told *i-D* in June 1988. In *Altered State*, Matthew Collin recalls the Sunrise Mystery Trip 88: 'As dawn broke, people frolicked with the horses and gathered flowers to weave through each other's hair.' It is all too beautiful, too Woodstock and astral-child Bolan. By the middle of 1988 the connection was explicit – people were talking about a new 'Summer of Love'. An editorial in *The Face*, July 1990, explained: 'The "Summer of Love" slogan first appeared on T-shirts around this time in '88 when the acid/Balearic boom was at its peak, when clubbers opened their minds and loosened their clothes and the party seemed like it would never end. Many of us felt it could never happen again.' Many 1988–1991 ravers/Shoomers may have falsely (or truly) believed they were experiencing a 'Summer of Love' based on not so much an informed reading of the late sixties but a nostalgic construct of the summers of 1967 to 1970. Its unlikely anyone would be calling for a 'Summer of Love' if they had read Joan Didion's *Slouching Towards Bethlehem*, which visits and examines late sixties San Francisco. Didion records the sexual exploitation of young girls on drugs and the 'High Nursery' where three-year-olds take LSD. She says the Summer of Love created the bedrock for a new submission, not freedom. Didion predicts Manson (Charles) when she describes late-sixties flower-power kids as weak and confused people who made themselves weaker and more confused through drugs – grown-up children running around looking for a leader.

The oft-repeated narrative of London acid house is of a 'secret' Paradise ruined or blown open by mass take-up and tabloid exposure. The truth of the story is an extraordinarily rapid mainstream exposure of a small drug-party sub-culture. There's probably a marketing parable in here somewhere, a story about the potency of certain cries and symbols as 'Acieed' and 'Smiley' travelled from Shoom – where they were private fetishes and battle cries – into the tabloids and the charts. If Shoom started around November 1987 (or January 1988) by August 1988 the game was up (or on). The clubs section of *i-D* noted in August 1988: 'When you get 2,500 people at The Camden Palace every Friday screaming "Acieeed!" and waving their hands in the air you know that the end is near. You know that what started off as a cry of dance-floor orgasm in Ibiza has now replaced "Wo-oh! Wo-oh!" as the sound of the suburbs. "It's ridiculous how fast acid house has crossed over," Colin Faver says.' Around the same time the *NME* used the TV show *The Hitman And Her* – the Pete Waterman-fronted clubland TV show – as a litmus test. 'Peter Waterman encourages the delirious mass of Sharons and Kevins to yell "Acieeed!"'

Of all the myths and stories of raving, very few DJs or writers have discussed the scene in terms of a mass, self-administered and unguided therapy session. Which is a very real possibility. And why it has sometimes been hard to shoehorn the history of dance-floor music into the pre-existing forms set by rock'n'roll – great LPs, tours, biographies, etc. – because in many ways the music isn't what the raving thing is about. And it should be obvious that a regular gathering where a group of people will take Ecstasy, and even large amounts of Ecstasy together, could or will be a very sensitive gathering. It is a drug that makes people open and makes them weak – nightclubs have always been 'killing grounds', places for sexual predators and perhaps drug and other criminals. As Dr Jerome Bell and Marsha Rosenbaum discovered when they interviewed a hundred Dallas Ecstasy users: 'The most frequently reported spiritual effect was a profound feeling of connectedness with all of nature and humankind.'

Speaking to *The Face* in November 1990 Danny Rampling explained why he was steering clear of what was then a huge and ever growing legal/illegal rave scene. 'I prefer to stay with what we started with – small parties. I didn't agree with the big raves, OK, it's fun to have that many people together, but it lost the whole meaning of the scene. The peace vibe and friendliness was taken away by the greed.' And perhaps more interestingly, if you believe that a room full of people on MDMA is really a therapy and not a club scene, Rampling explained why he closed Shoom. 'What we started out with was totally different to how it ended up. That upset me. I wish people had looked deeper and seen it for what it was – breaking down all those barriers and giving people a good time.'

There's always been a terrible duality about the acid-house experience – the high, obviously, always leads to a low – the 'innocent' scene becomes corrupt, the playground ruined, the Paradise spoiled. The fragile love or therapy space is crushed by a brute 'outside' reality. Media about the scene is nearly always in some kind of schism, terminally bouncing from one side of the contradiction to the other, never able to resolve itself. There was a genuine element of shock – those involved in the early days of acid house experienced violent change, initially into Paradise and then, just as rapidly, an equal and opposite force catapulting them in another direction. These conditions are perfect for nostalgia, argues Fred Davis in his *Yearning for Yesterday: A Sociology of Nostalgia*. Davis writes: 'Nostalgia thrives on transition, on the subjective discontinuities that engender our yearning for continuity.' 'Looking back,' wrote Sarah Champion in 1990 (in her book *And God Created Manchester*) 'it all seems so simple, so perfect, so naive. It was the very beginning. The beginning of something which would soon sweep the country. Something already taking hold in London. It was like the very first acid tests in the sixties. No one really knew what they were dealing with. In this pure, wonderful state, it could not last.'

Just as the tabloid/mainstream adoption of 'acid house' created violent discontinuity, similarly a growing awareness of the hidden costs of a drug culture stripped the astral glitter. Famously, Tony Wilson closed Manchester's Haçienda in response to the gangs; Sean Ryder discussed the changes with *The Face* in January 1990. 'E were great two years ago, y'know. It made everything peaceful. But now the violence is coming back in the Manchester clubs. There's too much of freebasin' going on. All the lads we know in London...it's the same.' Interviewed in Collin's *Altered State*, Terry Farley described a Sunrise party – Farley relishes the chance to play Dante, the 'good man' wandering in a hell of drug dealers shouting Es and trips while young girls fall to their knees and vomit. 'It was very cold and it was very obvious that it wasn't right. Something that had seemed all warm and cuddly at Shoom suddenly seemed really cold and rather nasty.'

The standard riff on Ecstasy and Thatcher or rave and capitalism is that the Ecstasy scene presented a loving, caring society and natural riposte to Thatcherite capitalism. A text like *Class of '88* by promoter Wayne Anthony, details the rave scene from a promoter's perspective – a distinction then emerges not between Thatcher and Ecstasyland but Thatcherite capitalism and 'rave capitalism'. Although years before 'corporate clubbing', it was obvious the Ecstasy utopia would be unable to withstand the forces of capital. The greed of the promoters, the cost of the tickets, the endless rip-offs, complains Richard Norris in June 1989 in the *NME*: 'This doesn't feel like the Second Summer of Love. This feel's like BIG MONEY.' The same bitter tears in *i-D* magazine two summers later. Matthew Collin notes: 'Everyone's making money and nobody has any idealism left any more, or so it seems.' A few years ago, when the 'rich lists' were announced, it was noted that Fatboy Slim made something like £10 million or perhaps £20 million in just one year. I don't know if anyone has managed to work out the exact value of the post-Ecstasy economy – the revenues taken and turnovers amassed in drug sales, record sales, clothing sales, drink sales (at the bars of clubs), advertising, design, production, media, A&R, plugging, promotion – what is interesting is the interconnectedness of it all, the complete entanglement of an illegal drug economy with a 'legitimate' business and entertainment machine. It is easier to speak in poetic metaphor than economic theory. The nostalgic dream of squeezing sunshine from a summer of love is an easier story than a discussion about the early phases of new capitalism.

Perhaps it is strange these youth cultures have any truck with nostalgia at all. But the history of acid house or dance music is built on a mythology of long-lost Edens – The Haçienda, Madchester, Paradise Garage, Ron Hardy in Chicago, the Belleville Three in Detroit, Alex Patterson at Land of Oz...by 1991 these were being routinely described as ancient tales from a distant and epic past – even though they had only taken place just months or maybe two years previously. Milan Kundera has noted that nostalgia is a characteristic of youth – it is a young person's 'historical emotion'. In his novel *Ignorance* Kundera writes: 'The more vast the amount of time we have left behind us, the more irresistible is the voice calling us to return to it. This pronouncement seems to state the obvious, and yet it is false. Men grow old, the end draws near, each moment becomes more and more valuable, and there is no time to waste over recollections. It is important to understand the mathematical paradox in nostalgia: that it is most powerful in early youth, when the volume of life gone by is quite small.'

Youth culture craves history – the nostalgias of youth are part of a game to appear more grown-up – to have experienced enough history to own the right to feel nostalgic. Otherwise what can you wax misty about when you're eighteen? Your first day at school? First cig? Potty training? First pill, shag, fight, holiday or acne explosion? So much of rave and dance-music history is described as prehistory, something that happened thousands of years ago. For a long time you couldn't open a music magazine or talk to a DJ or producer without reading the phrase 'back in the day'. The borrowing is from US hip hop but the intention is the same – to dignify a culture by using language that suggests a lineage that is centuries old. An attempt to build a history where none exists. Ancient history is invoked in an *NME* review of Sweet Exorcist's 'Clonk' from 1991: 'You'd have to go back past the early days of Acid House'. And something close to the time of Jason and the Fleece is conjured in an *i-D* piece of September 1991. Helen Mead writes: 'From the golden roots of the Shoom, Future and The Trip'.

The nostalgia for the ancient is also the nostalgia for the epic. By 1991, just three years after the initial acid-house 'summer of love', writers were reporting on the bleakness – although I sense they secretly enjoyed the drama of the story. If nothing else it was mythic. Writing in *i-D* in August 1991, Sarah Champion said: 'This year's Solstice celebrations are touched by hate and gloom: Milton Keynes supergig/rave Midsummers Night's Dream is cancelled; 6 bouncers are stabbed at The Haçienda, a man dies in a fight at another venue; and 94 people are arrested on drugs charges at a World Party rave in Lincolnshire. Where did the love go?' Graham Massey (then from 808 State) recalled his first rave/Ecstasy experiences. 'It was like the kind of feeling you only get in a war: everyone pulling together.' His point of referral is the Second (presumably) World War – the real or nostalgized picture of life in England during wartime – the sense of community said to exist (ironically) before the schisms of rock'n'roll, the sixties and the first youth cultures.

England is always in a permanent state of nostalgia for its Englishness. At the beginning of 1989 Mike Pickering (later of M People, then perhaps the key northern house DJ) told the *NME* that he and Graeme Park were working on a single to promote the Green Party. Pickering enthused: 'It starts off with the lines from "Jerusalem" about "this green and pleasant land".' It was a prophetic dream – within months the rave/dance culture aligned itself with the fantasy of England as Albion – all misty and green and Arthurian, itself a nostalgic fancy of the countryside. While there doesn't seem to be one clear, authoritative study that maps the drift to the rural in English youth culture, it is the late-sixties hippy culture and late-eighties rave culture that exchange urban for pastoral. The myths of the late sixties are flowers, festivals, farmhouses (the places to which one retreats) and fields. The rave culture similarly owns and broadcasts a mythology, mainly influenced by the 1989 Sunrise, Energy and Biology parties (or media accounts of those parties) of precious dawns and drug-soaked sunrises. Frequently, reports make a fetish of the dawn. A December 1990 story in *The Face* maps The Beloved's LP *Happiness* back on to the rave and rave-dawn – and marks the record as a collection of drug devices to trigger specific memories. 'But for those who were there when London first discovered house, it serves as a series of snapshots: the mellow dawn greeting of "The Sun Rising", the ecstatic vision of "Up, Up and Away".'

Raving reawakened a pastoral nostalgia said Bill Drummond in a July 1991 interview with US underground magazine *X*. Discussing the sleeve of KLF's *Chill Out*, Drummond said: 'The sleeve is a very very English thing. The Pink Floyd album ATOM HEART MOTHER, do you know that album? The sleeve with the cow's head on it? That's a very English thing and it has the vibe of the rave scene over here. When we're having the big Orbital raves out in the country, and you're dancing all night and then the sun would come up in the morning, and then you'd be surrounded by this English rural countryside…so we wanted something that kind of reflected that, that feeling the day after the rave, that's what we wanted the music for.'

With its sheep and trains and Elvis samples, *Chill Out* is a record that projects images of 'great lost railways', 'great lost journeys' and 'great lost decades'. There is 'music' on the CD but more than anything *Chill Out* is a kind of conjuring trick built from samples. And perhaps designed to entertain the MDMA-softened mind. It understands that tiny fragments of resonant sound can draw huge landscapes of memory. Back in the seventeenth century, when he first coined the word, Johannes Hofer said nostalgia operates by an 'associationist magic' – triggers that make us dream of 'home'. Seventeenth-century soldiers were driven to madness and tears, suggests Svetlana Boym, by a little scrap of something, a detail that set memory on fire. She writes:

Swiss scientists found that rustic mothers' soups, thick village milk, and the folk melodies of Alpine valleys were particularly conducive to triggering a nostalgic reaction in Swiss soldiers. Supposedly the sounds of 'a certain rustic cantilena' that accompanies shepherds in their driving of the herds to pasture immediately provoked an epidemic of nostalgia among a group of Swiss soldiers serving in France. Similarly Scots, particularly Highlanders, were known to succumb to incapacitating nostalgia upon hearing the sound of bagpipes.

To the extent to which dance is sample-based music, it tends to exist in a permanent state of nostalgia or nostalgic reference to other scenes. There are records that only make sense because of their relationships to other tracks, genres, scenes and times. There are records (and even whole genres) in sample and dance music that feed off and refer to dub reggae, US disco, UK punk, eighties MOR, South American tango, Brazilian batacuda. The possible aesthetic of a good filter disco track is that you enjoy and relish the trace elements or captured memory of Paradise Garage now held in the more modern frame. A vast swathe of dance or sample-based music creates meaning by sampling – often literally – the memories and mythologized images of youth and pop cultures past. Every record contains a trace of another life. Alex Patterson samples Minnie Ripperton's 'Loving You' (itself a poetic hymn to her husband and baby girl Maya), Mixmaster Morris steals Joyce Grenfell (a reference to a pre-modern England on the *Flying High* LP), Roger Sanchez mines Loose Joints' disco classic *Is It All Over My Face?* on his beautiful, hypnotic *Luv Dancin*. And the symbols of time and memory and magic are woven into *Chill Out*, *Selected Ambient Works Vol. 1*, *Flying High* and *OB-SELON MI-NOS* – a haunting music of ticking clocks, human breath, railway announcements, hums, clicks and curious fragments. A sound that suggests cultural memory in disarray or a literal rending of drug-memory: jumbled scraps and half-heard, barely remembered bits and pieces.

The records themselves are artefacts – a second-hand 12-inch with the name of a DJ scrawled across it in marker pen is potentially as sacred as one of John Bonham's drumsticks. Second-hand record shops are full of 12-inches that once enjoyed full mythic life at parties, clubs and raves. The scarcity of the records also invokes feeling. Any one tape of any DJ set will probably include records that have never been reviewed or documented. There are artists who have been and gone, their presences barely registered by music or any other media, and yet their records might have spun at parties and raves around the world and created intense, beautiful, hardcore, sexy drug meaning for tens and even hundreds of thousands of people. Dance music is a form made up almost entirely of lost or unknown records. Authorship is peculiar anyway in dance as records share a distinct sonic language and records are purpose-built to slide into each other in the mix. So fans may never know the name or the author of the record that rocked their world. Or more perversely have a favourite record and go to parties for years and maybe only hear that record 'played out' just once.

Blogger 1471 (www.norfolkwindmills.com) discusses 'the great lost Marc Acardipane track'. He writes that he has owned a copy of this record since he was sixteen but 'the *only* time i ever heard this played out was at 8am as the final record in a *Fabio* set in the jungle tent, although admittedly judgement was pretty seriously impaired by that stage'.

Dance music is almost purpose-built for morose nostalgics who will nurse and treasure their copy of one of the world's 'great lost records'. It is entirely possible that the bulk of a record collection might be a store of otherwise 'great lost records'. The record collector becomes something more than a consumer. If you have one of the only copies of a 'great lost record' you are an archivist and you keep the flame alive – your work as a collector is the only bulwark against the void and obscurity that would otherwise devour the record.

Perhaps the hardcore scene is best known for making a fetish of its own history and very is-ness – the often mocked 'Back to '91' and 'Back to '95' parties. This week I saw a poster that said 'Back to '93'. Hardcore continually revives itself, says 1471, because the scene never resolved itself. Instead there was a great vanishing. He writes: 'the interesting thing about rave is that true crossover never really happened, this was because the scene hyperventilated and then imploded spectacularly at some point during 1993, it was as though 500,000 people jumped off a cliff at once, some had built up two years or so too much class-A action. It was interesting to see the thing get really too mental in such a short space of time. Reynolds [writer Simon Reynolds] covers this well, hedonism for hedonism's sake, not even enjoyment towards the end, then paranoia, fear, overdose, the clubs shut down, the scene basically put itself into hospital.'

An Old Skool Web-ring lists forty separate websites that celebrate and document the hardcore scene. Tapes of Ellis Dee, Micky Finn, Ratty, Easygroove, Carl Cox, etc. are available from Old Skool Raves 1990–1993 (www.angelfire.com/music4/oldskoolrave/). Hardcorewillneverdie.com offer 'complete track listings of classic old skool sets from 1991 to 1994'. The archive splits hairs the outside world cannot even see – it works at microscopic intensities. Colin Dale tapes at BACKTO92RECORDS (www.backto92.co.uk) include *Colin Dale – Empire '91, Colin Dale – Passion Jan '92, Colin Dale – white light white heat, central park, portsmouth '91*.

Nothing that has been recorded can be forgotten. Svetlana Boym argues that the recording industry and modern capitalism have created industries of nostalgia. Boym says videotapes, cassettes, CDs and DVDs have created 'an eternal present' in popular culture. 'The widespread re-use of work produced in previous generations has now become the most striking characteristic of contemporary mass culture. More than at any other time in history, we can (if we choose – and many do choose) live large chunks of our imaginative lives in the past.' At time of writing the current vogue in London's Shoreditch is flyers and parties that celebrate 'acid' and 'rave' – they might be playing a gently ironic game but the old music is being played by DJs who were just toddlers when records like Phuture's *Acid Trax* were released. *Acid Trax*, arguably the first 'acid house' record, reached the UK on import in March 1987.

In a 2002 interview with Simon Reynolds, New York DJ Larry Tee – the inventor of the phrase 'Electroclash' – complained the New York nightlife had become moribund. 'It's *CADAVEROUS*! At New Year's Eve, Junior Vasquez had a room at his party—and not to knock Junior, he's given me some fine moments over the years—but in this room in the bowels of the club you could hear his New Year's Eve set from 1993.' The story points to the hubris of Vasquez and the presumed resonance of his archived sets. And also the distance the recording of a DJ set has to travel from being transitory to mythic or precious.

A Tony DeVit set was replayed at Trade years after the DJ had died. In 2001, Strut Records released *Larry Levan Live At The Paradise Garage* – Levan died in 1992. There's a morbidity to this remembering – which combined with the Vasquez story suggests a labyrinthine nightclub of the near future with level after level playing different mixes from mythic and long-dead DJs. The kind of thing the West imagines for Tokyo – a nightclub as monster archive or museum. The recordings would have to come from heavily mythologized sectors of the dance culture, Levan's last night at Paradise Garage (27 September 1987), Stika at Spiral Tribe, Rampling at Shoom or Carl Cox or Coldcut at Shoom and Frankie Bones perhaps playing the 'dawn' set at Sunrise from 4am to 8am in summer 1989.

Rave nostalgia is fuelled by rave myth. From what I can recall of the truth – as I knew it – the best was a human rather than divine paradise. And fragmentary – there are flashes of intimate connections and wild explosions with other human beings. To recall these experiences in exquisite detail is an engrossing memory game – and it is not quick. Svetlana Boym says nostalgia is a 'rebellion against the modern idea of time'. The nostalgic, she writes, remakes history according to their dreams and refuses to surrender to the irreversibility of time. But all remembering is engagement with the past – perhaps she means nostalgia is a focused or immersive remembering. Nostalgia is magical, writes Svetlana, because it can slow down a world that is moving too fast. Perhaps inhumanly fast.

Glossy style magazines have served as reference points and source material for this story. Perhaps I have a nostalgia for the power *i-D*, *The Face* and *NME* once had to make and mythologize youth culture. The media that reminisces nowadays is the Net: the Web and the blogs hold the fragments that make up the group mind. Our epitaphs will be written on html.

The forum at www.acid-house.net has been discussing the true nature of the original acid-house parties. A contributor calling her (or himself) 'acid ain't over' writes on 12 February 2003: 'From what I have read and experienced the closest you ever got to hearing what we would call acid house was at the RIP clink street parties. They did a night called acid transmission which was very underground acid.' A few weeks later, on 13 March, he/she adds an update. 'I went to the rip reunion parties at The

End (I think they only did a couple). Mr C, Evil Eddie Richards, Colin Dale, Trevor Fung, Kid Bachelor and Jazzy M played. Obviously didn't have the atmosphere of the original venue but it was very good. It looked like they still had some of the original banners.'

recommended listening

Armando – *151* (Warehouse)
Marshall Jefferson – *Move Your Body/House Music Anthem* (Trax)
Phuture – *Acid Trax* (Trax)
The Irresistible Force – *Flying High* (Rising High)
The Orb – *A Huge Ever-Growing Pulsating Brain That Rules from The Centre of The Ultraworld* (Loving You) (WAU! Mr Modo)
Marshall Jefferson presents Truth – *Open Our Eyes* (Big Beat)
Rhythm on the Loose – *Break of Dawn* (white label)
Blame – *Music Takes You* (White label)
The Beloved – *Blissed Out* (East West)
Omni Trio – *Deepest Cut Vol 1* (Moving Shadow)
Adamski – *Killer/Bassline Changed My Life* (MCA)
MFSB – *Love Is The Message* (Philadelphia International)
Tony De Vit – *Don't You Want My Love* (White label)
Taana Gardener – *Heartbeat* (West End)
Loose Joints – *Is it All Over My Face?* (West End)
Underground Solution – *Luv Dancin'* (Strictly Rhythm)
Electribe 101 – *Inside Out* (Mercury)
Carl Bean – *Born This Way* (Motown)
Various/The Loft – *David Mancuso* (Nuphonic)
Various – *Larry Levan Live at The Paradise Garage* (Strut)
Mystic Institute – *OB-SELON MI-NOS repainted by Global Communication* (Evolution)
Marc Acardipane – *The great lost Marc Acardipane track* (Unknown)
KLF – *Chill Out* (KLF Communications)
Fingers Inc – *Mystery of Love* (DJ International)
Frankie Knuckles – *Baby Wants To Ride* (Trax)

recommended reading

Sarah Champion – *And God Created Manchester* (Wordsmith)
Matthew Collin – *Altered State* (Serpent's Tail)

Svetlana Boym – *The Future of Nostalgia* (Basic Books)

Joan Didion – *Slouching Towards Bethlehem* (Random House)

Bruce Eisner – *Ecstasy: The MDMA Story* (Ronin Publishing)

Evelyn Underhill – *Mysticism* (Oxford, OneWorld)

Dr George Greer – 'The therapeutic use of MDMA', in *Ecstasy: The Clinical, Pharmacological and Neurotoxicological Effects of the Drug MDMA* (Kluwer Academic Publishers)

Dr Jerome Bell and Marsha Rosenbaum – *Pursuit of Ecstasy, The MDMA Experience* (State University of NY Press)

talking all that jazz

Mixmaster Morris

When I sat down to write this essay, it suddenly dawned on me what a tough job it was gonna be. To start with, there's a hundred years of history to condense into a few pages; and for a general audience, who won't be jazz buffs, you can't take any knowledge for granted. Jazz has been pushed to the margins in the last thirty years, so that most younger people regard it as a fossilized art form of little relevance. Yet it is perhaps the greatest contribution America has made to the musical world, and it's still influencing and inspiring musicians even today. Even if no one can define it or even agree where the word comes from…

The one thing historians agree about is that New Orleans was the place where it all started. Being a major seaport, it became a melting pot of races and languages, where African, European and South American cultures collided and interacted. While the English colonized the east coast, the French and Spanish settled in other areas such as Louisiana and along the Mississippi. Most of the population in the nineteenth century were Creoles – a uniquely New Orleans blend of African and French, with sprinkles of English, German, Mexican, Irish, Native American – a spicy jambalaya of a gene pool. And they were free from slavery long before the Civil War, unlike in other parts of the South.

Many of the local traditions were imported directly from Europe, like the Mardi Gras, a French festival that is still the highlight of the year. On holidays or at funerals, marching bands were popular but, although the instruments were familiar, the results were miles away from the rigid military bands of Europe. Firstly there was improvisation, not the solos of later jazz, but two or more instruments simultaneously embellishing a popular melody and adding new layers of complexity. And secondly there was the swinging, syncopated beat that was entirely absent from European brass-band music, with its marches, quicksteps and polkas.

Funeral processions would feature large black and Creole marching bands, who would play slowly all the way to the church, and then repeat the same tunes as fast rags on the way home again. And at Mardi Gras scores of bands would appear from nowhere, like carnival all across Latin America and the Caribbean. The king of this scene was the legendary Buddy Bolden, who died unrecorded and penniless in the asylum.

The rhythmic complexity came directly from African drumming, where polyrhythms – different beats overlapping each other – are a fundamental part of the music. The syncopated beats were present in the 1860s in styles like the cakewalk. Named because the best couple would win the eponymous cake, this was a colonial-era dance where black people would dress up like the slave owners and parody the high-and-mighty manners of the white man…But what turned this into a nationwide phenomenon was the birth of ragtime almost simultaneous with the dawn of the twentieth century.

Ragtime was essentially piano music with a heavy syncopation, and Scott Joplin was the undisputed master of it. The breakthrough came in 1899 with *Maple Leaf Rag*, which sold a million copies in sheet-music form as it swept across America and beyond. In these days every home had a piano, even if few had a newfangled phonograph. Even fewer 'honkies' could play this complex, difficult music. But even if they couldn't master the fiendishly tricky rhythms they could get the authentic sound from a pianola roll, effectively the CD of a century ago. That's definitely digital recording! Via these perforated rolls of paper, a cultural revolution was exported around the world, and they could be mass-produced…

Throughout the first decade of the century, Joplin and a host of lesser composers, turned out thousands of rags, which became the soundtrack of bars, brothels and bordellos across America. But Joplin wanted his music to be taken seriously as a black classical music, and was dismayed to have it associated with such low surroundings. Pianola players started pumping the machine too fast, playing Joplin's scholarly rags up to 30 per cent faster than he intended. The crowds loved it, but he hated it (because it was Edwardian happy hardcore, or the American equivalent). People started writing novelty rags, and cheap commercial rags, while the original creator starved in his garret. He put all his efforts into writing a ragtime opera, whose dismal failure (it only had one performance) left him a broken man dying of syphilis. And by the time the First World War broke out, the ragtime craze had run its course.

With the USA entering into the war in 1917, the government closed down the whole red-light district of Storeyville, putting hundreds of musicians out of work overnight. They responded by getting on boats and travelling up the river, infecting city after city with the new sounds. Many ended up in Chicago, which became the capital of the new music. The local press gave it a new name, 'jass' – a term that first appeared in 1914. As to its etymology, there are dozens of theories. It could be derived from the French words *jaser* or *chasse*, or the Mandingo word *jasi*. *Chasse* has the advantage of having a sexual implication, as most commentators agree that the word had an obscene origin (just like later forms such as rock'n'roll). There is even a theory that it comes from the jasmine perfume worn by local prostitutes. As to why 'jass' became 'jazz', I would like to believe the story that mischievous kids would often erase the first letter of signs advertising 'Jass Dancing', which is why the spelling was changed. See, the music business was about tits and ass even a century ago.

It was a white Chicago band, the ODJB (Original Dixieland Jazz Band), who made the first jazz records, in 1917 – and who became the first to travel to England in 1919, where they stayed for eighteen months, making a string of successful records. Many grown men have spent generous portions of their lives tracking down the actual dates, line-ups and track-listings of these incunabula of jazz. (What a lovely word that is.)

Prohibition started in 1920 and for thirteen years alcohol was completely forbidden in the USA. Overnight, millions of people became criminals, and crime boomed. Gangster-controlled speakeasies replaced local bars – by 1925 there were a staggering

100,000 of them in New York City alone! Mob bosses like Al Capone opened plush nightclubs, and paid huge sums to get the hottest band. Many historians identify this period as the birth of organized crime in America.

As the Roaring Twenties unfolded, more and more southerners arrived in Chicago, including a young Louis Armstrong. He played in many bands, most notably his own Hot Five (and later Hot Seven), whose records influenced musicians worldwide. The move to Chicago coincided fortuitously with the birth of jazz records – there are no recordings of the original New Orleans bands, so we can only guess what they sounded like. The northern bands developed a new style, where virtuoso soloists were a central attraction, and many of them became jazz legends, like Bix Beiderbecke, Benny Goodman, pianist Earl Hines, drummer Gene Krupa.

In 1929 the stock market crashed, the Depression arrived, and record sales fell by over 90 per cent as millions of people became unemployed. Radio boomed, giving free access to music – but black musicians were barred from the radio in favour of bland, all-white commercial dance bands (sound familiar?).

Something else was happening too. A young Jewish clarinetist, Mezz Mezzrow, who started out in the Chicago speakeasies, moved to New York. More than any other single figure, he turned the entire jazz world on to the demon weed, so much so that a 'Mighty Mezz' was widely recognized slang for a jazz cigarette. Nicknamed the Reefer King or even The White Mayor of Harlem, he did much to invent the pothead argot, a hipster slanguage that soon became the hallmark of jazz musicians, keeping them one step ahead of the police.

Surprisingly, weed was legal but virtually unknown until after Prohibition ended, when the notorious FBI agent Harry Anslinger started a vicious campaign which resulted in the Marijuana Tax Act of 1937. Anslinger personally popularized the term 'marijuana' to stir up American xenophobia against anything Mexican.

Musicians started to write songs about dope in this age of Reefer madness. Of course, they couldn't officially release such things but they could play them live in the speakeasies and gambling dens. Sometimes they even recorded them for private release, creating an under-the-counter culture in the same way that Blues singers would record highly sexual uncensored songs in samizdat editions. Dope smokers became vipers, and weed became tea, boo, reefer, gage – and a hundred more pseudonyms. Even the word 'jive' itself was a euphemism for dope, in song titles like 'The Man with the Jive' or 'All the Jive is Gone'; and the great Fats Waller recorded the classic 'Reefer Man', with lines like 'I'm the king of everything, I gotta be gotta be high before I swing' or even 'Well you know you're high when your throat gets dry'. It could have come from a Cypress Hill or Snoop Dog album.

On the musical front, a new style was being born in the dance halls of Harlem. The big bands were a world away from the 'hot' styles of Prohibition-era Chicago. Duke Ellington had been the resident bandleader at New York's Cotton Club through the late 1920s, and through radio he became a household name across the country. Mixing jazz and classical influences into an accessible calm style, he broke into the farthest reaches of the music world. He became one of the most successful composers in jazz, writing many standards like 'Take the A Train' and 'It Don't Mean a Thing if it Ain't Got That Swing', a tune which helped define what became known as the Swing Era. Ellington appeared in many films of the time, and Hollywood embraced swing with a passion.

Suddenly a huge new audience was flocking to the dance halls, to do the lindyhop and the jitterbug. Ellington, meanwhile, came to Europe in 1939 for a tour that inspired hundreds of musicians to start playing. A few months later the war began. Blackouts and curfews closed the clubs, and record pressing ceased in 1942, due to shortage of vinyl and a crippling strike by the American Federation of Musicians. However, many Swing bands went to war with the US military – at one point over sixty bands travelled with the US forces. The Nazi ban on jazz as decadent Negro/Jewish music only reinforced its popularity and its key role in the war effort. Allied radio stations beamed swing records to all corners of the globe.

The end of the war coincided with a revolution: the emergence of bebop and its greatest exponent, Charlie Parker. He grew up in Kansas City, but it was in New York that he made his name. Though he had been a successful sideman for a few years, 1945 saw him leading his own band for the first time, and also hiring a young man called Miles Davis. The new sound blew people away, many older people couldn't accept it as music at all, and most musicians had no chance of ever achieving the breakneck velocity and complexity of the improvisation. In fact some say this was the very idea – to create a new style which white musicians couldn't rip off so easily!

Within a few years, booze and heroin had taken their toll and by 1955 Parker was dead. Miles was in Rikers Island prison when he heard the news. He had already set off in a different direction, widely called 'cool' jazz, after his 1949 album, *Birth of the Cool*. With the masterful orchestral arrangements of Gil Evans, this and subsequent albums like *Kind of Blue* and *Porgy and Bess* became the cool sound of the contemporary salon.

Miles became the most successful jazz musician on the planet, and embarked on a career that was to last nearly half a century. Although he could have rested on his laurels he kept on innovating and taking risks, leading to Ellington's comment that Miles was the 'Picasso of jazz'. Continually reinventing himself, he took jazz into areas it had never been and his keen talent-spotting was to initiate the careers of many of the greatest jazz musicians alive today.

Pianist Thelonious Monk was another bebop graduate who created his own universe of sound. Watching rare footage of him, it's fascinating to see the way he hovers over the keyboard, as if he's never seen one before. Many people thought that he was crazy, or that he played 'the wrong notes', to which he replied, 'The piano ain't got no wrong notes.' He would often hit two adjacent notes, making what is a discord to some ears but in fact striving for extra 'blue' notes, meaning those in between the twelve of the normal scale, in the same way that blues guitarists bend a string. If only the pitch wheel had been around – but on an acoustic piano, of course, that wasn't possible.

Monk's distinctive compositions have become standards, especially 'Round Midnight', one of the most frequently covered songs in jazz history. The Kronos Quartet made a classic album of chamber-music arrangements of Monk's classic songs, something that contributed mightily to his reappraisal as a composer of the highest magnitude. Although he made records involving everything from quartets to big bands, I'd rather take his solo piano works, where you can hear more clearly exactly how fresh and original his playing is, even today. He seemed to hear things that nobody else did, as

evidenced in a famous anecdote. Taking a critic out on the lake in Central Park, he stopped rowing. 'Listen,' Monk said, 'we're moving through the water in 4/4 time and the birds are singing 6/8 over it.'

John Coltrane first came to fame through membership of the Miles Davis quintet in the 1950s, and played with Monk as well, before his landmark album *A Love Supreme* in 1960. Unsurprisingly, he was strung out on heroin most of the time, as were most of Miles's band. The folks in St Louis didn't know Miles was smacked out of his head, because there weren't that many junkies around town. But in Harlem smack was the currency. And Coltrane would sometimes fall asleep on stage, or pick his nose and eat it, to Miles's disgust. He played with an intensity 'so strong, it's religious', cascading sheets of notes that went on and on.

He favoured long solos, sometimes over an hour at a time, and instead of the fast-changing chords of bebop he developed a 'modal' style, based on scales rather than chord changes, like an Indian raga. He once said that he just didn't know how to stop. 'Take the fucking thing our of your mouth, motherfucker' was Miles's retort.

A critic asked him what he wanted to be in ten years. 'A saint,' he replied.

Sadly, he died far too young, at the age of thirty-seven, but his wife Alice continues to spread his message to this day. And in Haight-Ashbury, to this day there is a Church of St John Coltrane.

With her mystical harp improvisations, Alice Coltrane became perhaps the greatest female jazz artist of them all, although the number of women musicians to have made an impact in jazz is small, even compared to other forms. She became a Hindu devotee and adopted the name Turiya, and throughout the seventies made a series of amazing albums taking John Coltrane's legacy, and sometimes his songs as well, into ever deeper, more devotional areas. She also made the critics howl by overdubbing strings onto John Coltrane's recordings. Much of her recent output has only been released through her temple. (4 Hero recently invited her to perform on their album – her reply was that she would only do it if John gave permission, which meant a seance had to be organized! Presumably John didn't approve, as the recording never happened.)

Another protégé of Coltrane who is still active and touring is Pharaoh Sanders; as well as playing with both Coltranes (and also Sun Ra) he made a series of extraordinary albums for Impulse, perhaps the greatest being *Karma* (1968). Many of these featured the incredible bear of a singer Leon Thomas, who co-wrote a song that was to become the most famous anthem of the cosmic jazz era, 'The creator has a masterplan, peace and happiness throughout the land…'

As well as his rich singing voice and scatting ability, Leon developed an amazing yodelling style which is truly unique – this came about after he had a fall the night before a gig, and had eight stitches in his mouth so that he couldn't even open it! He later toured with Santana and Freddie Hubbard, and recorded a large canon of work, sometimes mellifluous, sometimes with a raw voodoo passion. Later he got to sing 'Creator' with Louis Armstrong, on the latter's seventieth-birthday concert – an amazing night that brought together three generations of musicians.

Lonnie Liston Smith was another member of Pharaoh Sanders' group and in the early seventies he made a series of classic releases for the Flying Dutchman label. These are essential additions to any ambient jazz collection. These albums are often described as cosmic jazz – a fair description, I would say. After the success of 'Expansions' (a dance floor classic to this day), he went in a more explicitly disco direction, and then he went down with the disco boat. This happened to so many talented jazz artists in the mid 1970s. They were forced by their labels to jump on the disco bandwagon, and most of them didn't last too long in that cut-throat world.

There seems to have been a magical period from 1969 to 1973 when the racks were filled with deeply cosmic releases, by these and many other musicians – Gary Bartz, Doug Carn, Marion Brown, Don Cherry, Charlie Haden, Cecil McBee, Roland Kirk, Dollar Brand, Andy Bey, and Azar Lawrence. It was a time when African-Americans were finding their own voices, in the wake of the Civil Rights movement and the huge social changes of 1968. All these records seem to have a shining, forward-looking optimism that some would call naivety; they practically glow in the dark.

Most of these albums have been damn hard to find in the last thirty years, unless you have a platinum Amex card, but now many are coming out on CDs, and the wonders of the Web make the private obsessions of the few available to the many. Particularly in Japan there is a sizeable audience for this kind of music, and large crowds turn out to see even lesser-known jazz artists of the 1970s.

Something else that was happening at the beginning of the 1970s was a concerted effort to mix elements of rock and jazz, which became known as fusion – a term that certainly covered a multitude of sins, but also carried a subtext of racial integration.

Miles Davis played a crucial role in this, as most of the major players in the fusion scene were graduates of his band, and he consistently picked black, white and Latin musicians with a refreshing colour blindness that shocked the brothers. (Miles even survived getting shot for working with white promoters in New York.)

In 1969, Miles made *In a Silent Way*, perhaps the definitive ambient jazz classic, and certainly one of the most unique – you know for sure that this record will be cherished and loved in another hundred years, something you can't say about many contemporary records. The unusual line-up featured no fewer than three keyboard players – the incomparable trio of Herbie Hancock, Chick Corea and Josef Zawinul. It also introduced virtuoso English guitarist John McLaughlin to the jazz world. (This essential album has not only been remastered recently but the entire sessions have been reissued as a triple CD set for those who can't get enough of it!)

Miles had finally dispensed with Gil Evans and his orchestral stylings in favour of an all-electric line-up – a heretical move that was as controversial as Bob Dylan's famous conversion to rock. Austrian Joe Zawinul had written the monster hit 'Mercy, Mercy' for Cannonball Adderley, and it was his Fender Rhodes playing on that record which attracted Miles.

Miles declared the acoustic piano obsolete, to the horror of many. Herbie was always a neophile, and took to musical evolution immediately; Chick Corea took a little more persuading. They added effects like the Echoplex (a tape-loop-based delay unit), ring modulators and foot pedals, creating a sound that was to change the shape of jazz for ever. Musicians with effects pedals and delays on stage meant the birth of a whole new style of improvisation, where you could modulate the tonal qualities rather than just riffing on a scale. Herbie took synthesizer playing to new heights with his ARP 2600 – doing things with the instrument that no one had attempted before.

What's more, Miles began to play with a pickup in his mouthpiece (instead of pointing his trumpet into the microphone), allowing him to process his sound like the keyboard players. The next year he released *Bitches Brew*, an equally seminal work that enraged jazz purists but became the most commercially successful of his career, mixing heavy funk, electronics and wah-wah pedals into the pot. The group played in rock venues like the Fillmore, and they played as loud as The Who or Cream.

For the first time, Columbia promoted it like a rock album, putting him on the cover of *Rolling Stone*, and the album entered the *Billboard* Top 40. Out on his own like never before, Miles was drawing inspiration from Stockhausen and Sly Stone, not to mention Jimi Hendrix. Miles and Jimi played at the legendary Isle of Wight Festival, and planned to record together straight afterwards – a mouth-watering prospect that was never fulfilled as Hendrix died in London a few days before the session.

It seemed like the whole jazz world was populated by graduates of Miles Davis University (a phrase widely used by its alumni). Herbie Hancock spent the early 1970s making wildly experimental electronic albums like *Sextant*, *Crossings* and *Mwandishi* that went way over most people's heads, before hitting pay dirt with the million-selling *Headhunters* album, which put a healthy portion of funk on the plate and led to The Headhunters band being a success in their own right.

John McLaughlin went on to form the Mahavishnu Orchestra, a blistering full-frontal assault of hard-driving rock and jazz propelled by master drummer Billy Cobham. They made three classic albums with the original line-up. Later on, McLaughlin's interest in Indian classical music led to him form the band Shakti. Zawinul & Wayne Shorter started Weather Report, which became perhaps the most celebrated jazz group of the decade, making seventeen albums and winning every award in the book before disbanding in 1985. Chick Corea and Lenny White went on to create Return To Forever, who were almost as big in the 1970s. A new music was born with limitless potential and possibilities, and the future looked bright.

But whereas all these bands started with impeccable credentials, the politics of the American music industry was to wipe out all this

good work. Fusion became a byword for self-indulgent pyrotechnics; the press and music industry backed artists who had technical skills, but not the subtlety and intelligence of the originators.

FM radio formatting in particular diluted fusion into 'adult contemporary' and then the style called 'contempo' or 'jazz lite'. Then, having removed anything with any balls, it emasculated the music even further to create the nightmare that is so-called 'smooth jazz', a style so bland and anodyne that it can cause a spontaneous lobotomy within seconds. There are hundreds of stations across America with this format, and they all feature playlists programmed by the same consultancy group, Broadcast Architecture.

The music covered goes all the way from Kenny G to Enya and back again. And again. And again. Music so bland it makes The Carpenters sound like Throbbing Gristle. Music so corporate it makes The Ministry of Sound seem dangerously risqué. Music that is to jazz what Vanilla Ice is to hip hop. And boy, is it lucrative – Kenny G's album sales stand at 47,000,000 units and rising. It's no wonder that teenagers in the USA don't buy into jazz, if all they get to hear is this washed-out musical Mogadon, designed to pacify you as you push your trolley around the Wal-Mart store.

I was born in the 1960s, but the music of that time passed me by as a child. Pop music was forbidden in my house; my parents made me listen to classical music for my own 'improvement'. Of course, this had exactly the opposite effect and I haven't been able to stand it ever since. My father did claim to be a jazz fan – but that only included pre-war music. Anything more recent was dangerous modern nonsense, a point of view shared by poet Philip Larkin (who also had strong views about parenthood!), or Tory wet Ken Clarke, nowadays reborn as a jazz pundit.

Lincolnshire in the early 1970s wasn't exactly the front line of the culture wars. There were no clubs or concerts, and the predominant youth style was a choice between Elvis and Abba fans. Neither of these attracted me, and I began to search for something that did. All the exciting developments in America might as well have been on another planet.

My first exposure to any modern jazz-based music was with The Soft Machine, who started as a psychedelic rock band, darlings of the UFO set in swinging London, but began to incorporate more and more jazz elements. Robert Wyatt's drumming was clearly the product of listening to too many modern-jazz albums, and their improvisations were so unlike anything else in rock it was clear they were getting inspiration from somewhere else entirely. Their golden era (1968–1970) was all too short though, and when Wyatt left the band, their sense of humour went with him and they soon became ponderous and pretentious.

From the point of view of a teenage punk rocker, jazz didn't seem to have much of a role in the new-wave period. Punk was predicated on non-musicianship, and most of the bands could hardly play three-chord rock, let alone bebop. The brass instruments were deadly weapons in the hands of the punks – Poly Styrene would honk away on her tenor sax, with gruesome results. The guy in A Certain Ratio could curdle milk with his trumpet playing, and the guy in Cabaret Voltaire who played the clarinet was no better, but as there were fifteen layers of echo and reverb on top it didn't matter.

One of the most exciting bands at this time was The Pop Group, from Bristol. When they split, half the band became Rip Rig and Panic, who took their name from a Roland Kirk album. Their enthusiasm almost (but not quite) made up for their untogetherness. When I saw them play at WOMAD in 1980, a very young and very pregnant Neneh Cherry sang and dad Don Cherry stood in on trumpet. Other members formed Pigbag, who finally cracked the top ten for one delirious moment. Sophisticated they weren't, but they brought a new youthful energy to the scene, in a similar way to New York bands like Konk or The Contortions.

Also on the scene was the American guitarist James Blood Ulmer, who was a protégé of the Ornette Coleman school of harmolodics – pretty damn funky but weird with it. He used to play on bills with post-punk bands like This Heat – and the album *Are You Glad to Be in America?* opened jazz to a new-wave audience. Like the man said, jazz is the teacher, funk is the preacher.

In the early 1980s I used to make music with a jazz drummer called Jim, who lived in Shepherd's Bush. We would go down to the front line (All Saints Road) to score some 'black ash', then go home and listen to his Miles albums. It was here that I first heard *In A Silent*

Way and *On the Corner*, as well as the lesser-known *Jack Johnson* and the rarities collection *Circle in the Round*.

Miles had been in semi-retirement and plagued by illness for the previous five or six years, but suddenly he announced a European tour. Well, there was no way we were going to miss that so we both went to Hammersmith Odeon to see him play. Miles spent half the evening letting his band jam, and then occasionally dropping a few plangent notes over the top. There was a suprising amount of humour and joking about – Miles extracting the urine from his guitarist every time he did a solo, and pulling strange grimaces – but it was still a mind-blowing night.

After this show I started going to see more American jazz artists when they came to London. Anthony Braxton, Sonny Rollins, Ornette Coleman, the Art Ensemble of Chicago with Lester Bowie, John Zorn's Naked City.

I found that free jazz was much more engaging live and in the flesh than on vinyl. You can't pause or fast-forward, so you just have to stay with it, or walk out. Which of course a lot of people did!

British jazz legend Lol Coxhill once told me a funny story about a free-jazz festival in Holland. He asked one of the organizers, 'What shall I play?' to which the guy replied, 'Oh, play anything you want.' So he got up and started playing 'Oh I Do Like to Be Beside the Seaside', at which point the organizer went red in the face and pulled the plug on him. One man's freedom is another's handcuffs.

Ornette was the pioneer of 'free jazz' – the term itself comes from the title of his 1960 album, but soon became shorthand for the unstructured improvisations of the turbulent 1960s. Yet there was far more to his music than the lack of conventional signposts. He began to play the violin, and to compose string quartets and symphonic works.

In the mid 1970s he formed the Prime Time Band, with a most unusual format of two drummers, two bass players and two guitarists – in effect two separate bands playing simultaneously, but in different time signatures. When I saw this band in London, a packed venue emptied in minutes under the harmolodic assault, leaving about two hundred hardcore aficionados grinning from ear to ear as all the 'normals' ran from the building covering their ears. After that, the atmosphere was just wonderful!

In the 1980s, I used to go to the old Recommended Records shop in Battersea, ground zero for London's avant-garde music scene. The name of Sun Ra was frequently invoked, in hushed tones of reverence, so I decided to check him out. Now Ra is perhaps the most prolific artist in jazz history, recording maybe four hundred albums over half a century, and some of these are very hard going indeed. So I went to see the Sun Ra Arkestra at the Fridge in Brixton, which was truly one of the most amazing shows I have ever seen. The whole band wore outrageous costumes – half Egyptian gods, half intergalactic travellers. Ra conjured up ear-splitting sounds from his minimoog while a myriad of percussionists set up a clattering polyrhythm on talking drums and congas. They played a thirty-minute version of Brecht/Weill's 'Mack the Knife', and then followed it with a medley of songs from Disney movies, like 'Pink Elephants on Parade' from *Dumbo*. And of course lots of their own songs, invariably about space travel and the cosmos. Finally the band marched off the stage, round the hall a few times, still playing with glee, and then out of the doors and round Brixton like the Interstellar Salvation Army, chanting 'Space is the Place…Space is the Place'.

Later the band returned to meet the audience – apparently the members got paid in white labels, which they were selling furtively like contraband goods outside the venue. These were the legendary albums off the label Saturn, some of which are now fantastically rare. Ra not only claimed to come from the planet Saturn, at the Berlin Jazz Festival he demanded a telescope with which he could study his home planet during solos. After that I was a convert and I made sure to catch every show the Arkestra played.

Joining the Arkestra was a full-time commitment: the musicians actually had to move into a communal house to ensure their availability round the clock, and abandon drugs, booze, sex and other music! The fact that great musicians like John Gilmore or June Tyson were happy to devote their entire lives to this regime indicated the magnetic power that Ra had over all those he touched.

A few years later, I somehow got booked to open for Ra at the Academy. I was beside myself with excitement. But hours before showtime, the promoter pulled out, even though a lot of advance tickets had been sold. The Arkestra went up to London University to play instead, and were on top form. The last time Ra played in London was at Ronnie Scott's, and by this time he was in a wheelchair, and paralyzed down one side. But he was playing the piano with one hand, and jamming away on the DMX, and the gleam in his eye was still there.

After the show I met him for a few poignant seconds. Somehow, we both knew that he wouldn't be coming back. Though he has now gone back to his home planet, you can experience the Arkestra at full blast in three amazing movies – the sci-fi epic *Space is the Place* and the documentary film *A Joyful Noise* (a perfect description of the Arkestra's musical mayhem), both of which are essential viewing. And the surviving members are still on the road, playing in 2003 at Lee Perry's Meltdown festival, and doing an impromptu five-hour set on Resonance FM.

By this time I was starting to develop an interest in dance music, at first through early hip hop and electro. Herbie Hancock smashed into the top twenty in 1983 with the single 'Rockit' and its innovative video, which cleverly circumvented MTVs colour bar (how odd to think that MTV was 100 per cent white when it started).

Miles was also getting into hip hop, and hanging out with Prince (they played live together at Paisley Parke) – it's a tragedy he died before he had a chance to fully explore these new arenas. Herbie also released hip-hop mixes of classics like 'Butterfly'. And hip hop was returning the interest. As samplers replaced the DMX, the producers started digging in the crates for jazz breaks, starting with Gangstarr and Stetsasonic.

Hip hop was the new thing, and the jazz scene seemed to be old and in the way. There was a more purist jazz-dance scene at venues like Dingwalls and the Electric Ballroom, and my memory of those parties is that you would get a small clutch of good dancers taking turns like breakers while everyone else stood against the wall, too intimidated to join in. Before Ecstasy, people were too self-conscious to cut loose, and they were more concerned with wearing the right hats and keeping their suits clean.

Then there was the ageing soul-boy scene, throwing weekenders on the south and east coasts. Like the American scene, they started with great records with real jazz pedigrees as well as dance-floor appeal – Lonnie Liston Smith, The Blackbyrds *Rock Creek Park*, Roy Ayers, Deodato, Eddie Henderson, Bob James's Nautilus – but as the eighties dawned it all started to get a bit sickly, like a big chunk of icing without any cake. The jazz roots dropped off, and the plant got sick, that's how I see it.

There's one artist I always had a lot of love for, the mighty Gil Scott Heron. I saw him play in the early 1980s to a crowd who just wanted to hear 'The Bottle' all night, and weren't into his political stuff. We would rather have heard the coruscating social comment of 'The Revolution Will Not be Televised' and 'B Movie'.

The only other time I heard such righteous fury was when listening to The Last Poets, another by-product of the Civil Rights era; their first record, *Right On!*, sold nearly a million copies in the ghettos, without proper distribution. One track is a hymn to James Brown, another is simply called 'Jazz' ('Jazz is a woman's tongue, stuck dead in your motherfucking mouth, you dig it?') It's a show-stopping, life-changing album that too few people have heard even today. They appeared in Mick Jagger's movie *Performance*, where they are scary and fascinating, declaiming from the roof of a car while the brothers try out their AK-47s. Even more prescient was the 1975 album *Hustlers' Convention*, truly the Rosetta Stone of hip hop, with songs about pimps, players, dealers and hoes. Later on, one tried to kill another on stage in France by stabbing him in the throat. Westlife they ain't.

Rather than the watered-down jazz funk around in the mid 1980s, I preferred the heavy funk of the JBs or Parliament, or the percussion overload of Troublefunk and the Go-Go scene. By 1985 I was playing on the Pirate station NETWORK 21 alongside Coldcut, and I loved their upfront, open-minded approach to the dance floor, based on funk rather than fashion. It's an attitude still prevalent at Ninja Tune today.

By 1989, I had my first DJ residency upstairs at Heaven in the room previously occupied by Alex Patterson, Youth and the KLF. This was the prime time of acid house, of course, and electronic music was busting out all over; the challenge was to find a relevant counterpoint for the chill-out room. In those days I didn't have many jazz albums, especially ones that would work in this context. I used to play *In a Silent Way*

all the time, even making my own extended mix – later someone in Europe did a bootleg house mix of this and I played that as well.

And I began to look for ambient jazz tracks that I could mix together with or over the top of ambient house records. In particular I would use Don Cherry's *Codona 3* album on ECM, and this worked so well that I began to buy more records on that celebrated label, particularly those by solo musicians (strangely, the idea of solo jazz performances seems to be a European one).

ECM was set up in Munich in 1969 by the great Manfred Eicher, and occupies a unique niche between jazz, classical and ambient music – with over nine hundred releases, you could spend a lifetime exploring their catalogue. I fell in love with the albums of Stephan Micus, David Darling, Paul Giger and others. Another outstanding ECM release was the Liberation Music Orchestra album, featuring Charlie Haden and Don Cherry performing Spanish Civil War songs. And their biggest success came with yet another graduate of Miles University, pianist Keith Jarrett, whose 1975 live album has sold over a million copies.

Next I started to add vibraphone soloists like Walt Dickerson; electric-piano solos like those of Eddie Henderson and Lonnie Liston Smith in his cosmic years; flute solos like Tony Scott's albums recorded in the Pyramids and the Taj Mahal. I began collecting all the Alice Coltrane records, particularly the harp solos, and the superb Ptaah the El Daoud.

Later on, I discovered the early works of keyboard prodigy and former Frank Zappa keyboardist George Duke, like 'North Beach' – a shimmering lake of piano echoes and rude feedback that Derrick May used to open his sets with. Marc Moulin's seventies classic 'Sam Suffy', with its much-sampled water drums, was another chill-out favourite – later I discovered the albums he made under the name Placebo, now reissued by Brighton's Counterpoint label.

Two maverick, genre-busting records that I used to play were Joni Mitchell's *Mingus* album, a heartfelt tribute to the great bass player, and underrated UK singer Annette Peacock's *The Perfect Release*, with its conspicuous drug references and in-your-face feminism, which always used to get people queueing up to find out what it was.

There were a few early US house records that had some real jazz content, e.g. Frankie Knuckles' 'Tears' and some of the Nugroove releases, especially those by the Burrell brothers. One that really blew me away was Bobby Konders' 'The Poem', which became a classic, even though 90 per cent of the credit is owed to the keyboard playing of Peter Daou, who solos for about six minutes over a sparse rhythm (and some Mutubaruka poetry). He went on to do a series of twelves under names like Vandal and Transonic with very flamboyant piano on all of them. It seemed such an improvement on the irritating muppet-like jangly pianos that were synonymous with Italian house at that time. In 1990 I played a live gig at the UFO club Berlin with Peter Daou, so I got him jamming on the piano while I improvised with three drum machines. It was insane but brilliant – wish I had a recording of it!

Even the Detroit techno artists began to show their roots. Underground Resistance suprised many with their ambient-jazz classic 'Nation to Nation', a record which instantly brings the early nineties back to life. Carl Craig did an outstanding mix of Incognito, which has been in my box ever since. Later on, of course, he went the whole way, forming a full-on jazz ensemble, The Innerzone Orchestra. Most recently he made the album *The Detroit Experiment* with a collective of Detroit jazz legends, including the mighty Marcus Belgrave – who experimented with jazz electronics in the 1970s on the legendary Tribe label – Bennie Maupin of The Headhunters and young turks like Amp Fiddler and Ayro.

Slowly I began to meet other people in London sharing a similar headspace. Kirk DeGiorgio, who used to run the A.R.T. label, obviously had a much bigger jazz collection than I could afford, and turned me on to lots of records I didn't know, like Julian Priester's *Love, Love* and Herbie Hancock's 'Nobu' – a solo electronic masterpiece from the super-rare *Dedication* album, a Japanese-only release recorded at the soundcheck of a gig in Tokyo. Later, Kirk did a fantastic series of radio shows for KISS FM called R Solution, along with 4 Hero and Phil Asher; the music on these shows was truly outstanding, in contrast to the lame commercial playlist they have today. His compilations with Ian O'Brien (The Soul of Science) are also highly recommended. Squarepusher, whose crazed jazz noodlings have a whiff of Pastorius about them, seems to have imbibed the spirit of Frank Zappa along with lots of Orange Sunshine. Because he is a genius he is also prone to acting like a prat.

A very important gig for me was New Year's Eve 1997, when I played at north London's Alexandra Palace. There were 25,000 punters in that night, and the chill-out room was myself, Gilles Peterson, James Lavelle and Tom Middleton. It was the first time I had played on the bill with Gilles, and also the first time I realized how much common territory we were occupying with our playlists! Rather than blindly opposing electronic music, he was prepared to look for the best of it, with an open-minded attitude that has served him well over the last decade. Talking Loud made some great records, such as U.F.O.'s 'Flying Saucer' or even Roni Size's 'Brown Paper Bag' as well as the classic 4 Hero albums, but somehow they never seemed to come to terms with electronic music.

Later I played with other UK jazz luminaries like Patrick Forge and Russ Dewbury, and had a similarly positive experience. These people aren't bandwagon jumpers or fashionistas, they are genuine music lovers, obsessed with the music above all else. Not historians trying to recreate the past, but visionaries trying to create the future, and we all owe them a debt.

Being electronic and being jazz aren't incompatible, its just that not many have really succeeded in combining the two in a satisfactory way. By the mid nineties there were more and more artists mixing jazz and electronica in some way, making a new type of fusion. There was Ludovic Navarre, who Laurent Garnier memorably called 'the funny old melon farmer', who sold 200,000 copies of his first St Germain album. In Munich there was the new Compost label run by Michael Reinboth, which started out on a left-field electronic tip, then in 1995 made the first in the series *Future Sound of Jazz*.

The sleeve notes are interesting: 'I call it hybrid system music because it is the combination of analogue ideas and sounds with digital steering. It's just the beginning!' There are shout-outs to Xenakis, Sun Ra, Can, John Peel, Black Dog, Lee Perry, YMO and Clara Rockmore, but no jazz icons at all. Another thing not present is any noodly solos; an underground electronica vibe persists throughout. This series is now up to volume 9 and still going strong!

Michael has an amazing collection of East European jazz releases, and was able to bring some totally unknown gems to a wider public, like the seriously unhinged Polish a cappella band The Novi Singers. His *Glucklich* series showed an equal passion for obscure Germanic Latino music and who knew that such a scene even existed before? And his good friend Rainer Truby has put dynamite under the Latin music stage, becoming a superstar across South America in the process (as well as having his own brand of wine!).

Another outstanding band on Compost is the Swedish crew Koop, who have an outstanding vibes player in Matthias Stahl, and a rare ability to write perfect pop songs with a real jazz flavour. Not to mention Michael's own group, Beanfield. Meanwhile Jazzanova have performed similar miracles in Berlin, once the capital of brutal unforgiving techno, raising the standards in programming and musicianship, and bringing a remarkably eclectic mixture of talents into their studio, including the superb singer Victor Duplaix, and jazz legend Doug Hammond, who used to play drums for Mingus, Donald Byrd and many more. Their JCR imprint continues to amaze with its open-minded A&R policy. Compost and JCR certainly aren't loved by everyone – one club in Germany recently sent me an e-mail telling me not to bring any of their records, and I got thrown off the decks in Ibiza for playing a Jazzanova record. But in a few years I reckon even they will be ready for it. They have brought an intelligence to dance music that is sorely lacking in the mindless thudding of commercial beats.

Other parts of Europe seem to be experiencing a similar phenomenon. Bugge Wesseltoft used to be an obscure ECM artist, but since he formed the Jazzland label he has won a Grammy, toured with Billy Cobham and created a style that's all his own. Norway's Jaga Jazzist are totally insane, if their excellent *Ninja Tune* albums are anything to go by. In Finland, Jimi Tenor started Puu Jazz to release obscure Finnish jazz cuts from the 1970s, while the man himself seems more than able to deal with any style of music, not to mention Nu Spirit Helsinki and many more.

Sweden's Esbjorn Svensson seems likely to be the next Scandinavian jazz superstar, with his band EST already in the album charts across Europe. And in a more dancey vein, Andreas Saag records as Swell Sessions and Stateless for labels like Jamie Odell's Freerange and Hollow.

Obviously, America is the home of jazz, so there are many artists growing up with their parents' record collection – one of those is hip-hop producer Madlib, whose jazz sensibility is no suprise when you find that his father played with Mingus and Dizzy Gillespie. After success with Lootpack and his alter egos Quasimoto and Dudley Perkins, he plunged headfirst into jazz with Yesterday's New Quintet. On his track 'The Jazz Cats' he lays his influences bare: 'I give props to Blue Note, Black Jazz, Impulse!, CTI Records, Milestone, Atlantic and Muse. There's plenty more that I could name but y'all won't put 'em to use.' Now he has a prestigious job remixing the back catalogue of the longest-running label in jazz history, Blue Note.

Travelling in America, you soon realize the ubiquity of jazz music. Which reminds me to mention the superb Ubiquity label out of San Francisco. Born out of the tiny but superb record store Groove Merchant, they have grown to become San Francisco's finest export. They are possibly the only label in the world to give a 100 per cent money-back guarantee of satisfaction with all their records! With compilations like *No Categories!* and artists like Ptaah, Quantic, As One, John Beltran, Roy Davis Jr, Nobody, Stateless, Theo Parrish, etc., I doubt they have many dissatisfied customers.

Chicago has some great stores too, like Jazz Mart, with over one million jazz albums in stock. Shopping in Chicago reminds you that the amount of jazz records that ever come to the UK is but a tiny fraction of what's out there. Chicago was also home of the legendary Cadet records, original home of the much-loved singer Terry Callier and the influential producer Charles Stepney, whose albums with Rotary Connection are reaching a wider audience now than they ever did on first release.

They also released the magnificent Dorothy Ashby, a harp player who is a million miles from Alice Coltrane, but beautiful nevertheless and a must for any ambient-jazz fan. Like so many holy-grail rarities, these have all been recently re-pressed, so now's your chance to grab 'em…I once spent a Sunday afternoon locked in Dusty Grooves, the legendary shop where you can find all those rocking horseshit-rare platters, and that was an education.

Twenty years on from *Wheels of Steel*, scratching and turntablism get slowly bigger, surely a direct descendant of the jazz solo, especially with the 'battling' aspect. At the earliest hip-hop jams, the most popular crew would win the other side's equipment, a tradition that jazz bands had back in the mists of time. DJs like Q-bert and Craze (who've both been DMC world champions three times, the maximum allowed) – have taken prestidigitation of the platter to a new pinnacle. Miami's Craze can play any tune you like, just using the first note of a song over and over while jamming on the 33/45 button and pitch slider. It's an awe-inspiring skill that makes jaws hit the floor. In Portland, Oregon I was booked to go on after DJ Craze. 'No, I'll go first!' I said modestly…but I'm no fool, I knew that whoever has to follow Craze is liable to be booed at very loudly – which is exactly what happened to the next guy.

Montreal's Kid Koala has taken ambient scratchadelia to another dimension, as well as forming the funky live band Bullfrog. His solos cutting up worn-out old jazz from the twenties recycle the Old Testament into a born-again beauty that's recycling at its best.

In the UK The Scratch Perverts have done something parallel without just copying US styles. Their extended routine of scratching without records is truly groundbreaking – and funky too. They have achieved what DJ Shadow talked about some years ago, each one soloing like a bebopper with vinyl and crossfaders. Wynton Marsalis might not like it, but Bird and Miles sure would have done. Just like free jazz, some deny that it's even music. But the kids love it – and it's in a direct lineage of avant-garde music from John Cage via Ornette Coleman.

So what's happening in the UK? Well, 'So What?' is of course one of Miles's most famous compositions, and even became a UK hit single in the early 1990s for Ronnie Jordan. Among that band was a young man who we now know as IG Culture. Together with 4 Hero's Dego, he founded the inspirational club The Co-Op, and released a string of amazing records under the names Likwid Biskit, Da One Away, Quango and now New Sector Movements. He and Dego are Miles and Bird, the most exalted archbishops of the West London thing. 4 Hero began in the rave days with their label Reinforced, being pioneers of jungle and drum'n'bass, but cast that aside years ago to experiment with the breakbeat further.

4 Hero became the vanguard of black exploration on the London scene, and even tasted mainstream success with the hit 'Starchasers' and introduced the world to jazz poet Ursula Rucker. They also toured with a huge (and expensive) orchestral section, some of whom were from the Big Chill's in-house string section, Instrumental. And I already mentioned their R-Solution show, which is a worldwide cult nowadays, traded on CDRs and websites around the globe.

Dego and Marc practically invented the fast-growing genre 'broken beat', or as IG would prefer to call it, 'bruckstep'. Rhythmically, IG's in a different league from anything in UK music that I have heard before; beats so black you can't see your feet. Instead of the machine-perfect sequencer, or repetitive hip hop, the beats are subtly refracted, with the downbeat not where you expect it to be. The beats are chopped up so they always change – check the work of Domu, another producer who's coming up fast. Dego's craziest stuff seems to come out under the name Pavel Kostiak, a name to cherish, I can promise you. His most recent album *At the Musicals* (!) has familiar titles like *The King and I* or *Chitty Chitty Bang Bang*. It's well out on planet mong, if you ask me, like a modern-day *Bitches Brew* – and sure to become a collectors' item, especially after I dubbed it the *Trout Mask Replica* of broken beat. Some of it sounds like The Mahavishnu Orchestra without the guitar solos. It's on Dego's label 2000 Black, itself named after a track by Roy Ayers.

IG Culture revealed his roots by doing a George Duke song on a recent B-side, and Roy Ayers made a guest appearance on the 2000 Black compilation. This fertile West London scene also contains more great musicians, like future star Kaidi Tatham, the nearest thing we have to Herbie Hancock over here, and a member of influential crew Bugz in the Attic, who amazed everyone at Eastnor in 2003, as did the sensational singer Bembe Segue, who was one of the highlights of the festival. The Bugz crew have a new CD out right now called *DKD*. (Dego, Kaidi and Daz-I-Kue.) Not many foreign crews have managed to emulate these quirky innovations yet…although Detroit's Ayro and Amsterdam's Red Nose District seem to be having a good attempt.

Other stalwarts of London's post-jazz diaspora include two talented Kiwis, one in the shape of Nathan Haines, creator of the Bemsha! club and now Easy Living, and the first UK artist to play at Kevorkian's influential Body and Soul club in New York. 'Impossible Beauty' sounds like a standard already, but he wrote it himself, with a top line of the sophistication of a Monk song. It even quotes 'Round Midnight' for a second, but it is catchy enough to be a future classic. The other one is pianist Mark de Clive Lowe, who is much in demand on the keys, as well as running new label Antipodean. Both are probably looking at Jamie Cullum and thinking 'Hmmmm…' Not to mention Jamie Odell, whose Jimpster albums have been a success. Mostly he's in the Bays as well, a perennial favourite live band at The Big Chill.

Ninja Tune have their own jazz hero in the shape of Jason Swinscoe, whose Cinematic Orchestra has amazed and delighted audiences across the globe, and whose album was voted best dance album of the year by BBC website visitors. I played a memorable gig with them in Central Park a few days before 9/11. They also blew people away at the fabled Montreux Jazz Festival, with the mighty Fontella Bass on vocals. And there are the complex stylings of Chris Bowden, who's also appeared with 4 Hero and The Herbaliser, whose horn section moonlight as The Easy Access Orchestra. Not forgetting aforementioned Jaga Jazzist and Poland's Skalpel. And of course demon vinyl hound Mr Scruff, who sampled the great itinerant musician Moondog to create the Ninja favourite 'Get a Move On'. And he made an album called *Trouser Jazz*, as well as entertaining songs about seafood. So he obviously shares some wiggy jazz-humour sensibility with the likes of Slim Gaillard.

And how could we omit DJs like Nik Weston, whose club Bite Your Granny is one of London's funkiest, and whose latest compilation *Sakura: Aural Bliss* is getting mad props from many quarters. His knowledge of obscure Japanese jazz is almost legendary.

Well, I have run out of time and space right now, so I have to bring this little essay to a close. Looking at US sales figures, jazz in total represents only 3 per cent of all record sales, that means 23,000,000 albums last year, including all those Kenny G records, and many back-catalogue sales. To put that in perspective, it's half the size of the Christian music industry, and a third as big as country music. On the other hand, it's one of the few sectors that's actually growing. Majors seem happy to exploit the back catalogues of jazz artists – after they are dead and not causing a nuisance by asking for royalties.

To the corporate world nowadays, jazz is synonymous with easy listening, that dreaded term that signifies music for people who aren't really into music all that much. Witness the millions spent on promoting artists like Harry Connick Jr or his modern equivalent, Jamie Cullum, dubbed the 'David Beckham of jazz' by some dumb publicist who ought to know better. Still, for a $2 million advance most musicians would gladly suffer such humiliation – his current album has sold 600,000 copies in the UK this year. And just by being twenty-four years old he's putting a young face on the scene, which isn't a bad thing. With people like Gilles pushing him in the right direction, maybe he will astound us – he certainly has the UK by the ears right now. He likes to sing about cocaine, but let's hope he keeps his nose clean.

In fact he's been seen as part of a new wave of easy listening. Now I always used to start my sets with a Laurie Anderson tune, that goes 'welcome to…Difficult Listening Hour', so you can guess my position. I mean, that was the point as I saw it back in the ambient days, to make radical easy listening, not smooth but spangly. So I want my nu jazz futuristic not nostalgic, thank you. We need a new Miles, not another Richard Clayderman.

Maybe the secret is the fact that for the first time over-forties buy more CDs than teenagers. Perhaps because they haven't yet worked out how to download them for nothing. Whatever you like at sixteen, you will be bored of at thirty-two. That's the way it works, and as you inexorably turn into your parents, your CD collection will start to contain things no teenager would ever admit to liking.

At least such mega-platinum sales will silence those who think that jazz has no place in today's marketplace, and maybe it will encourage some people to dive further into that well of inspiration. And when they do, they will discover a treasure trove of musical marvels that can easily take a lifetime's listening.

Happy hunting, folks!

recommended listening

Dorothy Ashby – *Afro Harping* (Cadet)
Roy Ayers/Ramp – *Come into Knowledge* (Blue Thumb)
Donald Byrd – *Steppin into Tomorrow* (Blue Note)

Doug and Jean Carn – *Infant Eyes* (Black Jazz)
Cinematic Orchestra – *Everyday* (Ninja Tune)
Alice Coltrane – *Ptaah the El Daoud* (Impulse!)
Alice Coltrane – *World Galaxy* (Impulse!)
Miles Davis – *In a Silent Way: The Complete Sessions* (Sony)
Miles Davis – *Kind of Blue* (Columbia)
Miles Davis – *Bitches Brew* (double CD, Sony)
George Duke – *Inner Source* (MPS)
Herbie Hancock – *Dedications* (Sony Japan)
Herbie Hancock – *Thrust* (Columbia)
Eddie Henderson – *Heritage* (Blue Note)
Bob James – *One* (CTI)
Thelonious Monk – *Monk Alone: The Complete Solo Recordings 1962–68* (double CD, Sony)
Marc Moulin/Placebo – *The Placebo Sessions* (Counterpoint)
Novi Singers – *Vocal Jazz from Poland 1965–75* (JCR)
Pharoah Sanders – *Karma* (Impulse)
Lonnie Liston Smith – *Cosmic Funk* (Flying Dutchman)
Lonnie Liston Smith – *Reflections of a Golden Dream* (Flying Dutchman)
Sun Ra – *Lanquiduty* (Evidence)
Leon Thomas – *Spirits Known and Unknown* (Flying Dutchman)
Various – *Message from the Tribe* (Universal Sound)
Various – *Reefer Songs* (Stash records)

house music: the haçienda must be built

Hillegonda C. Rietveld

Now this is how it started – Bam! Stop the clock…

'What is this?!' I shout as I fall off my stool. It's a Saturday night, somewhere at the start of autumn 1986, in Manchester, England. I'm in the DJ box of The Haçienda Club, there's smoky atmosphere, people milling and dancing down on the main floor, my then music partner Mike in control of the decks. The speakers…well, they just blurt out the maddest bursts of single-minded electronic disco energy. The biggest foot I've ever heard – that bass drum is going right through my body – bom bom bom bom, goes that big fat bass drum.

'Aaaaooououoooooouuuuueeeeeeeehhh' – the deep male vocal pitch ascends like a hyperbolic version of Gospel excitement, higher and higher, up to a queen's scream…' I want you! Yes I do!!!' – screams a throat thick with indulgent overtones. Wow! The piano jumps in, stabbing away in a sequenced Afro-Cuban rhythm. I try to dance while I sit and somehow my butt lands next to, rather than on, the seat of this high stool.

'Are you on drugs?' – I look up into Bernard Sumner's concerned face and scramble up.

'No! No, what…What is this music?!' I blurt out.

'Love Can't Turn Around', with Daryl Pandy on vocals: Farley Jackmaster Funk's over-the-top remake of a much more restrained and rather noodly Isaac Hayes's 'I Can't Turn Around' was my first introduction proper to Chicago House. This was madball assertiveness and oddball sleaziness in one, at a faster, more tumultuous pace than the usual dance music of that time. It seduced, but didn't mess around. Raw and fiercely camp, it was just there, straight in – bam!

And so my love affair with house music commenced; there was 'No Way Back', as a sultry Adonis track observed. It was time to 'Jack Your Body' with JM Silk. It was time to get that house music that sets you free. Marshall Jefferson's house anthem confirmed it was time to stop being a wallflower and to 'Move Your Body'. All of this music came from Chicago – catching the spirit of the time, it gained popularity in similar post-industrial enclaves of the UK, from where it was packaged and exported elsewhere. The Haçienda was one of the very first nightclubs in the UK to embrace this music wholeheartedly. Combined with house music, this club came into its own for a few intensely bright-burning years in the late 1980s and early 1990s. House in context of The Haçienda shows a strangely intertwined story of electronic disco and punk, rebuilding, rewinding, recreating; this became especially clear to me during dialogues with cultural critic Jon Savage in relation to my research on house-music culture. Chill and take a seat on the edge of a volcanic fault line that exists in the cultural politics of transatlantic dance-club music.

disco's revenge

In the beginning, the legend goes, there was Jack, a benevolent creature with community spirit who invited all into his house. To jack was the pelvic engagement with any animate or inanimate object available on and around the dance floor of a select set of Chicago clubs in the 1980s – people, speakers, walls; a precedent was set during Frankie Knuckles' Saturday night into Sunday morning DJ sessions at The Warehouse, itself modelled on a sexually experimental 1970s dance scene in New York. This was followed in 1983 by Frankie's sessions at The Power Plant and Ron Hardy's crazed nights at The Music Box, and Farley Jackmaster Funk's packed-out Friday and Saturday nights at La Mirage, while a host of other, more temporary, dance events started to occur. The trends were set by venues that mainly, but not exclusively, catered for African-Americans, as well as Latinos, and where it was hip to be gay. Promiscuously, just like disco and garage, which are part of the same dance-music family, house provided a welcoming democratic musical home; when you entered it, it became 'our house', changing and evolving as a consequence. Mr Fingers' sampled shouts on 'Can You Feel It' sum it up: house was a feeling, rather than a particular format – in 1988, Jack's manifesto was added to that particular tune. DJs played a wide range of dance music; depending on the DJ this could range through soul, funk, electro, electronic post-punk, new wave and a splattering of funky rock – whatever took the mood. Most important was the way in which the DJ presented this material, taking the crowd places in terms of emotion, of a feeling. Each DJ had a distinct style in this. The stately smooth soulful Frankie Knuckles favoured the soulful vocals of African-American disco, occasional Afro Beat and even the electronic Euro-trance sound of Kraftwerk; Knuckles brought with him a technique of careful programming and the full use of the available audio equipment. DJ Ron Hardy reputedly had a more chaotic style, crossing European post-punk with American dance whilst speeding up records and twisting the EQ settings to such physically shaking extremes, it made people scream. On local radio, the Hot Mix Five captured Chicago audiences during their lunch breaks with increasingly clever mix antics and tape edits. As a consequence, house took on a variety of sensibilities, which enabled a variety of culturally specific mutations in the years that followed its arrival from across the Atlantic.

Chicago was also the heartland of reactionary Middle America, where, in 1979, two years after Frankie Knuckles' arrival at The Warehouse from New York's disco dance scene, white rock-radio DJ Steve Dahl had instigated the 'Disco Sucks' campaign. Through his radio programme, he rallied a huge crowd to bring their disco records and get in for less than one dollar at the next baseball game at Comiskey Park stadium, where White Sox played a double-header against the Detroit Tigers. After the first game, in front of about 70,000 people and prime television, a riotous crowd of white men detonated a huge pile of disco records accompanied by great cheers, applause and a hysterical rush on to the game field – the follow-up game had to be cancelled that day, much to the disgust of many sports fans. Similar actions occurred elsewhere, encouraged by similar rock-radio DJs whose hatred was fuelled by reactionary values.

It seemed fun to destroy what had become the cynical milk cow of the major record industry – a monotonous disco beat attached to everything from pop songs to classical music – and to destroy the polystyrene artifice of upwardly mobile aspiring tackiness that the 'medallion man' of disco seemed to personify. Yet, disco was arguably a subconscious articulation of a meeting between youth and working class as well as, importantly, ethnically and sexually marginalized groups. While gay disco had held the flag for a shift in sexual politics, it was African-American and Afro-Hispanic dance music that fitted under the umbrella of disco, in addition to (later) Euro disco. Women indulged in a new-found freedom on the disco dance floor, unshackled from patriarchal couple dances and enjoying matriarchal African-American divas who freely expressed a contemporary female desire. Amongst the records on that pile in the stadium were classic examples of African-American R&B, from soul to funk. Yet, the initial development of the New York hip-hop scene was also based partly on a distaste for the disco clubs in that metropolis, despite its own roots in the disco twin-table mix technique that had been adapted to an MC-based sound-system format; neighbourhood disco clubs often seemed too violent while the sexually adventurous Manhattan clubs were regarded as too gay.

As my students pointed out during a seminar, destroying those records was, to some extent, comparable to the Nazi destruction of Jewish books and jazz records, a fearful reaction to modernity. 'Disco Sucks' was a hate campaign based on insecurities generated by changing cultural, social, economic and technical values. The increased dominance of studio-generated recordings over live music and the increased use of electronic studio-based musical instruments also produced a sense of unease. Not only was DJ-generated music the cheaper option during the economic downturn that followed the oil crisis of 1973, also copyright legislation had continually encouraged the development of studio-based composition. The macho guitar realism of rock, its concept of the live concert and album included, was threatened in the process. All of this seemed to add up to the argument that disco was rather superficial and artificial; it was like the ultimate escapist postmodern dream machine – and inevitable within this context. Although the tag 'disco' became un-cool, dancing to records did not stop as result of the actions of hysterical radio DJs and rock journalists; in the velvety darkness of specialist nightclubs, dance culture continued its developments.

In Chicago, disco rose from its ashes, bigger, better and bolder, as house music. Using affordable Japanese electronic-recording studio technology, bass and drum tracks were created to boost the rhythm sections of the DJ's record selections, or to spice up the existing repertoire. Chicago supported a burgeoning competitive dance scene that was a hotbed of funky minimalist electronic dance music. When house solidified into a recognizable genre in the mid 1980s, with that distinctive heavy-disco bass 4/4 beat, the funky electronic bass lines and insistent samples flirted with the metronome marching beat. There were explicit sexy vocals, with men pining for yet more of that sexy love game and women in the throws of ecstasy, similar to the disco format of the 1970s.

Over in New York, the underground dance-music crowd kept on dancing at a big selection of clubs, including trendy places like The Funhouse, with the energetic punky electro sounds of John 'Jellybean' Benitez, or Madonna's hang-out, Danceteria, with DJ Mark Kamins, as well as after-hours party The Loft with influential David Mancuso, giving us the more gentle Peech Boys' 'Don't Make Me Wait' or D-Train's 'Keep On' in 1982. In the UK, such dance-club music was marketed as garage house, its name borrowed from Larry Levan's DJ home, Paradise Garage; this club existed on the front line of many new social and cultural features – not only in the way of presenting dance music, but also as an early experiment in X (E for English readers) as a dance drug. It was also early victim of a mysterious disease, AIDS, which exploded like a silent demographic bomb in the mid 1980s. Unlike the raw, rough-and-ready tracks from Chicago, the New York material that Knuckles shipped in from the Garage and Loft scenes was more sophisticated, made for fantastic sound systems. The kind of sound that Manchester's The Haçienda's sound system, with its badly echoing, high glass-ceiling warehouse space, certainly couldn't provide; but this did not stop the Manchester club from embracing new urban American dance music wholeheartedly.

post-industrial haçienda

There are some parallel links between Chicago and Manchester: both early industrial cities in the world; both suffering quite early on from post-industrial economic decay; both sporting a long-standing ethnically mixed working class. In Chicago, this included a mix of African-Americans and Hispanics; in Manchester the predominantly white ethnic mix included the Irish, while from the 1970s onwards Jamaican and South Asian descendants were also starting to put their stamp on the city. Mancunian working-class hedonism generated mad nights out, not only on the white-dominated gay scene but also at the now famous, then underground, Northern Soul weekenders of the 1960s and 1970s. There are also parallels with Detroit, once home of Ford and Motown soul, in terms of inner-city economic shock, which left its heart deserted by the middle classes. Manchester's inner city is smaller than Chicago's and benefits from an additional huge student population and a thriving local gay scene, which stimulated its night-time economy, making it a space ripe for a new dance explosion.

Rob Gretton, manager of local Factory Records band New Order, provided a catalyzing opportunity. A whimsical 1980 reincarnation of intensely angry and movingly depressing guitar band Joy Division, New Order did not want to abandon Manchester when their income allowed them to do so, and as many successful musicians had done before. Rather, they wanted to return something to the place that had made them who they were. In tandem with finance from Factory Records, which had already experimented with a punk and new-wave night in neighbouring council estate Hulme, New Order set up The Haçienda Club, which opened in May 1982. Gretton was inspired by Toffler's *Third Wave*, which popularized the idea of a post-industrial information society, describing how manufacturing industries of developed economies were replaced by service industries and supported by new information technologies. The 'techno rebels' who took charge of such technologies would be the controlling pioneers in this. In parallel fashion, according to Savage, this book also influenced the middle-class African-American techno originators in Detroit, who borrowed the term in 1988 to market their music in competition with Chicago house, with the help of

Northern Soul aficionado Neil Rushton. Toffler's visionary ideas not only encouraged New Order's quest for the newest electronic-music technologies that eventually propelled them to stardom, but also supported the idea of converting a warehouse space in Manchester for entertainment purposes, a service provider within the local and global night-time economy.

The Haçienda's building was in a boat-showroom space on the edge of an abandoned part of Manchester. It was positioned in front of the narrow canal that ran through central Manchester, connecting the Rochdale Canal and Manchester Ship Canal, past deserted blackened nineteenth-century industrial spaces with hollow broken windows, wild green and yellow flowers sprouting each summer from their roofs and cracked walls. Mythology has it that the ghosts of Irish child workers, from its previous incarnation as factory space, still wandered about this rebuilt version.

As a cultural space, The Haçienda was modelled on the New York clubs that Factory Records' main band, New Order, had visited, such as Danceteria with its multi-storey ex-factory dance floors and, even more so, Paradise Garage. Also Mike Pickering, Rob's side-kick and The Haçienda's creative manager, had been there when we travelled there together, in the early 1980s, as electronic dance combo Quando Quango. Through these visits, Mike gained a PR contact in the mid 1980s, who sent him house music direct across the Atlantic before it hit UK shops, which helped his budding DJ career. Paradise Garage was housed in an old parking garage, to which the space returned after the club closed in 1987. It boasted two massive rectangular spaces, one for dancing and one for sitting around, serving no alcohol but water, doughnuts and fruit from bars decorated with big flower displays. The sound system, designed by Richard Long, was phenomenal – two decades later I still remember tangibly the fantastic hi-fi stereo balance that allowed for normal conversation yet moved the hairs on your arm. When we were there, the Fridays were mixed and Saturdays catered for a mostly male African-American and Hispanic gay crowd. Dance music and the friendly exalted crowd were the main focus, celebrating a hedonistic gay sense of abandon, supported by stimulating and psychedelic dance drugs – mythology aside, it was a truly inspirational place. Gaining some similar reference points at The Warehouse in Chicago, we returned with fantastic ideas of what a good club could be like.

Central to Ben Kelly's retro-modernist post-industrial design of The Haçienda was the dance floor – the stage was displaced into the sidewall. As part of the sound design, a special bass bin was placed low on the floor, just underneath the stage; this enabled the bass to 'grab' the feet of dancers on the floor, giving them an extra boost. Many locals were suspicious of what felt like an alien, cosmopolitan dance concept, with its pale-blue-painted brick walls, grey-painted concrete floor and lack of reassuring pre-modern flowery carpets. Initially, only fashion-conscious gays, art-school students and Factory Records fans with miserable poses turned up, huddling downstairs in the cocktail bar, named The Gay Traitor. Occasionally, a coachload from London turned up, with people who were curious about the well-publicized design. In those early years, VJ Claude Bessy displayed surreal samples from video nasties and rare B-movies, while DJ Hewan Clarke worked almost every night of the week, playing rare grooves and jazz dance steps, mixed up with visionary electronic dance like Klein & MBO's 'Dirty Talk'. Despite the dislocated stage, many musical acts, two or three a week, performed there on weeknights, such as Cabaret Voltaire, Divine, Grandmaster Flash and Kurtis Blow. To be honest, most of the time the place was cold and most of the (straight) guys kept their damp heavy grey coats on.

The Haçienda's membership form carried a little poem, or quote, that had provided the club with its name and mission statement. It was from a 1953 Situationist manifesto on urban space by Ivan Chtcheglov, which Rob Gretton had found in a book, lent by Factory boss Tony Wilson, called *Leaving The 20th Century*. This book had been republished in 1974 as part of an underpinning of the punk philosophy of Malcolm McLaren, the manager of the Sex Pistols whose background was in a London art-school education. Chtcheglov's extract prophetically declared that:

You'll never see the hacienda. It doesn't exist.
The haçienda must be built.

It was like a prediction of the democratic space of disco, where the people are important, rather than the performers. *Haçienda* is a Mexican word for the main house on a ranch or farm. The statement seemed to suggest that the people make the place; they build The Haçienda, they produce the dream, they build the house and they rock it down. It took at least four years to create such a momentum and, before it did, The Haçienda was nearly bankrupted. Until 1986, that is, when its luck turned and house music arrived in the UK from Chicago, New York and Detroit, marketed as, respectively, house, garage and techno, finding a new home, a place to root. The European avant-garde idea of a *haçienda*, as a space made by the people that inhabit it, and the African-American notion of house, as a democratic sonic dance space that depends on interaction between groups of dancing people, seemed to click like long-lost partners.

acid house
When the first wave of house-music party activities seemed to slacken in Chicago in 1987, a selection of its main protagonists went on tour and visited The Haçienda on a cold Monday evening in March. These included DJ producers Frankie Knuckles and Marshall Jefferson (sporting gold-lamé shoulder pads), as well as artists Fingers Inc and Adonis. To put this into context, this was one month after electro outfit Mantronix had made an appearance and just two months before local indie band Happy Mondays played on The Haçienda's stage. We had some serious catching up to do, as these Chicago guys seemed to have had their party already: Adonis wailed 'We're Rocking Down The House' while we were still building up to it!

Later that year, Chicago house music's bass line started to wobble, modulate and inflect, the opening shot of a host of abstract tracks based on the Japanese-produced Roland bass line and drum machines, announcing a psychedelic dance crossover with electronic post-punk that eventually caught the European imagination even more. Chicago-based Phuture called it *Acid Tracks*, when they'd found that their Roland 303 bass sequencer had a random mind of its own when left unprogrammed; not only that, it produced a syncopated sequence that was actually danceable. In line with an African-American political sensibility also found in bebop jazz, which celebrates the 'wrong' notes in between the slave master's system, this machine's particular ramblings were recognized as art. Well, a fantastically weird inflection to dance to anyway, so way-out that no one has quite managed to ever reproduce it. Ron Hardy loved this track; his drugs'n'sweat-soaked DJ sessions at Chicago's African-American dance club The Music Box were perfect for this sound. Here Hardy took his crowd over the hill of Frankie Goes To Hollywood's 'Pleasure Dome', a gay chart anthem from Liverpool that was his usual opening tune, mixing up electronic punk with home-grown house music. Acid house articulated an altered sense of reality that only made sense on a subconscious level, late at night, when the brain has phased out in a blinking string of micro-sleeps.

On the other side of the Atlantic, British indie music journalists were twiddling their thumbs at the time, muttering gloomily that music would be going back to the future, plundering the past and leaving nothing new but regurgitated archive material, in faint echoes of a pessimistic analysis of postmodernity. Few may have read Stuart Cosgrove's 1987 sleeve notes for FFRR's *Acid Tracks* compilation, which showed futuristic foresight into acid house, which was only to explode a year later in the UK and West Europe, leaving a musical legacy of techno, rave, trance and jungle galore:

> The sound of acid-tracking will undoubtedly become one of the most controversial sounds of 1988, provoking a split between those who adhere to its underground creed and those who decry the glamorization of drug culture. Either way, the sound has settled in Chicago and is providing House's second generation with their own identity. Jack is dead welcome to the weird world of trance-dance.

On the dance floor in Manchester, most of us did not know the finer details – we just danced the night away to these new batches of tunes.

halluçienda

At first, clubbers on The Haçienda's dance floor just amazed themselves, dancing, tentatively, to the new psychedelic beat, which only occasionally made its way on to the local soul radio programme. In London, pirate radio DJs like Jazzy M spread the word, inspiring local kids to make their own material; a house compilation on London-based Warrior Records featured some rocking bass lines, which nevertheless lacked that modulated acid sound, that sense of total abandon, displayed by Chicago's African-American electronic acid tracks. In Manchester, The Haçienda DJs programmed those instrumental tracks as filler, between big vocal tunes. Over the weeks and months, we danced into a tighter and tighter spiral of beats 'n' bass line, slowly developing an addiction to this acquired taste and by 1988 the club filled up with crowds that queued patiently around the corner to get in. As a lucky side effect, this padded out the hard-surfaced dance space, improving the sound quality and warming its cold damp air – in turn, this made the club even more attractive.

Acid house took centre floor on The Haçienda's Friday nights, in Manchester a traditional lads' night out. This was interspersed with techno house from post-Fordist Detroit; for example, Rhythim is Rhythim stated in abstract pure energy that 'It is What it is' – no words needed, just your participation required. The high warehouse glass ceiling dripped, rained even, with condensation from hot sweaty bodies as straight boys embraced each other in this homosocial setting, dancing and jumping to their hearts' content like they'd just won the World Cup. In tone-deaf mysterious swoops, playing around that 4/4 beat, Pom-pom Paing-paing Pam-pam-pam Pom-pom, some Mancunian genius called Gerald named it 'Voodoo Ray'. Meanwhile, these happy twenty-four-hour party people from Salford supplied love-to-dance drugs all weekend that left people smiling into Mondays, when in the cold cutting day, the radio s'expressly doctored the house. Poing Poing Poing Poing.

In London, an additional psychedelic club concept developed that fitted the mood. Paul Cons, a sexual activist who had joined the creative team of The Haçienda, had been partying in acid-house clubs like Shoom and three-day warehouse-party extravaganzas in early 1988. He returned full of new ideas about the Balearic mix that, like early house music, was a hotchpotch of all music that felt good to dance to, this time inspired by the sexually liberated dance clubs of holiday island Ibiza. On Wednesdays, he installed Ibiza-inspired HOT night, featuring a tiny pool occupied by new playboy-fresh-from-Ibiza Danny, while huge beach balls bobbed over a dense crowd in beachwear. Like Saturday nights, this was a night for loved-up sweet soul vocals of garage and stately, deep house productions à la Knuckles. This musical selection attracted a more diverse crowd that included a significant amount of women and gay boys. The garage house sounds of Arnold Jarvis suggested we'd 'Take Some Time Out'. The atmosphere felt light and full of love, much like its lofty predecessors from a decade earlier in the underground dance scene of New York. DJ philosophy was delivered by Jon Da Silva, who applied what he had read about programming specialist Larry Levan's and mix pioneer Walter Grosso's DJ techniques – both were DJs who created narratives with their music selections, like artists using ready-mades.

Also in the summer of 1988, Graeme Park joined The Haçienda's roster – a skilful mixer who had introduced house to Nottingham. He liked to superimpose an 'a cappella' on top of the instrumentals, a DJ trick developed in New York that was not yet common in the UK. He managed to blend vocals and rhythm tracks from separate records or various of New York's MAW (Masters At Work) productions with three turntables at once, in effect re-editing and remixing live, dancing around in the DJ box with his hands floating free. The crowd had never heard anything like it – they were elated! Not surprisingly, he won the national DJ of the Year Award in 1990, and again in 1991. Occasional guest spots showed the American club DJs to be good at this too, but they were no threat to the local DJ establishment, as the visitors were The Gods from far, far across the waters – an inspiration, rather than a comparison. Away from DJ-box politics, to the dancing crowd it was ALL GOOD, totally fantastic stuff, to dance to your heart's content, hands in the air just like you don't care, surrounded by friendly faces. By 1989, after swaying like one family to Ce Ce Rogers' 'Someday', all agreed in complete unison with Ten City that 'That's the Way Love Is'. In particular, from summer 1988 to summer 1990, it all clicked, clicked so neat, slotted so finely into place, that funky bass line and loving feeling, away from the gloomy rain and economic deprivation into the embracing matrix of an incessant deep electronic heartbeat. Boom boom boom boom.

mobile home

English clubs like The Haçienda were only granted licence to be open till 2am. In disorderly fashion, in New Order's 'Fine Time' spirit of winter 1988, the low-ceilinged cellar was taken for just one night – we danced from midnight to almost noon, enveloped by the perfect bass and tweet of an oversized stadium PA like hypnotized moths caught in the light. Non-stop house beats spiritually erased boundaries, walls, limitations, niggly irritations. Erased were the daytime doubts that this house might be a bit too monotonous, too selfish, too hedonistic. Everything was all right, check check check this out, yeahh, jumping, pumping, yeahh. 'Work It To the Bone' with the rhythmical minimalism of LNR. The night is long, 'A Day in the Life', as New Yorker Todd Terry summarizes with pushy orchestra samples. One guy rediscovered his childhood epilepsy by gazing into the strobes on E – he was carted to hospital, while dancing feet erased the vacant spot with the bloodstain as the beat carried on. Nothing could take away that amazing sense of BEING. By 5am, in the chill-out room, legs and feet poked out upwards from between huge bean-bags screen-printed with *DIS-ORDER*, people recovering from too much of everything, vaguely realizing that only music, not alcohol, can carry you through such a nightly marathon. 11am, walking along Whitworth Street towards The Cornerhouse, black skirt and black tights splattered with yellow paint and mud from the dusty floor, a change in dress code seemed necessary, towards more casual, funky, baggy all-night dance clothes.

Empty warehouses, unregulated by the local law-enforcement agencies, were fine to carry on the party into the mornings, long after the clubs were closed. In major cities, sound systems were hired, down south from reggae crews, but up in the north of England from the usual PA folk. We danced till dawn; feeling fast yet wading slo-mo through strobe-lit smoke, losing all sense of dimensions, of time and space. Free at last, free at last! Alice had her *Adventures in Wonderland*, in an *Altered State*, 'Living the Dream'. The music played forever on and on and with Sterling Void we realized and knew, in every fibre of our being, that 'It's Alright'. The faces of friends blurred and our hands rose to the heavens, as we became brothers and sisters who sang with Anthony Thomas that we'd make it to Joe Smooth's 'Promised Land'.

Like newly-weds we were in love with nothing but the feeling of just being, there, in the here and now, for eternity. Chilling out after hours in The Kitchen, a squatted council flat in Hulme, walking distance to The Haçienda, chatting, dancing, hugging with perfect strangers and feeling so, oh so safe. Just like that E provider on acid, who on New Year's Eve had recklessly stuffed his car doors with banknotes and happily left it unattended outside a warehouse party on a bleak deserted factory terrain strewn with lorry tyres. Feeling fine, despite the dripping workhouse spaces, the puddles on the floor, the dirt on the yards outside, the lack of sanitary provision, the grey wet Sunday dawns in stifling parochial towns. It was even OK when the car driver could not decide what side of the road to drive on, needing one person to keep an eye on the traffic lights and another to change gears for him, as he pushed pedals and did the steering quite ably. In it together – sing along now, La-di-dahhh.

It seemed kinda idyllic, really, in those days of almost naive innocence, but the bumpy ride was only just around the corner. Things were not as nice as it seemed, the smoke curtain was hiding more than tired burned-out faces and rusty concrete wreckage. Where there's high-risk get-rich-quick business, the extreme professionals get in on the action: from tabloid journalists to machete-swinging drug swindlers exploiting the night-time economy; and from Conservative government MPs to a specially assigned police force attempting to regulate the ensuing mayhem, imposing an ill-fitting daytime mentality on a night-time cultural logic. A well-documented moral panic set in by the winter of 1988 and sensational front-page headlines announced that cops fled discos and young girls were seduced at mass orgies. It was the best marketing campaign the entrepreneurs could have hoped for. Mass media attracted young mass audiences who were signified by the figure of the so-called Acid Ted, who went crazy for the night at what tabloids dubbed 'raves'. By summer 1989, party organization, DJing and dance-drug dealing had become serious career options. Large dance events took place in the countryside where police forces were thin on the ground, taking over villages and country lanes. Convoys of cars could be spotted at weekends on the M25 and M62, the M6 and M1. More at home in that outdoor festival terrain, and politicized by state antagonism, anarcho crusties like Spiral Tribe got in on the action, as well, all into the pleasure-dome tent, dancing to that evolving house music.

Stoke-on-Trent was an example of how an old small-town disco became the centre of the weekend universe, the front line of Haçienda-house hedonist DIY philosophy, building a mythological space, a situation, and inviting all to join in. Here, in a little club called Shelley's Lazer Dome, Delight provided house music with E galore. Many of The Haçienda's regulars ended up going there, as the Manchester club closed between February and May 1991, because door staff had been threatened for the first time with a gun. Just over a month after it reopened, in June, six doormen were stabbed and the local police had sealed off the club that summer night, effectively locking all in for the night, not to let them go till dawn, one by one, under a hovering helicopter between rows of riot-gear-clad police and barking police dogs, each clubber photographed on police video. Manchester had been Madchester, but in that year it became Gunchester and local police did not make it easier for its dance clubs. At Delight, Mr Scruff's manager-to-be Gary McClarnan learned his trade in at the deep end, managing a new and upcoming DJ, Sasha, who had been Jon Da Silva's protégé – the three of them also lived in the same building in Manchester. Sasha was a handsome long-haired DJ who later often appeared on the front covers for *MixMag*. At Delight he really started to make his name – he had the crowd go wild to his DJ selection of Italo piano house, uplifting tunes that made everyone throw their hands in the air just like they did not care. The place was heaving, wall-to-wall, people dancing on chairs and tables, even those tiny one-pole cocktail platforms on which people swayed and balanced precariously to and fro. The only place to sit was under the washing basins of the toilets, a meeting point for London, Manchester and Durham. Walking from the sunny-lit sauna of the dance space into the dark winter air, cones of steam emerged from people's heads – we were cooked! Together with The Haçienda, this was a source of inspiration for party organization Renaissance, who set up around the time The Haçienda celebrated its tenth birthday and who, in the late 1990s, managed to set up in Ibiza and go global with cleverly marketed merchandise.

Close convoys of delighted folk would carefully find a way back home through snowed-under motorways. At service stations like Knutsford, the party continued, bam bam bam bam. That raver who could not choose what to buy from the service counter and ended up buying five drinks: 'Erm…I'll have this one. No, I'll have that one. Oh, I'll have them all!' Some were unable to stop and danced on to a portable tape player, while copies of dancezine *Outa Control*, covertly financed by Delight, exchanged hands. Straight guys hugging – boys in it together. Yet it all felt like a threat to the people who worked there, especially the law enforcers and security people. There was something quite anarchic about this liberal reinterpretation of space; a service station was for people to be processed – fast and functional – it was not for lingering, and most certainly not for fun and bodily motions which seemed innocent to the people who made them, but which looked like an orgy with coats on to the lone security man looking in from the outside. At some point in 1991, also there – a temporary night closure occurred, 'to keep the acid house from coming in'.

come with me

'Disco Sucks', so the threatened rock fraternity observed more than a decade earlier. Disco was thereby placed on the lower ranks of the sexual pecking order. Suckers were those bottoms, those New York rent boys, those punks on their knees whose ripped jeans patched up with safety pins were, as I learned from Savage, part and parcel of their occupational hazard. Sucking dick gets no girl pregnant, leaving lovers free to move on without papa having a say in the matter. One big extended raving house family in a nomadic home mobilized by the car and the telephone did little to promote the patriarchal nuclear family either. Queer pale punks as well as sexually experimental African Americans and Hispanics, it seemed, had been at the vanguard of a wider social change that no original rocker could hope to stop, however big their dynamite stick. It was like history had repeated itself after all, but differently, like a spiral that had gone full circle, but one step ahead. This time, there was no glamorous Donna Summer and no glam rock. Situationist DIY punk ethics and disco's blurry sexual politics had been married to a hedonistic fun that was not even aware of 'no future', or any whichever future – instead, time is now, a forever present, caught in the beat. Some took this sense of freedom to the feminine realm of 'handbag music'. For others, it was more the Day-Glo psychedelic raving acid-trance part that had inspired. The more gloomy punks indulged in the repetitive machine rhythms of techno, giving up sex, it seemed, for cyborg sacrificial consciousness. Jungle appeared via rave, as a cross between house and ragga in the inner city of London, to become breakbeat-driven drum'n'bass, in many different flavours. In a way this development is comparable to the emergence of hip hop in the 1970s, as disco's Jamaican sound-system-based sibling. Some of the drum'n'bass producers temporarily merged with a speeded breakbeat take on New York's garage, to produce jittery UK garage in the late 1990s. And so we dance, on the beat, breaking the beat, into new rhythms of the times.

Almost speechless and appearing like a noisy repetitive bump in the night, this house-inspired dance culture seemed to maintain a sense of a dark underground, an intense secret, an intense sense of unspoken conspiracy, which was its ultimate seduction. House records seduced; building blocks for DJ antics, they existed without recognizable performers as pure yearning studio constructions of loving bliss only available on black vinyl in mostly blank sleeves. This lack of presence sucked you into the club, onto the dance floor, around the country, into the record shops, every week, again and again, begging for more, more, more, in order to get closer. This void sucked you into its mystery, its faraway secret origins, deep into the ur-mother's heartbeat. Finally, in 1992, I managed to get myself on a plane to Chicago, for my pilgrimage. I went to my Mecca – The Haçienda had merely been a temporary temple of worship. Or so it seemed. Because, as I found out, house music is promiscuous and curious, it is an exchange between many influences, from funk to punk, from gospel to Latin music. The original clubs that had thrived a decade earlier had gone; Hardy was dead from drug abuse. Knuckles had returned to New York, where AIDS had created a vulnerability in its once buoyant dance-club scene – the illness and untimely death of many hardcore hedonist dancers had produced a gap which few could fill. The producers I met in Chicago were mostly African-American heterosexual males, who produced deep house for an English market, rather than a local one, which they said had been dead since around 1987 when the main radio-mix show shut down, illegal parties were clamped down on and important clubs closed.

Interestingly, they were just as curious about me as I was about them – in their teenage years, they had felt inspired by the electronic music that came out of Europe, from the UK and Italy in particular. Instead of finding the magical source, I had found myself on the other side of a transatlantic musical exchange, like being reunited with an extended musical family. Singer Daryl Pandy, a big diva of a man with a big taste for cheesecake, worked on advertising tunes directed at the African-American market for producer Vince Lawrence, who had once rewritten those lyrics for 'Love Can't Turn Around'. They worked in a punk-like basement loft decorated by Vince's translucently pale partner Evie with the surreal resin casts of real people she had acquired from a New York artist. Chicago's new DJ generation, such as Derrick Carter, were caught between deep house, the arrival of Euro-American rave culture and extreme techno noises from the European Continent. The vinyl-pressing plant, which had made a lot of the early house tracks possible and was home to the infamous Trax label, was close to the White Sox Comiskey stadium, pressing crackling vinyl from second-hand recycled records in a dusty place with a rattling air conditioner. A Corvette with a taped-up smashed back window was parked outside, belonging to the owner, Larry Sherman, a tired-looking man who gestured me to come in with a laid-back 'Welcome to the house that Jack built.'

outro

So close to an imagined mythical source, it seemed that there was jack all left of my love dreams but a little heart-shaped dollop of vinyl I picked up from the dirty factory floor. The Haçienda must be built, over and over. House music is like a crossroads of sensibilities that travels with its dancers, with the process – it is its demand for the engagement of the body with the music that is most important. I fell from my high stool in 1986 because I felt an intense energy that I could not quite explain at the time – now I realize it moved the air like a camped-up queer punk version of gospel and Farley's bass 'foot' to boot. I may have encountered the format of house prototypes earlier, but never executed in that powerfully over-the-top way. That creative pulse preceded acid house, which since has propelled a globally dispersed post-industrial generation into dancing the night away en masse with an intensity that resigned disco to the chill-out room. House was like a stone thrown into a big pond, and the circular waves are still criss-crossing back and forth, phasing each other into new shapes. In New York the signs were there in the early 1980s, when I looked from the stage into the wide-open eyes and big grins of several thousand enthusiastic African-American and Hispanic gay men at Paradise Garage. By the early 1990s, house music gave me the strength to DJ in front of several thousand strangers on a swaying platform in Rotterdam. It inspired me to research my PhD and to publish yet many more words on dance culture. Like any love affair, after the honeymoon is over it's not always that easy to maintain the original spark in the relationship. There are plenty of bleakly dull repetitive moments, when that repetitive beat drills my head without touching my heart, creating a hollow feeling without the excitement of syncopation. There are also those moments when writing seems to make little sense, when it is good just to exist in the music – moving, flirting, playing – here, in the now, where time is forever. Stop the clock. Bam!

recommended listening

Adonis – 'No Way Back' (Trax Records)
Adonis – 'We're Rocking Down the House' (Trax Records)
Black Noise – 'A Day in the Life' (Champion Records)
A Guy Called Gerald – 'Voodoo Ray' (Rham Records)
Farley 'Jackmaster' Funk feat. Daryl Pandy – 'Love Can't Turn Around' (DJ International)
Marshall Jefferson – 'Move Your Body' (Trax Records)
Marshall Jefferson feat. Ce Ce Rogers – 'Someday' (Atlanta)
LNR – 'Work it to the Bone' (House Jam)
Phuture – 'Acid Tracks' (Trax Records)
Rhythim is Rhythim – 'It is What it is' (Transmat)
JM Silk (aka Steve 'Jackmaster' 'Silk' Hurley) – 'Jack Your Body' (Underground)

Joe Smooth, feat. Anthony Thomas – 'Promised Land' (DJ
     International)
Sterling Void feat. Paris Brightledge – 'It's Alright' (DJ International)
Ten City – 'That's The Way Love Is' (WEA International)
Various – *Chicago House 86–91* (Saber Records)
Various – *Classic House 1* (Master Cuts)
Various – *Classic Acid 1* (Master Cuts)
Various – *The Garage Sound of The Deepest New York* (Republic
     Records)
Various – *The Garage Sound Volume III: The Third Generation*
     (Rumour Records)
Various – *History of House: Tracks from the Channel Four Series 'Pump
     Up The Volume'* (Channel Four)
Various – *The History of The House Sound of Chicago: From the Very
     Beginning* (BCM Records)
Various – *The House Sound of Chicago, Vol. III, Acid Tracks* (FFRR)
Various – *Jackmaster 1* (Westside Records)
Various – *Jack Trax: The Third Album* (Indigo Music / Precision
     Records)
Various – *Jack Trax: The Sixth Album* (Indigo Music / Precision
     Records)

recommended reading
Ivan Chtcheglov – 'Formulary for a New Urbanism', in Christopher
     Gray (ed. and trans.), *Leaving The 20th Century: The
     Incomplete Work of the Situationist International* (Rebel
     Press)
Stuart Cosgrove – Sleeve Notes for *The House Sound of Chicago,
     Vol. III, Acid Tracks* (FFRR)
Jon Savage – 'Machine Soul: A History of Techno', in *Time Travel:
     From The Sex Pistols To Nirvana: Pop, Media and Sexuality,
     1977–96* (Chatto & Windus)
Jon Savage, with Hillegonda Rietveld (eds) – *The Haçienda Must
     Be Built!* (IMP)
Alvin Toffler – *The Third Wave* (Bantam Books)
Matthew Collin, with John Godfrey – *Altered State: the Story of
     Ecstasy Culture and Acid House* (Serpent's Tail)

Sheryl Garratt – *Adventures in Wonderland: A Decade of Club Culture* (Headline)

Hillegonda C. Rietveld – *This Is Our House: House Music, Cultural Spaces and Technologies* (Ashgate)

Hillegonda C. Rietveld – 'Living The Dream', in Steve Redhead (ed.), *Rave Off: Politics and Deviance in Contemporary Youth Culture* (Avebury)

eclectic electric
– 1979–1983 –
a post-punk posting

Alan James

Music and memory.

Like scent, the faintest whiff of a note or a melody will transport us to a time and a place in the past. Music and time travel. Music is about identity, and expression and self-awareness and, at its most primal, about communication. It's also a great channeller. Picture a huge valve radio with exotic destinations on its dial but set to the BBC's Light Service. A small boy can hear The Beatles jangling out of the machine. At first, it's the sound that he responds to. It has formed itself a separate signal and stood out from the heartbeats, traffic, rattles, whistles, the general soundscape of growing up, the ambient drone of everyday life. But it is still recognizable as music – a familiarity with nursery rhymes and hymns helps with that; it has a power and a fascination far and away beyond the everyday. This raw and exciting syncopated thud. It's cutting through the static into a new world. The boy's mother shortly finds him attempting to remove the back of the contraption with the intention of crawling in to meet The Beatles.

How did I know what they would look like when I got there?

I remember distinctly wanting to find out what they looked like, how they could fit such a small stage in there. How was it done? Where did the sound come from when it didn't come out of the radio speaker? When I first heard and saw a record it seemed like a magical talisman. There's still an element of the conjuror involved in creating all that three-dimensional cacophony from this trick of aligning a microscopic point in a groove or sticking a guitar into an amplifier.

Later, in Weston-Super-Mare, or some such seaside resort, I remember walking into an art-deco café on the front. The most amazing, modern, alien-sounding music swarmed up out of the domed jukebox and around the curved, nautical walls of the white building. It was glittering and sharp and had an incredible hard and shiny edge, which was flattered by the architecture.

Music and space.

This was Joe Meek's incredible production of The Tornadoes' 'Telstar', although I didn't know it at the time. Joe Meek was like a British Lee Perry, one of the first producers to use the studio like an extra member of the band. I had *heard* music before but it was the first time that I had l*istened* to it. Later I saw the four members of the group in silver astronaut suits playing their one-hit wonder on a grainy black and white TV screen. They were The Kraftwerk of the sixties in one zany spotlit moment. Almost unbearably new. A glittery and unavoidable future.

The next time I heard anything so unrelentingly modern was probably about ten years later. A lot of music got taken to the bridge, or maybe underneath it, between times. Yes, I'd listened to Faust and Tangerine Dream and Yes, and to other progressive outfits. Started getting a bit clever with Hatfield and The North, Zappa and Beefheart. And then I got a seven-inch with Fast Product embossed on the roundel and dropped 'Being Boiled' by Human League down on an unsuspecting Grundig. Forged and cast in Sheffield it probably gave that city the beginning of its reputation as a sort of UK Detroit. Cabaret Voltaire were not slow in joining the production line soon after. This was a grungy, squelchy, low-core, solid vinyl slab of future funk that kicked all of the punk guitar bands firmly into touch. It was a record with a bad attitude. I wish I had stolen it off my friend's brother. In fact it was this sibling whom I had had to restrain from kicking in the television set a few months earlier, as 'Whispering' Bob Harris from *The Old Grey Whistle Test* sat cross-legged on a beach in Malibu interviewing Supertramp about their latest concept album.

'Being Boiled', along with Big in Japan's 'Big in Japan', was the most exciting record I had heard since Television's 'Marquee Moon', Père Ubu's 'Dub Housing' and anything by U Roy. And it was British.

Punk had hit Hull in 1977. I first noticed it when Stuart Cosgrove came back from London in a pair of drainpipe jeans. That term I promoted The Damned and The Adverts in the student union. Captain Sensible said we were a bunch of middle-class wankers. At that time we felt very left-wing so, as you can imagine, we were jolly annoyed. But of course by then the punk earthquake was merely an aftershock in Hull. It's sacrilege to say it but both the Pistols and The Clash were really just pub rock'n'roll bands; the music wasn't new but the attitude was. In London things were already starting to move on. The 'White Riot' tour was mere tyre tracks around Britain's pubs and clubs. But Mick Jones had already done a show in Liverpool with The Clash and given Pete Wylie a guitar to play with, and the word was spreading.

One of the most important after-effects of punk was that it shifted, however ephemerally, the focus of the music industry from London to the provinces. Factory started in Manchester and was the most vociferously anti-metropolitan of them all, but that story is so well known that it hardly needs revisiting. Postcard Records emerged in Edinburgh. There were countless others. Music began to take on regional shapes and forms. As indicated, Sheffield had pre-techno electronica; there were jazz-funk-reggae hybrids in Bristol; and ska and reggae merged with fast guitar punk in the West Midlands to create the 'Two Tone' scene. Liverpool was planning an early to mid eighties chart takeover based on big soulful vocals, poetic lyrics and jangling Searchers-style guitar. Roger Eagle had taken his massive, and immensely influential, record collection to the seminal nightclub Eric's, where he would DJ and promote some of the new bands which were cropping up every week. Nothing new for that city, of course; there were hundreds of bands practising in cellars and school halls at the time of The Beatles.

Then came something called post-punk. Post-punk must not be confused with new wave, which was much more pop-orientated and involved shiny suits and skinny ties. The Knack was new wave and we don't really want to go there. The Americans loved new wave but they soon got better and produced Sonic Youth and ESG. Post-punk was perhaps more art-orientated in its approach and involved a pushing and testing of musical boundaries. It may have had a correlation with postmodernism. In music its best reference, perhaps, was as a signpost to another path. It meant, more than anything else, a time to experiment. A time to get busy.

If punk was crap it was a fertilizer. The period stretching from 1978 to 1983 gave birth to a sprawling, eclectic and creative brood of British bands and musicians. Scritti Politti's first single, 'Skank Bloc Bologna', was put out by a nascent Rough Trade Records which was then still just the one shop in Portobello Road. It carried detailed instructions on how to make a group and cut a record. The budget for the recording was printed on the sleeve. The band functioned like a commune from their Camden flat. There was a flux of musicians, artists and polemicists who spun round Green Gartside's hub. They had picked up the advice offered by Mark P's Deptford delta-based *Sniffin' Glue* fanzine. It was the time of the by-now-famous DIY ethic. Learn three chords and form a band. Make a record and then get all your mates to come round and paste the individually designed artwork onto the bags one by one. Find someone who knows John Peel's number and give it a go. Customize your school shirt or buy a Nepalese army one from Lawrence Corner. Just go out there and do it, design for a living. Design for living. A lot of the earlier groups had members who had been to art school; actually it became a little bit of a cliché. I remember a group from Bristol who sang a song about this, but alas, without irony. This new-found confidence (arrogance – Rick Wakeman might have said) also led to experimentation and openness to influence. The punky-reggae hybrid of the mid-to-late seventies had started something interesting. African percussion and Roland Kirk blowing came in, as did jittery white-boy funk and rap. Everyone listened to heavy-dub reggae but funk, soul and Fela Kuti had their place too. Rhythm became incredibly important. The Slits sang, 'Silence Is A Rhythm Too'. The roots of such influential nineties bands as Massive Attack can be seen at this time. Everyone was referencing his or her music in a postmodern frenzy. Each week the pages of the *NME* had a bewildering list of new bands that just kept coming and coming.

Bands like Scritti Politti and Bristol's The Pop Group operated like political cells. This was still a time of left-wing radical activity. By the end of the seventies, Margaret Thatcher's Conservative government was firmly in control. We had a police force not a police service. People were regularly having nuclear nightmares. There was a fascination with ideas around control, surveillance and censorship. A visit to a gig or club could quite likely also result in sharing the room with a bunch of infiltrating Nazi skinheads. Both Scritti and The Pop Group were heavily influenced by reggae and dub. Scritti were attracted to a more Apollonian, cerebral, Gramsci-fuelled methodology whilst The Pop Group brought a funked-up beatnik Dionysian fire to the party. They were both sides of the same coin. In Leeds, The Gang Of Four took their socialist agenda to the studio and their live work vanguarded a post-Clash future for music and politics. The Au Pairs came rattling out of Birmingham with their song about gender, 'It's Obvious', with the rallying chorus, 'We're Different But Equal'. Writers like Paul Morley, Ian Penman and Chris Bohn were trailblazing like no one since underground scribes Charles Shaar Murray and Mick Farren in the sixties. They gave all of this regional energy a national showcase. The *NME* had something like 250,000 readers in the early eighties. *Sounds* fielded great writers too and added another six figures to the readership. These opinions cut a swathe across a whole generation of music lovers. On the radio, the only essential soundtrack to what was happening was the John Peel show, although the pirate Dread Broadcasting Corporation (DBC) had just started up in Ladbroke Grove, West London.

Now living in London, I got a job as booker at the University of London Union (ULU). The venue was relatively unknown then, set in a quiet backwater in Bloomsbury, opposite RADA. This was 1979 and there was a great sense of flux, fear and opportunity in the air. There was a guy called John Cullen already installed there who was good at lights and the technical side of things. One night, as we plotted whether we could get away with a pink and blue wash over The Slits, he told me that he knew he wanted to be a techie from a very early age. He said that his father had found him sitting at the table with the kitchen clock in pieces around him. Apparently he had been attempting to move the hands forward an hour so that teatime would come earlier. I felt that we would make a good team.

At that time there were 47,000 students in the collegiate membership of the student union so we felt that there would be one audience there and the rest could come in from the town. The hall in Malet Street was a square wooden box with a balcony, a 20'x20' stage with screen, cyclorama, fly tower and a backstage area. The dressing rooms had bulbs around the mirrors and the foyer had a Stanley Spencer mural, which the University had forgotten it owned. There had been concerts here before but these were mainly internal affairs that didn't blip much on London's cultural radar. Within three years this hidden Bloomsbury perch would become part of a network of venues, including the YMCA in Tottenham Court Road, the Railway Hotel in West Hampstead, the ICA, and the Electric Ballroom in Camden, which would play host to a fertile sprawl of performance activity which punk's DIY culture had helped to kick-start. It wasn't long before the sort of experimental bills pioneered on this circuit began to appear at the bigger venues like the Lyceum and Hammersmith Palais. A few years later, in the mid eighties, the venue found itself with a new ents programmer who had just completed a philosophy degree at University College across the road. His name was Ricky Gervais.

The promotional programme began with a judicious co-production partnership with cult promoters Final Solution. Their underground contacts brought many excellent bills to the stage. An early flurry of triple headliners set the agenda with combinations of Joy Division, A Certain Ratio, Scritti Politti, Durutti Column, Section 25, Cabaret Voltaire, This Heat, Delta 5, Prag Vec, Swell Maps, Z'EV, Fad Gadget, The Associates and others. Killing Joke came on a Tuesday night and frightened the living daylights out of everyone. Very soon the programme was running weekly and achieving some pretty special results. Jamaican artists like Culture and Michael Smith would play alongside 23 Skidoo, Aswad and The Au Pairs. The venue became one of the few places in London where new bands could break through. Bills like The Raincoats, Marine Girls and The Impossible Dreamers were enthusiastically received. The Marine Girls later became Everything But The Girl. The Slits played a magnificent show whilst the floor space played host to the Manasseh sound system. Out on the mixing board would be the likes of Adrian Sherwood or Grant Showbiz. Sherwood did the most full-on show with just him on the outboard and Keith Le Blanc on stage with a gigantic and perfectly miked drum kit. Meanwhile round the corner at the YMCA it was possible to have seen a triple bill of Echo and The Bunnymen, Teardrop Explodes and Orchestral Manoeuvres in the Dark for a nominal £1.50 ticket price.

As ideology-based politics began to fragment, and the emergence of the 'issue' allowed a newly politicized music business to line up behind causes. The miners' strike, Nelson Mandela and Steve Biko all had their theme tunes in the eighties. Many figures from all aspects of the industry lined up to be counted. At ULU we even did a Rock Against Racism gig with John Martyn accompanied by Phil Collins on drums. Later, in the most materially obsessed decade of the last century, groupings like Red Wedge sounded out against Babylon and gradually became absorbed by it. The Revolution was televised. The raggle-taggle Thompson Twins in their 'eight-piece in long overcoats' phase did CND fundraisers at ULU every other month. We became the home for RAR, CND, *City Limits* magazine and Rock Against Sexism benefits. We eventually started wearing badges saying 'Rock Against Everything in General'. We had George O'Dowd as a regular because he lived with Marilyn in the famous Warren Street squat, which was just round the corner. We put on Bauhaus, sold out, and people were rioting outside for tickets, proto Goths jumping up and down on car roofs in genteel Bloomsbury. A 'Culture Club' graffito appeared on the front of the building and no one had the faintest idea what it meant. We assumed it was the logo of yet another countercultural movement and that they would be on the phone next week asking for a benefit to be organized soon.

An underground stream sprang forth in the same period. The new synth axis around Stevo's Some Bizarre label reversed into darkness and began the tributaries that would culminate with groups like David Tibet's Current 93, Steve Stapleton's Nurse With Wound, Coil, Psychic TV and Test Department. Test Department were taking the bashing of metal to a much more agit-prop level and their ferocious but compelling performances railed against the superpowers and the soon-to-be-imminent government-planned decimation of the mining industry.

The turn of the decade also saw the rise of The Comedy Store and other similar venues. Post-punk was interested in the way that bands approached their relationship with playing live. So the cabaret style of performing became popular for a while. Along with this came the notion of multi-media billing. Richard Strange began his series of events in Soho called 'Cabaret Futura', named after the Dadaist interventions at the start of the century. An early cabaret incarnation at ULU was called The Rhythm Club, which was promoted in Bristol first and transferred to London and would typically involve bands like Maximum Joy and The Electric Guitars playing alongside DJs, comedians, short films, poets and jugglers. Groups were also questioning their physical locale a lot more. It was at this time that the notion of playing in different and unusual locations became prevalent. Paul Morley and Wah's Pete Wylie had invented the concept of rockism in the *NME*, questioning the whole 'paying your dues' skank and the excessive tour values of boring old rock and roll. The new wave of groups not only questioned rock and roll but also the very architecture of the tour and the stage. Later Echo and The Bunnymen would consider touring Britain by ship and playing on beaches, Bill Drummond would eventually propel them along ley lines or, more famously, in the psycho-geographical shape of a large floppy-eared rabbit. Bill Butt filmed a brilliant winter video of the band at Buxton Opera House. New Order grew out of Joy Division and despite an early appearance at the Forum in Kentish Town they were notoriously choosy about the type of venues in which they played and the frequency of those appearances. It was at this time too, fired by the populist articulations of punk, that bands began to question the student-venue circuit. A circuit that was considered as being the only way to break a band in the seventies became viewed as closed and elitist in the new regime. Usefully, ULU welcomed non-students at the time.

One group who played at ULU in this period arced across to the WOMAD Festival in Shepton Mallet in 1982. It was 23 Skidoo. This was a Camden band that started out as just another jabby 'white boys on funk' group but then started to delve deeper into the possibilities of rhythm and sound. Yet another group to take its name from a William Burroughs text, they had hit upon the notion of the urban gamelan, the instruments being a collection of found and purpose-designed objects: everything from Indonesian gongs to oxyacetylene gas cylinders and the tried and tested Tibetan thigh-bone trumpet. Their arrival at a world-music festival seemed as obvious as any other mad collaborative idea at the time. The juxtaposition of their performance with an actual twenty-five-piece gamelan orchestra from Java raised no one's eyebrows.

The people who had put together the Rhythm Club events at ULU had also started an interesting audio magazine in the West Country called *The Bristol Recorder*. In the summer of 1981 I was invited to a meeting in a West London synthesizer studio of another side project, then given the working title of Rhythm 82. This was probably the inaugural meeting of what soon became WOMAD. Bristol, which was still home to The Pop Group, was just about to produce post-punk's first major stab at the real charts when Pigbag took their 'Papa's Got a Brand New Pigbag' groove monster onto TOTP in early 1982. *The Bristol Recorder*'s crew of Thomas Brooman, Bob Hooton, Martin Elbourne and Stephen Pritchard were an eccentric mix of students and punks who went to interview Peter Gabriel in Bath. He ended up posing them a question instead: 'Would it be possible to produce the context in which musicians from all over the world could meet on one stage to play their own stuff and to collaborate with each other where desirable?'

In the end the 1982 WOMAD Festival at Shepton Mallet had five stages and was held over the weekend of a national rail strike. The eclectic spirit of the times was reflected in the line-up. Echo and The Bunnymen and The Beat played alongside The Burundi Drummers and the master Kora player Alhaji Bai Konte. Don Cherry joined his stepdaughter's band Rip Rig and Panic; up on stage Neneh was flying: 'come on you guys, dance! I'm pregnant and I'm dancing'. The Beat were riding high in the charts at the time and were mobbed by hundreds of school kids who were taking part in a music-education project tied in with the show. The fabulous Prince Nico M'Barga, with possibly the largest pair of platform-heeled boots in the southern hemisphere, brought Nigerian highlife music to the stage in truly spectacular form. The Musiciens du Niel floated gypsy pipes and strings across the heads of the audience and were there to meet them on the way out too, selling the same instruments and other exotic artefacts. My mum had her first curry at the age of sixty and my dad grooved to The Chieftains in a field.

The reverberations from this weekend have rolled down through the years. The world-music scene now, with its Radio 3 DJs and World Music Awards, is a very different place from how it was two decades ago. Despite the support of the *NME* and a few stalwarts on the London fringe-music scene, most people thought the idea mad and probably only tagged along because of the presence of the altruistic Peter Gabriel.

My main job at this event was to produce the visit by the Drummers of Burundi. WOMAD's programming director Thomas Brooman had witnessed this ground-trembling ensemble up close at the Rennes Festival in France the previous year. Despite making a strange impact on British culture via the sixties freak hit 'Burundi Black', and having their trademark rhythm pirated by Malcolm McLaren for the backbeat to Bow Wow Wow, the group had never played in the UK. Actually, many people had heard the ensemble before: their percussive force had formed the underlay for Joni Mitchell's 'Jungle Line' track from her hit album *The Hissing Of Summer Lawns*. On the Friday night after their triumphant first appearance at the festival the whole of the campsite rang out to the sound of the Burundi beat: people hit drums, fences, corrugated iron roofs and dustbins, anything they could grab at and worry with a stick or their bare hands. On the next day's appearance they came down off the stage and played on the grass, surrounded by hundreds of spellbound new fans. The huge drums were hollowed out of specially cultivated trees and weighed a ton. These would be balanced on heads and played above and then flipped down onto the floor without missing a beat. Those not drumming flailed about in mimetic choreography and large Masai-like vaulting leaps. As the drumhead sound got louder and louder it was punctuated by clacking strokes on the sides. Chanting vocal exhortations drove the performance on and on. The late and much lamented Pete De Freitas, the excellent drummer for the Bunnymen, ambled over to invite some of the drummers to jam that night. 'We're Echo And The Burundi Men,' deadpanned Ian McCullogh. The Burundi rhythm became the sonic thread for the event. Despite severe financial difficulties in its aftermath, WOMAD was a watershed event for the eighties. In the last months under the editorship of the far-seeing Neil Spencer, the *NME* printed a front-page image from the festival and an enthusiastic review from Vivien Goldman. In those eclectic electric days world music and post-punk noise were on the front page of the country's biggest broadsheet music paper.

Earlier in the visit I had managed to secure a support slot for the Drummers at The Clash's major gig at what is now the Brixton Academy. After much to-ing and fro-ing with the band's manager, the elusive Bernie Rhodes, we were on the bill and due to start the sold-out show for the main attraction. Last year Joe Strummer passed on and I found myself writing these words to send to whomsoever I thought might appreciate them. It's a nice way to leave this episode, I think:

> Twenty-four drummers from Africa, first time in the UK, cramped into a dressing room along with various tour personnel, eyeing a desultory plate of twelve sandwiches and six half-cans of lager. Promoter not interested in negotiating an increase to the supplies that are so necessary to power their stamina-sapping performance. Yours truly with insufficient funds to finance thirty meals. Joe Strummer pops his head in to say hello and clocks the meagre hospitality. Grabs my arm and walks me into the room opposite. Together we bring platefuls of food and drink from The Clash's rider in for the Drummers. Everyone sits down and has a feast.
>
> Later on the Drummers are playing to 5,000 pogoing new fans while Strummer and Jones bounce gleefully in the wings.
>
> The driver takes the exhausted Drummers off to the hotel while I stay back to watch The Clash play an excellent show. Wandering back to our room, I am aware of a commotion in the corridor. The Clash are coming offstage accompanied by streams of well-wishers. Their tour manager cordons off the band. As they pass by Strummer grabs me again and I find myself in the dressing room with four members of the band, steam rising from their backs, having a drink. The five of us, for different reasons, are lost for words.
>
> Joe Strummer was a great guy.

Michael Morris was working at the ICA and had continued their programme of quaintly titled 'Rock Weeks'. These 'Rock Weeks' had consistently showcased the best in new talent on the alternative scene; they became a barometer of what was likely to be kicking up some dust in front of music-industry chequebooks. The programming on this one was hardcore. German industrialists were in on the coat-tails of DAF and Einsterzende Neubaten and were determined to take it one step further. This was the era of big men hitting metal with lumps of metal. An apocryphal tale around the show always delighted me. These groups were not resistant to wielding an oxyacetylene torch or two but tonight the band were actually jack-hammering through the ICA stage. Through the spray of splinters the venue's programme manager was in deep discussion with the venue's technical manager, the splendidly named Lurker, about what to do.

'Look at that, what can we do?'

'We'll have to pull the plug.'

'We can't do that, it'll be like censorship or something.'

'Well, it may be art now, but it won't be art first thing on Monday morning.'

The ICA had invited me to curate one of these 'Rock Weeks' in 1983. Preliminary meetings led to a suggestion that the project should turn into a mini WOMAD, and Thomas Brooman, Bob Hooton and I started to work on the programme. In the baking hot summer a series of double bills featuring combinations like Test Department and The Aboriginal Artists of North-east Arnhem Land rolled out and saved the WOMAD name for posterity. One of the things I remember most about this series was a lunch we had in the ICA bar with Peter Gabriel, at which he explained that very soon we would be able to buy music down fibre-optic cables, thus cutting out record labels and shops. What a whacky idea, we thought, in that unfortunate way that you often sideline the ideas of the eccentric English visionary. Who had the last laugh?

In the same year I co-promoted a series of concerts at The Everyman Cinema in Hampstead with The Fall's manager Richard Thomas. Our basic premise was that each band should choose their favourite film as a support act and so Barry Adamson (*Man with the Golden Arm*), The Go-Betweens (*Whistle Down The Wind*), Psychic TV (films by Antony Balch and Derek Jarman) and Virginia Astley

(*Elvira Madigan*) did. The spirit of the times meant all of the shows would sell out, and the unusual formatting was welcomed rather than spurned. Thomas Brooman and I spent one dusty afternoon scooping up handfuls of trailing ivy from Highgate Cemetery to drape over Astley's piano.

I used to go out a bit. People started to do parties. They were word-of-mouth affairs and often involved unlicensed venues. *The Face* would write about the scene in their famous 'Hard Times' issue, which did as much for the sales of Levi 501s as it did for taking underground culture into the streetlights. There was nothing really that much different between these runnings and the shebeens of Notting Hill, which had been operating since the fifties. Or the classic New York rent parties with Kool Herc jacking his decks into the nearest lamppost and inventing hip hop in the process.

It's 1983 on a Saturday night in Battlebridge Road just behind King's Cross Station. A bevy of Victorian gasometers curtsied in slow motion across the street. This was the warehouse sector, the sort of locale that looked like it actually knew hard times. The streets were still cobbled and film crews didn't need much dressing to create an artful Dickensian feel or a dodgy atmosphere. It became the locale for Mike Leigh's film *High Hopes* and has now disappeared like Boadicea's grave and Harry Potter's train under the latest tectonic shift in inner-city plates. In those days it meant queuing for two hours to get in; in four years' time you'd be able to get to Paris in less. A long line of people dressed up in everything from ripped jeans to thrift-store romanticism pay £2.00 to get in and £1.00 for a can of Red Stripe. Up on stage Rip Rig and Panic's Sean Oliver and Neneh Cherry are at the decks dropping everything from Sequence through Sly and The Family Stone to Ornette Coleman. They may have called the night 'Miss Pibb's Hot Sty'; there was certainly a band of that name which flowed out of Float Up CP, who fell out of Rip Rig and Panic. Sean onstage in a kilt with his bad-ass bass held low – God rest his soul. This was the warehouse party in its proper configuration, cheap, tasty and a health and safety officer's worst nightmare. The gathered tribes were there because the music and the vibe were right and there was no West End club malarkey. It was a crowd which was cool without trying too hard. There was a connection between this scene and the one which The Wild Bunch brought together around the same time at the Dug-Out in Bristol, with the some of the same faces visible at both parties. There were raves like this going off all over the country and with Spiral Tribe's Mad Max celebrations just around the corner, this was the beginning of the specialist club circuit and the genesis of an uncommercial rave culture. Five years later this response to colour bars and prices – but actually, most importantly, just the shit music – in London's West End clubs, would become the mainstream. As the man said, 'When the going gets weird the weird turn pro.'

Then came The Smiths: it all started with a phone call from Mike Hinc at All Trade Booking. In a strange twist of fate Mike had been responsible for the early editions of Rock Weeks at the ICA. He was now one of the most adventurous booking agents in Britain. The Sisters of Mercy and Australian band The Laughing Clowns were booked to appear at ULU on 3 May 1983. The Smiths had only played five gigs in their short life but interest in the demo tape was so hot that a London showcase was needed. I had at first thought that the bill would be clunky, but Mike was very persuasive and the show came together with the band going second on. They played a fast and furious set with James Maker joining them on stage for interpretative dancing. It must have been one of the last gigs he did with them. The set list included 'Hand In Glove', 'What Difference Does It Make?', 'Reel Around The Fountain' and 'Accept Yourself'. It was only their second gig in London but you could see the beginnings of a fan base at the front. The showers of flowers had not yet become de rigueur. In the audience were their future record company (Geoff Travis from Rough Trade), publishing company (WEA, I think) and manager (Scott Piering, who was then doing press for RT) and the gig got them their first John Peel session via an impressed John Walters. A young Mixmaster Morris, then a student at King's College, played some tunes between the bands. What stuck with me was that after the show a very polite Morrissey came to find me and thank me for the gig. This was unusual because it rarely happened; the promoter usually got thanked by the tour manager or whichever musicians you bumped into on the load-out. It seemed a very decent thing to do. And quite at odds with his later reputation, if you believe what you read in the music papers.

I was to see the next three or four Smiths London shows, and the intensity grew very quickly. It really happened for them in a six-month period from early 1983. They were expertly corralled and guided on their way by Geoff Travis. I spent a short time working for Mike Hinc at The Rough Trade warehouse in Blenheim Crescent and one day we were passing by Geoff's office. He had a contraption which connected a record or tape player into a transistor radio so that you could hear exactly how your test pressing might sound if broadcast. I had a strange sensation of déjà vu but dismissed it at the time. The ringing guitar was the first thing that grabbed me but as the whole tune unfolded you knew that 'This Charming Man' was going to catapult the band fully into the limelight. Later on Scott Piering, who was by then the Smiths' administrator invited me to do various tasks – including designing and selling T-shirts for the band – on a short Welsh tour and then a tour of Ireland.

The Irish jaunt was wild. The band didn't just want to do Belfast and Dublin, so we hit Waterford, Limerick, Cork, Letterkenny and Galway. Three of the group had family in the South. Two days on and one day off meant you could get out a bit and see the local sights. We drove around in the ubiquitous Mercedes splitter, and I remember passing a parked-up and battered old green van whose occupants were engaged in a slow motion flow of t'ai chi in the adjoining field. It was the then completely unknown support act James, around the time they had just released 'Hymn To A Village', and Morrissey liked them. The vibe appealed to me at the time; it was possibly the most un-rock'n'roll tour in the world although our party credentials were improved by the presence of the legendary Grant Showbiz on the outboard sound desk.

I was sitting in the bar of the Dublin hotel at the start of the tour reading *Strumpet City*, Oliver Plunkett's great sprawling novel about the capital. Morrissey spotted a fellow bookworm and we struck up a slight acquaintance over this. I was asked to do the breakfast security accompaniment for him on the grounds, I suppose, that we could talk books. The threat of zealous fans storming over the buttered toast never really transpired. The concerts drew the most incredible response from audiences, however. Walking into the dressing room was like a visit to Interflora. The last live band to have played in Waterford was seven years before, so all the town turned out and went crazy from the word go. First on, James got a great lift from the crowd but the mayhem for the main attraction was highly impressive, if not to say hysterical.

This was the pre *Meat Is Murder* Smiths and they were doing all this off the back of the singles collection, *A Hatful Of Hollow*. Whether you connected with the music or not you couldn't help but be amazed by their dedication and application. Johnny Marr brought virtuoso guitar playing back to the forefront of British rock and pop and influenced countless bands to follow. It was a raw exciting live band, tight at the back and flowing up front, but I'm going to freeze-frame it there because, in this moment, post-punk was over. The airbrushed eighties had already begun to take hold and some of the earlier pioneering bands were starting to cross over. Scritti Politti were no longer an anarcho-syndicalist collective, Green had gone solo and was writing pop songs. Very good ones too. The Human League was soon to be just Phil Oakey looking for new members in the local disco. Everyone bar The Smiths was signing to major labels.

Nostalgia is big business, but the eighties we now see packaged up and touring the cocktail circuit is not the full story. It wasn't all about glamour and transparencies. I started to think about this article when I heard about a club called 'Nag Nag Nag' in London's Shoreditch, comedy-haircut capital of the south-east. 'Nag Nag Nag' was Cabaret Voltaire's most volatile single, it was 'Being Boiled's' electro-punk cousin. Then Soul Jazz Records began to release the back catalogues from some of the better bands on the eighties scene. A little earlier, on 'Block Rockin' Beats' the Chemical Brothers had rinsed the break from 23 Skidoo's awesome early 12" 'Coup'. Even earlier, Nirvana was about to ask The Raincoats to re-form and join their world tour; Kurt was a huge fan apparently. The new underground was rediscovering the old underground.

The period which followed punk saw an incredible variegation in British music. The fact that the *NME* could put WOMAD on its front page was a barometer of this open-mindedness. Nowadays, specialist music is niche-marketed into specialist outlets. You will read about your jazz music in the jazz magazines. No one believes in scattergun marketing. Perhaps not since the late sixties had there been such a wide and enthusiastic interest in new music. The early eighties scene started to make it possible to live with an increasingly eclectic record collection. It set scores of people off on audio discovery trips. It opened the sound gates to a whole new world. Music was no longer regimented into pop, rock and disco. The first sampling processes began to appear, going overground with David Byrne's and Brian Eno's 'My Life In The Bush of Ghosts' and ex-Can man Holger Czukay's beautiful 'Persian Love Song'. Sound collided and colluded with sound and into light and visuals. When Cabaret Voltaire played at ULU in 1981 the entire stage and the band were covered by a psychedelic coloured spinning light wheel and tape loops sputtered found sound into the mix. The Human League live at The Marquee in 1980 manipulated moving images with the music and their projectionist was a member of the band. This notion of converging media had been revived in the post-punk years, as it was in the sixties.

Ginsberg, Burroughs and Gysin organized the first truly multi-media shows in Paris in the late fifties; they had in turn picked up elements from Dada and Surrealism and passed them forward for future generations. In 1979 Final Solution produced The Final Academy in Brixton, an event that celebrated Burroughs's work but prefaced the eclecticism of the next few years. Burroughs was the guru for this generation as Kerouac and Ginsberg had been respectively for the fifties and sixties.

The 1983 Glastonbury Festival featured a line-up with King Sunny Ade, Curtis Mayfield, Moving Hearts and The Beat all on the same bill. In 2004 the festival, along with WOMAD and now The Big Chill, presents line-ups that are rarely bound by commercial convention. Here are programmes of bands, artists and multi-media creators which convey that spirit of experimental Zeitgeist that has had its periods of intensity down the ages. As it did in those short three or four years at the turn of the 1970s when anything seemed possible. Even the impossible.

recommended listening

A Certain Ratio – 'Shack Up' (Factory)
Au Pairs – *Playing With A Different Sex* (Human)

David Byrne and Brian Eno – *My Life In The Bush Of Ghosts* LP (EG)

Big In Japan – 'From Y to Z and Never Again' (Zoo)

Cabaret Voltaire – 'Nag Nag Nag' (Rough Trade)

The Drummers of Burundi – *Les Maîtres Tambours du Burundi* LP (Arion)

Durutti Column – *The Return of the Durutti Column* LP (Factory)

The Gang Of Four – *Entertainment* LP (EMI)

The Human League – 'Being Boiled' (Fast Product)

The Fall – *Perverted By Language* LP (Rough Trade)

James Blood Ulmer – *Are You Glad To Be In America?* LP (Rough Trade)

Joy Division – *Substance 1977–1980* LP (Factory)

Michael Smith – *Mi C'Yaan Believe It* LP (Island)

Misty In Roots – *Live At The Counter Eurovision 79* LP (People Unite)

New Order – 'Ceremony' (Factory)

The Pop Group – *For How Much Longer Must We Tolerate Mass Murder* LP (Y)

Rip Rig and Panic – *God* LP (Virgin)

Scritti Politti – 'Four A Sides' (St Pancras Records)

The Slits – *Cut* LP (Island)

The Smiths – *Hatful Of Hollow* LP (Rough Trade)

This Heat – 'Health and Efficiency' (Rough Trade)

23 Skidoo – *Seven Songs* LP (Ronin)

Various Artists – *Raindrops Pattering On Banana Leaves* LP (WOMAD)

Wah! – Nah Poo *The Art Of Bluff* LP (Inevitable)

Young Marble Giants – *Colossal Youth* LP (Rough Trade)

the eighties: or 'my life in england (part one)'

Stuart Borthwick

In 1982, as a know-nothing twelve-year-old, I fell in love with pop. Whereas previous generations had fallen for The Beatles, and where a subsequent generation fell for the beats, breaks and bleeps of dance music, I submerged myself in the chart pop of the time. And of the bands around at the time, I found none more appealing than Tears for Fears. The Christmas 2003 release of a Gary Jules cover version of the band's first big hit, 'Mad World', reminded me of the special nature of the band's early work, and got me thinking about the musical legacy of the 1980s.

In some respects, Gary Jules's relatively straight acoustic version of 'Mad World' deflects attention away from the extremely strange nature of the original Tears For Fears release, and the even stranger fact that 'Mad World' was a top-ten hit in 1982, with all the accompanying press releases, videos and promotional appearances that this entails. 'Mad World' was a synthpop song taken from an album (*The Hurting*) that was written so the band in question could make enough money to go into psychotherapy. This might signal that something strange was going on. The nature of the treatment, based on Dr Arthur Janov's primal therapy (whereby patients experience 'rebirth' and relive their infancy), confirms that here we have, fully formed, a crackpot band with a dream, a fantasy, a vision and a plan. In 2004, Tears for Fears would be laughed out of the charts and out of the *Top of the Pops* studio, yet twenty years ago they were welcomed with open arms by a pop audience that was, well, just a little bit more open to suggestion than nowadays. In thinking about the Gary Jules cover version, we can begin to see how utterly different the current pop era is from that of twenty years ago, and how, in some respects, the modern pop age is inferior to the previous one. What follows is not to be taken as a rose-tinted nostalgia trip. In the last twenty years we might have lost truly adventurous pop, but we gained a whole lot more. However, we still lost something, and it is the nature of this loss that concerns this essay.

Tears for Fears consisted of two childhood friends from Bath – Curt Smith (so far, so good), and Roland Jaime Orzabal de la Quintana (you don't get many of those on *Pop Idol*). Fey and introspective, yet egotistical and out there, Smith and Orzabal made great pop stars. Their interviews were impossibly intellectual for their record company's target audience (i.e. me), and carefully detailed their *très bourgeois* loves in the home counties, whilst name-checking obscure psychological concepts (I thought 'the primal scream' was a bunch of indie kids from Glasgow). As a twelve-year-old at the time, I joyfully jotted down the references that Smith and Orzabal kindly provided. Whilst I could certainly dig the obscure Teardrop Explodes tracks that they raved about (and I thank them for inaugurating a lifelong love of Julian Cope), I also bought Dr Janov's book, and dived head first into a solipsistic pit of despond that was not of my own making. When I should have been growing up, I was listening to music that was encouraging me to regress to a childhood state. Talk about an intellectual dead end! At the time, though, this did not seem abnormal to me; indeed, it was kind of expected. I just thought, 'This is what pop stars do, this is what pop stars think, in the world of pop this is normal. My friends think I'm weird, but I'm not, *I'm normal.*'

In retrospect, I was living in an age where, post-1977, the pretensions of progressive rock had been bruised and battered by punk, but, pre-1987, they had yet to be finished off by the dance revolution. This was an age where it was OK for bands to dream, to shout and to scream (quite literally) about what an awful time they had at school, and where it was acceptable to make videos detailing one's existential angst through references to swarms of bees and

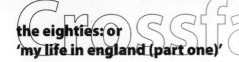

staring out of the window looking all moody. It was also perfectly acceptable to dress up in fashions that were so ridiculous as to invite concerns regarding the psychic health of all concerned (for Tears For Fears it was all karate slippers and long rats' tails).

In the late 1980s, I moved north and became a house evangelist. By 1990, I truly believed that house and techno had superseded all the daft frippery of the early 1980s. However, come a few years later, with house and techno in stasis, I began to have my doubts, and I began to realize that something was missing from the dance scene. I can remember the precise moment that this feeling kicked in. 1993 saw British techno duo The Grid (Richard Norris and Dave Ball) develop one of those club tours that was popular at the time (cf. The Shamen's early tours, the Midi Circus and the Megadog's outings). If my memory serves me correctly, The Grid's tour visited the Merseyside Academy (shortly to become Cream), with DJ Andy Weatherall providing the support. By the end of the night, the crowd had been whipped into the proverbial frenzy by The Grid's fantastically psychedelic beats, and were followed by Weatherall's dirty techno. Like a bolt out of the blue, Weatherall played Heaven 17's 1983 hit 'Temptation'. The track is quite literally hysterical. Starting with portentous vocals set upon eerie synthesized strings (the kind that make you worried, the kind that you hear in spooky films), the opening twenty-two seconds are a study in the art of anticipation. Sure, it's overblown and preposterous, but, by God, when the beat kicks in and the (fake) choir sings a decidedly dodgy biblical message, it works. On the podium at the Merseyside Academy, I revelled in it. The Grid were fantastic that night – but this, this is what it is about. It's all froth and bombast, of course, just overblown chart pop, but for some reason I preferred it to the techno that Weatherall had been playing. The house and techno scenes of the time were seen as being at the cutting edge of musical experimentation, and the 1980s were beginning to feel like a bad dream, full of vapid, mindless pop. But it didn't feel like that to me at the time, and it's not how I view it now.

The music of the 1980s may sound vaguely trite now, but we have swallowed the utilitarianism of dance music, and we are now less prepared to accept off-the-wallisms than any previous pop generation. Pop fashion is a case in point. In the 1980s, it was perfectly acceptable for a band to change their image completely with each new single. It was perfectly acceptable for pop stars to dress in the most ridiculous attire, with the most preposterous haircuts known to man. Nowadays, most bands stick rigidly to the new sartorial conformity – either down-to-earth laddishisms or six-pack sexy for men, and even less choice for female performers, who are simply expected to be sexy. In the early 1980s, the madder the clothes and the bigger the hair, the better. A Flock of Seagulls were laughed at heartily in 1982, but that was part of the fun. Nowadays, they would be rejected as looking that little bit too strange. Such an attitude entirely misses the point – pop stars *should* look strange. It's their job. I blame Oasis. Oasis themselves are clearly stars. Well, Liam is anyway. I was never sure of Bonehead, or the bloke who will remain forever in my mind the guitarist in Ride (dull, worthy indie labourers of the early 1990s). However, those who followed in Oasis's wake just looked too normal. The Doves are a case in point. I like the albums, but oil paintings they ain't. Neither are they stars, as they are simply too normal, not strange enough to light up the charts. Noel Gallagher was recently quoted as stating that contemporary music was 'getting weird'. Surely that's a good thing?

All the wacky psychotherapy would have been irrelevant had the music of Tears For Fears not lived up to the image, and relistening to it now we can see how it all gelled within their first few singles. 'Mad World' itself starts with synthpads, electro-glockenspiels and moody minor chords, before surfing a line between weirdness and old-fashioned songwriting. Most definitely, this made for repeated listening. Neither musically extravagant, nor sparse and spare like some of their contemporaries, Tears For Fears had the best of both worlds, appealing to the critics and the kids in equal measure.

After 'Mad World', the band's next singles followed in the same vein. 'Change' had the same vague air of dissatisfaction as its predecessor. The follow-up, a re-release of their first single, 'Pale Shelter' (an eventual top-ten hit in April 1983), returned to the theme of the band members' childhood upbringings (one can only wonder what their parents thought of the meticulous chronicling of minor childhood upsets). Musically, 'Pale Shelter' also performed a useful service in adding to the synthpop palette, through its use of an

acoustic guitar (in hindsight, maybe the use of a 'real' instrument actually signalled the beginning of the genre's decline).

Whilst the record company were sure that they were on to a winner, and flogged *The Hurting* to death, there were worrying signs that all was not well in the gardens of Avon. Firstly, a couple of years in the record industry had put the band off the idea of investing the profits of their musical endeavours in primal-therapy sessions. Secondly, the introspection that made the band's music so effective and charming (what their label called 'redemptive pop', and what the band would later call 'depressing') began to be replaced with a more straightforward (read 'dull') pop style. The fulcrum moment was the release of 'Mother's Talk' in 1984. Opening with assonant synth strings, orchestral stabs, and what sounds suspiciously like a breakbeat, this could be the intro to an Afrika Bambaataa track of the time. However, a few seconds later, we hear a blustering kick drum stage front, and the kind of 'chugga chugga' arpeggiated lead guitar that became briefly popular in the mid-to-late 1980s, following synthpop's eventual decline.

After a while, all was lost. Why? My theory is that the band tasted commercial success and stopped dreaming, stopped coming up with mad ideas and just thought, 'we're a pop group, and we make pop songs'. Out went the highfalutin psychotherapy, out went the pain and the anguish, and out went the dream. In short, out went everything that made Tears for Fears conceptually interesting. All that was left was well-crafted, if slightly bombastic, pop songs. Without a concept, an ideology or even a plain old idea, Tears for Fears descended into overwrought popisms like 'Everybody Wants to Rule the World', and vapid love songs like 'Head Over Heels'. By the end of the decade, the band that first appeared in 1982 had become an unrecognizable world-touring pop monster, but they'd lost their *raison d'être* in the process. The decline of Tears for Fears serves as a metaphor for all that was brilliant about chart pop in the early 1980s, and all that went wrong as the decade went on. Lying in the background of all great pop music is a grand scheme, a plan or a scam, and a fanciful notion of redemption through music. Lose that, and the house of cards falls.

Seeing as I have already mentioned Heaven 17, it might be worthwhile elaborating on the noble sons (and daughters) of

Sheffield's synthpop scene of the 1980s. For some reason, Sheffield has always played a central role in the production of techno. Maybe it is something to do with Sheffield steel, with the idea of a stainless shiny surface that remains ever-present, and which covers a brutally unforgiving foundation. Whilst they were definitely techno, The Human League (of which Heaven 17 were a part) tried as hard as possible to not sound like Kraftwerk, and, largely, succeeded. Rather than mimicking Europe's leading lights in electronic music, the band's aim was to draw upon the intellectual resources of those bands that had been untouched by punk's primal approach to music – principally Roxy Music and David Bowie. The resources drawn from these sources were musicological, sartorial and follicular. Both Bowie and Ferry had great clothes and great hair, as well as great music. Both were peaking in terms of creativity in the late 1970s. Knowing that a distinctive haircut could be as important as a distinctive sound (and why shouldn't it be?), Phil Oakey developed a lopsided haircut that was based on Veronica Lake, Hollywood's most popular pin-up of the 1940s.

The Human League's glamorous look (well, glamorous for Sheffield) was set against sequencing and synth technology that arrived courtesy of a hire-purchase agreement (very eighties). Early electronic fumblings and mumblings gave way to a purer pop sound. All that was now missing was an ideology upon which to hang the brittle sounds of their '100 System' synthesizer. Bob Last of Scotland's Fast Product record label provided this with the band's first press release, put out on what was then a very 'futurist' computer printout:

SCENARIO: In the summer of 1977 The Human League was formed due to the members finding no conventional channels for their immense talents.

BACKGROUND: None of The Human League have any orthodox musical training, but prefer to regard compositions as an extension of logic, inspiration and luck. Therefore, unlike conventional musicians, their influences are not so obvious.

CONCLUSION/MANIFESTO: Interested in combining the best of all worlds, The League would like to positively affect the future by close attention to the present, allying technology with

humanity and humour. They have been described as 'Later Twentieth Century Boys' and 'Intelligent, Innovatory and Immodest'.

The faith shown in the band by the label was nothing short of remarkable. Despite signing them in early 1978, Bob Last did not feel it necessary to actually meet the band until some six months after the release of their first single, 'Being Boiled'. Perhaps faith in the idea of The Human League was more important than the immediate results of the band's musical undertaking. Having said this, if as the owner of an indie label in the late 1970s you had heard 'Being Boiled', you too would probably be somewhat reticent to meet the producers of such an infernal record.

The press release quoted above shows a certain degree of arrogance on the part of label and band. Modesty was never on the agenda for either party, and why should it be? The best bands have always been aware of their greatness, and the best record labels (Island, Creation, Factory, Virgin in its prime) have never been backwards about putting their bands forward as leaders of their specific generation. The Human League's strength was that their self-awareness was also combined with a Yorkshire humility that meant they never complained when, following a decline in sales, they reached their lowest point in the late 1990s, playing on the corporate Christmas-party circuit.

In 1980, The Human League split into two factions. The first became Heaven 17 (who developed a corporate chic based around pinstripes and brollies), and the second revolved around Phil Oakey's hankerings after fame. Fancying himself as a bit of a Svengali (which made a change from just fancying himself), Oakey recruited two seemingly anonymous girls from a seemingly anonymous Sheffield disco, and embarked on The Human League's most successful period yet. Once Oakey had tasted success with singles drawn from their first two albums, *Reproduction* and *Travelogue*, he refused the path that read 'difficult third album' and took the path paved with gold. For The Human League, this was clearly the best path to take. Diving headlong into an unashamed commercialism, the band had a string of hit singles ('Don't You Want Me', 'Mirror Man', '(Keep Feeling) Fascination') and one of the best-selling albums of the decade (*Dare*). No underground credibility here, just great music. These singles were the equal of their more sparse early experimentations, and *Dare* sounds as fresh now as it did then.

Unfortunately for Oakey, the band did not heed the unspoken diktat that electronic groups should not comment on contemporary political affairs. Oblique and profoundly dodgy references to the alleged 'decadence' of Weimar Germany were OK in the early 1980s, but not the situation in the Middle East. The release of 1984's 'The Lebanon' saw the League's cultural stock plummet, and it has never fully recovered. Luckily, their musical legacy remains entirely untouched by their current lack of credibility.

Operating on the other side of the Pennines, another 1980s group was keen to debunk the myth that life was grim up north. Three debut singles, three number ones, and a rapid implosion amidst egotism and arguments about the money – that's the way to do it. Frankie Goes to Hollywood had a variety of essential elements that made them the surreal deal. Firstly, they had a form of Scouse cheekiness and irreverence that meant that they could cope relatively easily with whatever the media threw at them. Secondly, they had a marvellously meaningless agenda provided by Paul Morley, chief semiotician and propagandist at their record label ZTT. Thirdly, they were packaged to perfection with wonderfully constructivist twelve-inch record covers, posters, slogans, and oversized Katherine Hamnett T-shirts that captured the plutonium paranoia of the time. Here was a band that matched musical experimentation and eclecticism with outlandish attire. Amidst the sexualization of a culture that has continued apace since the early 1980s, Frankie Goes to Hollywood managed to top even McLaren and Westwood in terms of outrage. The fact that, despite the leather chaps and impish grins, half the band were as straight as they come must have confused a hell of a lot of people. Finally, they had a futuristic techno sheen provided by producer Trevor Horn. Experimenting with polyphonic synthesizers and sampling keyboards, and applying the cut'n'paste ethos of postmodernism to musical structure (later to become one of the key defining features of house and associated musics), Horn crafted a sleek and shiny technofuture amidst Holly and gang's tales of gay sex and nuclear Armageddon. You

just know that, should their like be seen again, broadcasters would ban 'Relax', only properly this time, and the government would ban 'Two Tribes' under public-order legislation, whilst simultaneously claiming the royalties for use in a 'civil defence' television commercial.

That I refer to the music of Heaven 17, The Human League and Frankie Goes to Hollywood as techno might surprise some. Most think that techno was invented in Detroit, but if anyone other than an anonymous programmer at equipment manufacturer Roland can claim to have invented techno, it is the likes of Heaven 17 and The Human League, and not any of the Detroit DJs that subsequently idolized them. Depeche Mode are another example. Take four fey boys from Romford, Essex (Vince Clarke, Dave Gahan, Andrew Fletcher and Martin Gore), give them a few synthesizers, and out comes a pre-formed perfect pop group that would go on to have twenty-one top forty hits in the 1980s alone.

In 2004, Depeche Mode are little more than a slightly gothic, slightly scary, electro-rock band (when bands have ideologies, big ideas, manifestos, it's best when they are original ones). Nonetheless, back in 1981, it came as a bit of a shock to hear 'Dreaming of Me' and 'New Life', the band's first two singles. Wrapping their musical output in a shiny futurist ideology, this new-fangled techno was an electric shock to the system. The release of the band's third single 'Just Can't Get Enough' coincided with a period in time when cultural wits were beginning to suggest that we had already heard all the possible sequences of notes within the Western musical scale, and that we were condemned to listening to them over and over again, for evermore. The simple seven-note melody of 'Just Can't Get Enough' showed that this form of glib postmodernism was wrong, and that there were brand-new melodic patterns that were utterly distinctive and unexplored. At a time when musical complexity was particularly prized, 'Dreaming of Me', 'New Life' and 'Just Can't Get Enough' showed that monophonic melody lines, and clean and crisp drum machines, could be as powerfully evocative as literary lyrics and angry guitars. It is this that made Depeche Mode the forerunners of the techno revolution of some years later.

The general progress of a band such as Depeche Mode would be to jettison the simplicity and youthfulness of their early approach and move towards a more 'mature' sound and structure. This would be a particular imperative of a band that had recently lost one of their key writers (Vince Clarke left the band after their debut album *Speak and Spell* to form Yazoo with Alison 'Alf' Moyet). Yet Depeche Mode resisted this temptation for another album, and released *A Broken Frame*, another album chock-full of simple melodies and broken Essex hearts. In many respects, Depeche Mode's first two albums are symptomatic of everything that is great about English pop music. It is almost as if the simpler the song, the more profound its effect. This simple approach produced music that is both inherently artistic and immediately accessible to a wide audience. Combine this with no fear of success, and we have the key to the great music of the early 1980s.

The simplicity and essentially 'pop' nature of Depeche Mode's approach soon gave way to the incipient rockisms of their third album, *Construction Time Again*, and accompanying tour. On this album, the love theme of much of the Mode's early work gave way to commentaries on industrialism bound in a more sombre, reflective mood. More angsty, and therefore allegedly more meaningful. By the time of their seventh studio album, 1990's *Violator*, the band from Basildon had become US rock gods, and had lost some of their essential charm in the process. However, one must applaud the way that, following this success, Depeche Mode still lived the dream. In particular, keyboard maestro Martin Gore developed a nice line in PVC fetishwear and leather skirts that would have made Madonna blush, whilst lead singer Dave Gahan developed a heroin addiction that would have killed many of his predecessors (indeed, the stories are that he was brought back from death's door on more than one occasion).

In the early 1980s, the likes of Depeche Mode and The Human League were often compared unfavourably with their more fashionable peers in bands such as The Beat, Selector, and The Specials. Whilst bands like The Specials and The Human League appear to be polar opposites (the former dour and miserable, the latter shiny and aspirant), beneath the surface they both tell the same stories of lost nights in bad discos, the feeling of being an outsider in a not-so-brave, not-so-new world. The same can be said for Madness, who surfed the line between youth-cultural credibility and mass appeal. Indeed, the thing to note about Madness is the extent to which they

led dual lives, appealing to three distinct audiences – subcultural, mainstream and teenage. The nature of these audiences shows the gulf that exists between the 1980s and the current decade.

In the beginning, the band relied upon the fanatical support of a range of interlinking subcultures. Punk had fractured, and from amongst its ruins sprang new wave, a mod revival (spurred on by the release of the film *Quadrophenia*), a ska revival, and oi! (a brutal male-only street-guitar sound that descended into violence and despondency). Drawing upon support from all these subcultures, Madness began updating the 1960s ska sound, adding little pop touches, and their first single 'The Prince', released on 2-Tone, went to number sixteen. No mean feat for what was essentially an indie band playing music then seen as woefully outdated. Despite accusations of revivalism, Madness's radio-friendly sound and accessible promo videos meant that they soon drew themselves to the attention of mainstream broadcasters and audiences alike, with their next nine singles all going top ten.

In turn, this subcultural fanaticism bought them to the attention of a whole new audience, and it was the nature of this audience, and the band's relationship with them, that serves to highlight the gulf between the chart pop of today and the chart pop of the early 1980s. The vast majority of this new audience consisted of Madness fans who were under sixteen. Such was the size of this audience (it became difficult to ignore in the circumstances – school classrooms would be suspiciously empty when Madness were in town), the band began playing weekend matinees for the under-eighteen audience. Could you imagine it today? With songs about rubber johnnies? Sure, boy and girl bands play gigs for pre-teen and teen audiences (in sterile enormodomes like the MEN Arena in Manchester or Wembley Arena), but when was the last time such a band also had a twenty-something following, a mainstream radio following and credibility?

The three audiences of Madness were catered for in equal measure in the videos accompanying the band's hit singles. Firstly, the subculturalists looked towards Madness for ways of subtly updating the 1960s look, settling on a kind of mod/skinhead hybrid that also drew on a Teddy boy lineage. To this day, a black Crombie overcoat, based on the original Edwardian style, with the red lining of the breast pocket pulled up to form a faux handkerchief, sets my heart a-flutter and reminds me of Madness (rather than Edward VII). Secondly, for the kids, the videos were bright and cheerful. Essentially pantomime, the Madness videos softened a generation of lads that could easily have gone the other way. Thirdly, the grown-up audience could marvel at the subtle comic gestures, the band's mimicking of Tommy Cooper's fez, or the suits and bowler hats seen in other videos. There was something there for everyone.

As the story of Madness shows, the 1980s were a time when credibility and success were not seen as mutually incompatible opposites, and chart success did not equal creative bankruptcy. Nowadays, a band's appearance on *Top of the Pops* is as likely to be rewarded with sneers and accusations of selling out. In the early 1980s, an appearance on *Top of the Pops* was cherished. Madness might still play annual 'last ever' concerts in London, tarnishing their lustre with every gig, but in the 1980s they were unassailable. Maybe they were a lads' band, and maybe their refusal to reject explicitly the boneheads in their audience led them to alienate their female fans. Maybe they were derivative, and once they had tried to develop a more grown-up sound (around the time of 'Michael Caine') they had lost some of their naive charm. Maybe, by 1985, they had run out of steam after six years in the charts, and maybe their albums had become patchy affairs (e.g. *Mad Not Mad*). But in 1985 they had released six studio albums, and had amassed fifteen top-ten hits, with a further five singles reaching the top forty. How long did it take Oasis to go off the boil? At best, three albums. Oasis's third album, *Be Here Now*, is not as refreshing or engaging as its predecessors, *Definitely Maybe* and *(What's The Story) Morning Glory?*, and by the time of their tenth single 'Do You Know What I Mean?' the band were in irreversible decline. Yet Oasis were seen as the great white hopes of the 1990s; they were supposed to rescue British music from the pincer movement of American dance music and American grunge. Eulogized like no other band since The Sex Pistols, Oasis had everything to play for, yet they blew it. Were Oasis really any better than Madness? For me the answer is no (no matter how much I love 'Wonderwall'). The comparison is made all the more poignant by the fact that Madness were by no means the best band of the 1980s.

They were simply a good band (by anyone's criteria), who over a five-year stretch produced twenty quality singles and a range of visually interesting and amusing videos.

At roughly the same time that Madness were spearheading the ska revival, another post-punk act was combining teen appeal with musical experimentation and stylistic extravagance. Starting off as Pistol devotees (Jordan was an early member, Malcolm McLaren their 'image consultant' at a crucial point in their development), Adam and the Ants were the epitome of pop stars from 1980 through to 1983. During this period Adam Ant and his merry men had three number ones ('Stand and Deliver', 'Prince Charming', 'Goody Two Shoes'), and a host of supporting singles ('Antmusic', 'Kings of the Wild Frontier', 'Young Parisians', 'Deutscher Girls'). What do I want from a pop group? Infectious rhythms, lyrical obscurantism, fantasy, fetish and fashion. Mystique and melody in equal proportion. Where are their like today? Where are the pop stars that are prepared to (forgive the pun) stand and deliver complete nonsense with utter conviction? 'Antmusic for Ant People', accompanied by a look that combined a piratical fetish with Native Americanisms? 'Stand and Deliver', accompanied by the dandyish of highwaymen and the pantomime of 'Prince Charming'? I'll have some of that, thank you very much. This was their secret of success – Adam Ant sold us a sartorial, sexual and musical manifesto that was at once profound yet meaningless. Is that not the quintessence of rock'n'roll, of postmodernism, of everything anyone who loves pop believes in? There's a wonderful line in a Bill Drummond song from the mid 1980s that sums up my attitude to such views – 'you say it's all so shallow. It's like deep-sea diving for me.'

On relistening to Adam Ant's hits, the one thing you notice is the truly adventurous nature of the music. From the perfectly timed drumstick play on the opening few bars of 'Antmusic', through to the Glen-Miller-on-speed meets Dixieland boogie and Burundi drumming of Adam's solo number one 'Goody Two Shoes', this is out-there pop. When was the last time that happened in recent years? When was the last time that the teen market's favourite pin-ups of the year produced provocative music that pushed the proverbial envelope? Were the early Westlife singles influenced by African percussion?

But where are Adam and the Ants in the pantheon of pop, where are they in the musical history books? Well down the page, that's where. Whilst the histories of hip hop give Blondie rightful praise for popularizing rap vocals with their 1981 single 'Rapture', any mention of 'Ant Rap' as a possible contender for the best early rap crossover receives blank looks, despite the fact that Adam's rapping is *better*. Sounding like a cross between The Fall and The Bronx, by rights this should have got nowhere near the charts whatsoever, yet it spent ten weeks in the top forty, peaking at number three.

The fact that Adam Ant stopped being dandy and showing us he is handsome, and ended up a figure of ridicule in the tabloid press in January 2002, shows the reprehensible attitude our culture has to the psychic fallout that so often accompanies the fame and fortune of our pop stars. When news filtered out that Adam had gone berserk in a north London pub, the nation seemed to be pleased that one of its former pop stars had fallen so spectacularly from his pedestal.

The Music Industry (capital letters, because it's scary like that) sucks them in, steals their ideas, exploits them to the hilt, and spits them out, damaged and occasionally destitute. Dave Gahan, Boy George, Adam Ant, Kevin Rowland. All casualties, all victims of a vicious industry. But what do we do? Laugh at the tabloids' tales of heroin overdoses, madness, and pub shoot-outs, or laugh at them when they dare to wear anything so outrageous as *women's clothes* at Reading Festival. The shame of it.

My point is simply that, in 2004, our credible musicians are afraid of the charts, and all of our chart stars have lost their credibility. Our pop stars have also lost the ability to shock and surprise, or simply lost the ability to act like stars. We leave it up to acts from other countries to ham it up (Madonna, Kylie, Marilyn Manson, Eminem), whereas we have to import Hollywood stars to sex up our bands (e.g. Coldplay). What is really surprising is that so few people have noticed this phenomenon, and that no record company has stepped into the breach and mopped up the millions of sales that could be made by a new, credible (or even an incredible) band. Just look at The Darkness. With reheated seventies riffs and a sack full of leather catsuits, The Darkness walked away from the 2004 Brits awards having conquered all, without even breaking into a sweat. There was simply

no competition. In 2003, no other British band had any sense of edge, let alone danger. The Brits are not exactly renowned for showcasing credible artists, but the line-up at the Brits in February 2004 was pretty good in comparison to previous years – 50 Cent, Gwen Stefani, Missy Elliot, Outkast and Beyoncé. Not bad, eh? They're all American, though. Other than The Darkness, what was representing this side of the Atlantic? Katie Melua and Jamie Cullum, Busted, Muse, and Duran Duran. Oh dear. The most rebellious thing that occurred at this Brits ceremony was that Dido did not turn up, as she was rehearsing for a forthcoming tour. Rock'n'roll, this is not.

In the late-1980s rush to embrace the star-free world of house music, the world of underground credibility, we lost faith in the stars. In retrospect, we did truly lose something. The dance world of the 1980s survived according to an underground ethos that frowned somewhat on 'showing out' (as Mel and Kim said in 1986). As a consequence, everyone over the age of ten has lost faith in the singles charts and abandoned *Top of the Pops*.

The performances of our musicians on television music shows are now ruled according to the tyranny of the choreographer. But choreographers never come up with any original ideas; they merely enable performers to act out their fantasies. When the performers have no fantasies and no ideas, then the results are dull. House and techno are brimful of ideas, but they are not the kind of ideas that translate well onto the small screen or onto the radio. Equally, when in the early 1990s the music industry reasserted its authority over the star-free worlds of house and techno, they ushered in an era of superstar DJs who have no real star qualities. I could list the DJs, but you know their names already. These men (always men) may be superstar DJs, but are they superstars in the sense of being outstanding performers? Or are they just outstanding DJs? Surely, the world where superstar DJs are essentially anonymous is both a contradiction in terms and the worst of both worlds?

The British music scene has also lost the ability to churn out great albums, year after year. To be fair, twelve-inch remixes took over as the default mode, as we took an American formula (house) and created a behemoth called 'dance music'. I blame New Order. Has there been such a mythologized group as New Order? Equally, has there ever been such a challenging and innovative group as New Order? Now that everyone has seen the film *24-Hour Party People*, they know the basic bones of the story, so there is no need for repetition. What is worth noting is the extent to which New Order straddled the different epochs of 1980s and 1990s, fitting neatly into both eras' modes of working. Appearing on *Top of the Pops*, but refusing to mime. Having the best-selling twelve-inch single of all time, but managing to engineer it so they made no money. Building the best house club in the world, but still managing to shut it down in the face of police pressure, reopen it, and then sell it off before it had broke even. Being perfect stars for the era by refusing to be stars at all, by refusing to play the game.

Without disrespecting the enormous significance of their musical output, it is the legend of New Order that is of most importance, containing as it does the finest tales of heartbreak, bereavement, bankruptcy and barking lunacy. As individuals, though, the band were and remain relatively ordinary. Like Morrissey and The Smiths, New Order made for difficult, awkward stars, but like Morrissey and his protestations of shyness, you suspect that if they really didn't like it, they would have stepped off the stage a long time ago (indeed, one band member appears to have done so, and few have noticed). You'd never get the great stars of the 1980s punching photographers, not unless the photographer absolutely refused to take a picture of them.

With their faceless techno epics like 'Blue Monday' on albums such as *Power, Corruption and Lies*, New Order were the beginning of the end for a particular era in pop. New Order took a particular road. Unfortunately, the road that they took leads our pop stars to be afraid of doing what they do best (i.e. being pop stars). This is the road that leads to Coldplay and Travis, anti-stars who are as dull as dishwater.

Perhaps what is needed is faith, even if that faith is in nothing in particular. Pop stars should clearly believe, if only in themselves. For example, the dialectic struggle between belief and self-doubt within the career of Dexy's Midnight Runners is an example of how faith is the dynamo of all great British pop. After a false start that saw the band adopt a proto-New Romantic look well before The Blitz Kids (the look was jettisoned after homophobic attacks from fans of The Specials, who they supported on an early tour), Dexy's Midnight

Runners came up with three great looks for three perfect albums. Debut album *Searching For the Young Soul Rebels* contains urgent, driving rhythms and furious fire, soundtracking a look that said New York docker meets northern soul raver – pork-pie and woollen hats, brogues, single-breasted leather jackets, or the kind of coats that used to have 'NCB' on the back (ask your dad). *Searching For the Young Soul Rebels* also came complete with a manifesto, a grand scheme, a plan, a scam and faith. Scattered throughout the album are references to the famous Dexy's flame – the intense burning desire to search for a new soul vision in the face of the kind of synthpop celebrated earlier in this essay (for a full insight into the cataclysmic clash between the new soul vision and synthpop, listen to Adam Ant's 'Goody Two Shoes' and picture its subject matter – Mr Kevin Rowland).

Searching For The Young Soul Rebels eventually spawned a number one single with 'Geno', and a million young men (and some women along with them) began riffling through the racks in second-hand-record stores for the music of Geno Washington. As Rowland opined in promotional interviews at the time, this was soul power: 'we don't want to see ourselves as missionaries but we do have something to put over: we really would like to see an end to rock, punk, heavy metal, ska, country and western, reggae, everything'.

This quotation is a clear example of a band on a mission. To believe in Dexy's Midnight Runners, to have a faith that was lit up by the Dexy's flame, was all. No wonder the most apt comparison made at the time was between Rowland and the Reverend Al Green, who by the early 1980s had rejected the pop world entirely, and whose career had turned towards the production of entirely sacred texts.

No sooner had Rowland sparked a new soul revolution than the band had split up amidst acrimony. Rowland soldiered on, and with a new line-up toured a 'Projected Passion Revue', which many feel was the best touring band of the 1980s. Even though they turned in remarkable performances, this band was also rent asunder by Rowland's cantankerous nature. Following a further split, Rowland put together a new band whose style was influenced by former member Kevin Archer's interest in Irish music. The new band promptly adopted a Celtic look and sound that has subsequently drawn such ire that it makes me sad at the undercurrent of Gaelophobia inherent in English musical discourse. Lyrically, 'Come on Eileen', the number-one single on their second album *Too-Rye-Ay*, is as complex and elegant as anything from the 1980s. The fact that 'Come on Eileen' is also musically accessible should raise it to the pinnacle of twentieth-century pop, rather than condemn it to weddings and Radio 2. The fact that it contains (gasp!) instrumentation not usually found in Western pop (i.e. fiddles) is a reflection on the limited palette of much subsequent pop, rather than Dexy's perceived low cultural capital. The fact that *Too-Rye-Ay* also contains the best soul song of the post-soul era (the glorious affirmation of 'Let's Make This Precious') as well as a host of other timeless classics ('Plan B', 'Liars A to E', 'Until I Believe in My Soul') seems to be lost in time.

Depressed by success, and fighting as many band members as he fought demons, Kevin Rowland retreated to yet another new line-up, and produced what for this author is the finest album of the decade. *Don't Stand Me Down* is deeply profound, yet hilariously funny. It's an album of conceptual contrasts set amidst musicianship of the highest order. The album's structural complexity and lyrical poignancy are a match for any of the high cultural values of the greatest classical music.

I always feel deeply uncomfortable describing this album, stuck in the prison house of language, unable to describe how I feel. Best leave it to a pro then, music journalist Chris Roberts writing for *Melody Maker*:

> A forty-five-minute, seven-song record, it's brave, bold, passionate, inquisitive and swaggering. Rowland confesses, as is his style, but also attacks, accuses, curses. He swoons with love and rages with curiously specific frustration. No Live Aid clichés here. He ups the ante by entering into constant asides and dialogues with sidekick Billy Adams, displaying worry and doubt and great lashings of male vanity. Like any Dexy's record, *Don't Stand Me Down* is as volatile and voracious as an ego in full effect. Records without egos are negligible, unassuming, self-effacing backdrops. *Don't Stand Me Down* goes where only egos dare.

At the time, few agreed with this, the album sunk like a stone and yet again the whole package was misunderstood. How the beautiful tailoring of the Brooks Brothers clothes that featured on the album cover and accompanying publicity shots could be mistaken for estate-agent chic is beyond me. No wonder Rowland descended into an abyss for a decade afterwards.

Kevin Rowland is back on form now, though, and Dexy's Midnight Runners are the only band of the 1980s that have managed to re-form and retain any sense of integrity (Duran Duran don't count, because they had no integrity in the first place). The band's comeback tour of 2003, entitled 'To Stop The Burning', had something that the big revival tours did not. It had credibility. The fact that the band had something new to say was an essential part of this credibility. A whole new package was provided for our delectation – there was a new look (French 1930s gangster), a new sound (more reflective, more contemplative, with two lead singers instead of one), a new message, and a couple of new songs, including the wonderful 'My Life in England (Part One)'.

Go West, Kim Wilde, Paul Young, Human League, ABC, T'Pau, China Crisis, Curiosity Killed The Cat, even Heaven 17, have all appeared on 1980s revival tours entitled 'Here and Now', yet it doesn't sound very 'now' to me. It sounds a bit 'eighties' to me, a bit 'ironic'. It sounds like blind unthinking postmodernism. It sounds like a music devoid of meaning and ripped from its original context. Born amidst the turbulent onslaughts of Thatcherism, the music of the 1980s represents a high point in the evolution of English musical identity, yet this same music now seems destined to be remembered as somehow less significant than the music of the 1990s, the 'dance decade' that seemed to sweep away all that had preceded it. Britain is supposedly better off now than it was then, and this revivalism seems too corporate, too moneyed and too straight. We need to rescue the music of the 1980s from the condescensions of this prosperity, to rescue the music of the 1980s from the phenomenon of 'the eighties'. Say the word 'eighties' now, and the musical images that spring to mind are those of big hair and bigger egos, bad clothes and bad vibes in nightclubs, vapid pop playing to vacant dance floors. That wasn't how I remembered it. I remember a glorious few years whereby chart success did not necessarily militate against credibility or quality. It is a paradox that, in a world which contains SchoolDisco.Com, ironic poodle metal nights in certain trendy east London districts, Capital Gold FM and fly-by-night Electroclash clubs, the music of the 1980s is in bad need of a revival.

recommended listening

Dexy's Midnight Runners – *Searching for the Young Soul Rebels* (Parlophone)
Japan – *Quiet Life* (Hansa)
Madness – *Absolutely* (Stiff)
The Specials – *More Specials* (Chrysalis)
Adam and the Ants – *Prince Charming* (CBS)
Depeche Mode – *Speak and Spell* (Mute)
Heaven 17 – *Penthouse and Pavement* (Virgin)
Human League – *Dare* (Virgin)
New Order – *Movement* (Factory)
Soft Cell – *Non-Stop Erotic Cabaret* (Some Bizarre)
Teardrop Explodes – *Wilder* (Mercury)
Dexy's Midnight Runners – *Too-Rye-Ay* (Mercury/Phonogram)
Yazoo – *Upstairs at Eric's* (Mute)
New Order – *Power, Corruption and Lies* (Factory Records)
The Style Council – *Introducing the Style Council* (Polydor)
Tears for Fears – *The Hurting* (Mercury)
Julian Cope – *Fried* (Mercury)
Frankie Goes to Hollywood – *Welcome to the Pleasure Dome* (ZTT)
Dexy's Midnight Runners – *Don't Stand Me Down* (Mercury/ Phonogram)
The Smiths – *Meat is Murder* (Rough Trade)
New Order – *Low Life* (Factory Records)
The Smiths – *The Queen is Dead* (Rough Trade)
The Justified Ancients of Mu Mu – *1987 (What The Fuck Is Going On?)* (KLF Communications)
The Happy Mondays – *Bummed* (Factory Records)
Stone Roses – *Stone Roses (*Silvertone)

juju, jit, punk and politics

Guy Morley

This is a story about how music became a force for change. African music formed a significant part of the picture, acting as a rallying cry for some of us involved in the counterculture throughout the eighties.

For me, the journey started as I bumped and jostled around the Freshers' Fair at North Staffordshire Polytechnic where the array of stalls and wackily dressed students nearly put me off being a student altogether. After a trawl through the activities on offer, I ended up affiliated to the Caving Society – a brief dalliance – and to the Animal Rights Society, which never got going but ended up as a longtime passion of mine. Other students joined anything from the Hockey Club to Kurdistan Students' Communist Party.

Most shockingly, one of the more outspoken bunches of zealots at the Fair was the Conservative students. On their stall they had button badges saying Hang Mandela, Socialism Sucks and On Yer Bike. Their Monday Club leanings and far-right bigotry provide an insight into how polarized views were back then. The Tories wanted Mandela strung up because they viewed him as a just another terrorist who was a threat to the state (and the status quo). For some other people on the left, the ANC's reliance on armed struggle against apartheid conflicted with their own support for pacifism. However, trade and cultural boycotts were less controversial and became an acceptable mass movement which contributed to the overthrow of the apartheid regime. I remember marching into Barclays bank to close an account I had held since I was a child, telling the clerk the bank was responsible for murder and racism and could she inform her boss.

The cultural boycott had another consequence: it focused attention on South African music. In the UK we had access to many exiled musicians – Dudu Pukwana, District 6, Dollar Brand all had a profound impact on British jazz. The boycott should have embargoed all South African music but migration unintentionally brought the township sound to us. This was a time when Paul Simon was lambasted for breaking the rules of the boycott with his *Gracelands* album in which he collaborated with Ladysmith Black Mambazo. More obvious targets were Queen – who might seem innocent now – fronted by the posthumously outed Freddie (who incidentally was born in Africa), because they played the infamous leisure complex Sun City.

A generation of young people were politicized by their opposition to Thatcherism and to the get-rich-quick culture of the time. Political ideals were part of youth culture in a way that is not in vogue now – then the fashion was politics. I began to pick up on politics through bands such as Crass and Chumbawamba, and from the emerging 'straight edge' scene in the US. At school the sinking of the Belgrano during the Falklands war had a huge impact on me, and the miners' strike with the recession of the early eighties politicized me as a student. I was energized by records with titles like *Pictures of Starving Children Sell Records* – a great reaction to the sticking plaster of Band Aid and Live Aid. Sir Bob perhaps had some impact on the thirty-something generation who would later vote for New Labour in 1997, but Live Aid was what it was – a well-meaning but ineffective sticking plaster. I hated Red Wedge (the tour to support the Labour Party, featuring Paul Weller, Billy Bragg and Jimmy Somerville, to name a few). But then again, I hated power and party politics. I conscientiously objected to voting even though I fought for the principle of one person one vote in South Africa.

Under the Conservatives class politics were alive and well; the Tories were out to put the boot in. The rhetoric of the time was in-your-face, worn on T-shirts and button badges. Like those on the right, the left pushed slogans of their own. Microdisney named an album *We Hate You White South African Bastards*. The times did not demand subtlety or complexity. The sanctions movement gained pace, and

gay-activist white South African Ivor Toms was sent to prison for refusing to be drafted into the South African Army. The year before the Tories brought out the poll tax, they put the anti-homosexuality Clause 28 into the Local Government Bill, controversially banning all mention of homosexuality in schools. All amounted to one thing – whose side were you on?

My generation of politicos and refuseniks appropriated reggae. We dug the Clash and the Ruts DC. We learned about animal rights and SUS laws through dub poets such as Benjamin Zephaniah and Linton Kwesi Johnson. We made our own fanzines to sell at gigs, and liked Tackhead, The Pop Group and Mark Stewart because Adrian Sherwood's On-U Sound mixed reggae with attitude.

This is all part of how African music began to fit the picture for me: it was the same process of politicization – we were all under attack and this brought out a strong sense of solidarity with other people who were facing hardship and oppression. Reggae often made a direct link by referring to Africa and in particular South Africa. 'Africa must be free by the year 1993,' sang Hugh Mandell, The Special AKA released 'Free Nelson Mandela' and Tapper Zukie 'MPLA'. It might have been white punk bands that got us into reggae, but once there we found it was not just Bob Marley. We picked up on African reggae artists like Alpha Blondy, whose album *Apartheid is Nazism* fitted the sentiment.

Early WOMAD festivals reflected this broad range. If you look at their programmes from that period, there is a tremendous diversity to their line-ups, from the Drummers of Burundi and TPOK Jazz to The Fall, Blurt and New Order. WOMAD had a big impact by providing youth culture with opportunities for new experiences; the Glastonbury Festival would not have developed their Jazz World Stage had it not been for the audiences going to WOMAD.

Another important factor at this time was indie UK label Rough Trade, mostly noted for its massive and productive alternative output, from the Young Marble Giants, The Fall, The Feelies, and Robert Wyatt to the big sellers such as The Smiths. Rough Trade also released African music like the fantastic rough-edged *Soweto* compilation or soukous by guitarist Pablo Lubadika; they also distributed other labels' artists through the 'Chain with No Name'. For me, in Stoke-on-Trent, and, by and large, this was the same everywhere else in the UK, this meant record shops could sell good African music and for the first time there was the wider will to buy it.

The cultural boycott of South Africa had an effect that energized the African scene abroad in a different way. It pushed a focus on other southern African music and with it came the discovery of one of the best African bands of the time. This band became the semaphore that guided me into African music. The story goes like this.

Richard Attenborough was filming *Cry Freedom*, the story of murdered anti-apartheid activist Steve Biko. For obvious reasons it was filmed in the neighbouring country of Zimbabwe (ex Rhodesia). It was here that the deputy stills photographer on the film met and heard the legendary Bhundu Boys after a tip-off from a friend that they were playing a local gig. The Bhundu Boys took their name from the children who acted as runners for the liberation army in the fight for independence from Ian Smith's white rule in Rhodesia. She fell in love with the music, quit the shoot and became their tour manager. Later, with Gordon Muir, she brought them to the UK. The Bhundu Boys lived in the UK for a year and this is when I saw them at Glastonbury, promoting their classic album *Shabini*. Live, the music was magic, upbeat and joyful – a performance that won over everyone who heard or saw it.

There was already a good feeling about the band, as John Peel and Andy Kershaw had been plugging the album endlessly on their radio shows. For the Bhundus the experience must have been extraordinary. A UK crowd was weird enough but a bunch of drenched hippies at the biggest festival? At the time Glastonbury was supporting CND and had asked WOMAD to organize their prototype world-music stage. Biggie Tembo, the lead singer, took full control, unfazed by the strange crowd and their odd dancing, and a magic began to work.

A touching common feeling transcended the differences in language. Even though many of the songs were not overtly political there was deep sharing. When I say 'overtly political', remember that the bands I was into sang about smashing the state and eating the rich. The Bhundu Boys' songs covered everything from relationships and lonely hearts to politics and wars and it was the combination of the music and the harmonies that brought people together.

The music was rough enough to get that feeling of rock and roll. It was a fusion pitched somewhere between chimurenga (popularized by Zimbabwean Thomas Mapfumo) and a looping hi-life or soukous sound (hi-life is Ghanian and soukous is from Congo/Zaire). They called it jit, and this music became a real force in Zimbabwe played by different bands like the excellently named Marxist Brothers or the very political Sungra Boys. Zimbabwe had not long had independence, and an optimism shone from the music even though there were tribal conflicts and near civil war involving pro-Nkomo dissidents in Matabeleland and accusations of atrocities against them by Mugabe's forces.

Having seen the Bhundu Boys, I picked up on more Zimbabwean music. Worth finding are Jonah Moyo and Devera Ngwena, whose silky-smooth harmonies remind me of the Beach Boys. One of the great aspects of Zimbabwean music is the breakdowns put into the songs: instrumental sections that are much more than middle eights – glistening grooves filled with guitar twists that make you want to dance.

The Bhundu Boys tried to recapture the spirit of those early UK gigs – if you were lucky enough to see them around you would not forget the experience – but sadly trouble beset the band. Biggie Tembo, the lead singer, had mental-health problems and eventually got forced out of the band. Afte unsuccessfully trying a solo career he went into depression and hanged himself. Over the years, several members of the band have died of HIV-related illnesses, but a version of the band continues today with their guitarist, Rise Kagona.

I took much of this humanist feeling into my own political activity. I got involved in the anti-apartheid movement and the peace movement. At a civic reception for the Mandela Freedom March in Stoke and Stafford I made a speech likening the Tories' Clause 28 to a measure under the apartheid regime. This drew ridicule from some of the 'good' people of Stafford, including the local newspaper, the *Evening Star*. However, most of the marchers I spoke with supported this comparison, including a Durham miner and a jailed South African political activist, called Indres Naidoo.

I became involved in anti-fascist activity, aligning myself with Anti-Fascist Action rather than the Anti-Nazi League. Later in Manchester a group of us got together to form Freedom of Movement as an attempt to politicize the dance-music scene with an anti-fascist message. We organized club nights, and people such as DJ Justin Robertson helped get special guests. We wanted clubbers to understand that the cultural diversity enjoyed in many nightclubs, and the party scene, was a potential target for racists and fascists. We wanted to get them to make a stand against the BNP and the like. We released an album of remixes from a cover version of Consolidated's *This is Fascism* by the New Fast Automatic Daffodils. The remix included Fun<da>mental, Lol Hammond and Charlie Hall from the Drum Club, Coldcut and David Holmes. For me it was the first recording for the prototype Yam Yam (the recording name I share with Rick Turner). We remixed an Afro-house-styled version under the name of United Spirits of Rhythm; the name was a pastiche of the United Colours of Benetton, a brand slogan thought up by ex-situationist (radical Marxist anarchists) Gianfranco Sanguinetti.

Seeing a Zimbabwean band in a muddy field at Glastonbury had helped me join the dots. Circumstances of time and place came together and I could see the wider context much more – that's how it came together – politics and music. I believed music could change the world. The jury might be out on that, but it changed my world.

Seeing the Bhundu Boys had another effect: it made me want to chase the music. I reinvestigated the African music I had heard and seen, and I found out more about how African music fitted – its influences and its range and genres. I have explored a lot of music through African music, from jazz to funk, soul, even to do-wop and country blues. Very often I discovered the African versions first and then sought out original artists. Tracing the roots and influences of African music opened up so many new interests. It was a bit like the way some people rediscovered funk through those hip-hop artists that sampled them. I know that Cymande and Mandrill would not be so well respected had De La Soul and their like not used them.

There was a common production value between Western alternative or indie music and some African music. Single takes, cheap equipment and non-studio recording gave a really similar feel. African music had a natural ability to sound DIY. Even though it's very different from Western alternative music there were rock influences in it that further helped identify it with alternative culture, not pop culture.

However, for some African artists, who were big pop artists back home, being labelled as 'alternative' by us in this country was not always easy to handle. The culture shock cut both ways. For us, it was mostly about feeling our way around paradoxical cultural clashes between our 'right on' views and some aspects of African culture.

For instance, I remember talking about vegetarianism with a dancer from The Real Sounds of Africa during his warm-up for an ANC benefit one night in Stoke. As we got talking he said he was utterly bemused by the amount of veggies he met in the UK. When I explained that I wasn't just a veggie, I was a vegan, he smiled and looked at me as though I was really odd – and maybe I was a bit, then!

At another gig by the great Palm Wine guitarist S. E. Rogie, from Sierra Leone (he had been rediscovered after a period as a taxi driver in London), the audience were treated to truly beautiful music. Yet he did not win many friends with North Staffs Poly women's group when he said in a segue between songs, 'Girls don't become women until they have had children.' Still he was given the benefit of the doubt, maybe not so much down to culture but perhaps due to his age – he was approaching his seventies.

Sometimes finding out about the subject matter of songs affected the way we perceived the music and the musicians. For example, hearing songs that celebrated female circumcision was a challenge to our 'liberal' values, but it was necessary to look behind the happy music and beyond language we did not understand to hear in context what was being said. We also needed to understand that the most crucial challenge to patriarchal establishments was coming from within African society itself. Today, Oumou Sangare, the celebrated singer from Mali, takes a big stand for women's rights on everything from circumcision to polygamy. She remains a hugely popular artist in West Africa.

In countries across Africa, musicians in turn took Western influences and worked out what was relevant to them. It's no accident they picked up mostly on black music. Slavery and migration kicked off a whole other evolution: the music became less African and more its own genre. The advent of the radio age took ex-pat music back to Africa. African rumba went to Cuba and became salsa. Mento and Niabingi rhythms in the Caribbean developed ska, calypso, rock steady and reggae. You can hear one-drop ska guitar licks in West African music. Calypso developed into socca, which in the French-speaking parts of the Caribbean fused well with Congolese music. The whole thing got filtered through black music in the US, especially through R&B, blues, jazz, disco and soul. Black British communities played their part – as reggae was strong, developing its own style called lovers' rock – and provided a home for some English-speaking Africans from Ghana, Nigeria, Kenya, Tanzania and South Africa to discover black British music.

All these styles and influences in music were welcomed back home in Africa – a sharing of black culture and black music. It is no surprise that hip hop is big in Africa today. Colonial music such as Portuguese fado and French chanson also influenced music in Africa. The music of Cape Verde and Angola has a heavy dose of fado, and you can hear French influences in the music of the great political poet Franklin Boukaka and Cameroonian Manu Dibango.

Perhaps it is not obvious, but country and western was also popular and an influence. Jimmie Rogers was a big hit across large parts of Africa. Country music has working-class roots and Jimmie sang about the ordinary person and about common feelings. Country music also had religion and this gave it a righteous audience. I was thinking about this as I watched the US alternative country band Lambchop recently (they're Nashville's most messed-up country band); seeing the five Lambchop guitarists get into a groove was like watching the interplay of an African guitar band. There is a subtlety to the feel the players produce when repeating a riff or chord sequence – minute changes produce texture and an extraordinary emotional response. Kurt Wagner from the band says he particularly enjoys music by King Sunny Ade. I could see why. Synchro System, Sunny Ade's band, mix juju and other Nigerian music and a large dose of funk with pedal steel guitars all pitched somewhere between Hawaii and Nashville.

Perhaps the biggest influence on African music was the return of the rumba. Cuban music became very popular and its fusion gave birth to Africa's greatest dance music, soukous – but more about that later.

African music sounded alternative enough for me to get into – perhaps the attraction of Western pop to African people was that it sounded different from roughed-up African music. Whatever it was, the catalyst of the Bhundu Boys and my growing love and knowledge of African pop music made me reappraise how I thought about music.

Long before the Bhundu Boys at Glastonbury, I saw Fela Kuti, now rightly acclaimed as a post-acid-jazz icon. The show was promoting his album *Black President*, a Fela classic: three songs made up his whole set. I loved the politics – an anti-capitalist precursor to the anti-globalization movement as he railed at the American multinational ITT in 'International Thief Thief' – but at the time I didn't get the jazz-funk thing.

Fela Anikulapo Ransome Kuti was brought up in a political, middle-class family, his mother an early Nigerian feminist. He was sent to England in 1958 with the family intention of studying to be a doctor; instead he enrolled in music college, but dropped out after getting bored with Western classical music. He returned to Nigeria to reform his band, Koola Lobitos, in which he took to the fusion principle by blending black American music à la James Brown with his own sound. In Nigeria, Ghanaian hi-life music was having a big impact and Fela brought them all together in what he dubbed Afrobeat. For a while he lived in Los Angeles and was politicized by the Civil Rights movement. He took the Afrocentric view of the world promoted by activists such as Malcolm X.

Despite all this I had huge feelings of ambivalence towards him due to his sexism and his over-the-top polygamy, although he would have viewed my objections as quaint Eurocentric arrogance. It's sadly ironic that his mother was such a political force – she was known as Beere and, as a proud socialist and founder of the Nigerian Women's Union, was among the first African women to visit the USSR, China and other countries behind the Iron Curtain. Tragically she lost her life when soldiers threw her out of a window during a junta raid on Fela's compound in the Kalakuta republic. Fela's stance brought him into direct confrontation with the military government, and he suffered raids and imprisonment for championing the poor and dispossessed. These frequent military raids meant also that many of Fela's recordings were lost forever.

On his *Black President* tour in the early 1980s I stood and watched him with a small group of striking miners. Fela had his wives with him – all twenty-two of them – and the rest of the band made over forty on stage. His megalomaniac barking of orders at his band as he berated players who stepped out of line was uncomfortable. However, he produced a fantastic spectacle that could not be rivalled, even by George Clinton and the Brides of Funkenstein. I caught on to his music when the album *Underground System* came out, recapturing the Africa 70 energy that I had missed in the eighties incarnation of his band called Egypt 80. Then I discovered his earlier classic material and the music of his brilliant drummer, Tony Allen. After his HIV-related death, Fela's reputation just grew and grew, a potent mix of uncompromising politics and the anarchic ramble of his sound. With the popularity of the funk and jazz thing, Fela now rightly has the status he deserves. In fact, he has spawned an industry.

As I began DJing, I found that discerning dance floors, despite not being able to hack a twenty-minute Afrobeat track, could not resist artists who sampled Fela, such as Branford Marsalis, who produced a version on the track he did with Maya Angelou, 'The Caged Bird Sings', or Italian-house crossover pioneers, the Kwanzaa Posse, on 'African Vibrations'. Afrobeat still has a big hold over West Africa. Today Fela's sons, Segun and Femi, are well known and there is a groundswell of younger bands bringing other elements to the party, like rap; New York has its own Afrobeat scene analogous to 2-Tone and ska with bands such as Kokolo, Femme Nameless and Antibalas; and the current fashion for the Afrobeat sound is eclipsing some of Africa's older generation of brilliant guitar bands.

It took me a while to get going as a DJ: I had been so involved in politics that partying and DJing at first struck me as a diversion from the struggle. But then I saw the opportunity to use music as a subversive tool. Organizing and playing at benefits and broadening cultural horizons through music seemed logical – part agitprop and part subversion. On one occasion I remember mixing 'Merry Crassmas' – a nice Crass sample wishing that people who ate turkey for Christmas would fucking choke on it – into a King Sunny Ade track.

As well as the Freedom of Movement anti-fascist stuff I mentioned earlier, we organized benefit after benefit for groups we were involved in or supported such as ActUp (the HIV direct-action group), trades' unions, hunt saboteurs, the peace centre, Artists for Animals. The list went on. In the end I learned that you did not have to be outside mainstream culture to try and change it and, like everyone else, I wanted to party…

I discovered soul and funk in part through Fela's music. '2000 Black' took me to Roy Ayres but via Fela I discovered bands such as Ghetto Blaster, Wganda Kenya from Colombia, and Matata. From this I got into funk and jazz, which happily took me away from the four to the floor progressive house scene that could have become a rut. The sort of funk I got into related heavily to African music: Plunkey and the Oneness of Juju, Cymande, The Last Poets, and Afro Francophile hip hop like Soon EMC and Senegalese rapper MC Solaar.

I played all this at the Cubop nights in Manchester's Home nightclub. Most of the music there was orientated around jazz funk, rare groove and acid jazz. But the African music I introduced got a great response on the dance floor: the West African thing really worked. Ghanaian music was just so funky, full of horns and swinging 6/8 rhythms. You had to play the funkier tracks for the dance floor. E.T. Mensah, responsible for inventing hi-life, had a son called Joe who had lived in New York and understood well the funk aspect to Ghanaian music. His tune 'Funky Talk in Hausa' was a big hit at Cubop, as were tracks by Peter King, a Nigerian multi-instrumentalist. On his album *Omo Lewa* were a couple of killer tunes – 'Congo' and 'Afro-Funk'. Some South African music went down well at Cubop; among this was Hugh Masekela's album with Ghanaian musicians, *Hedzoleh Soundz*. I was slightly frustrated, though, because it was hard to drop something a little more adventurous, such as a Mahotella Queens' track. Most other African music – Senegalese or Malian, East African or Central African, like soukous – would not work with that crowd either.

But some great crossover dance tracks helped fill the gap. Manchester band Yargo had an early Justin Robertson remix of their song 'Love Revolution', which had a great sample from Black Soul's track 'Mangous Ye'. Every rule needs an exception and my favourite crossover tune was, strangely enough, Malian. Sali Sidibe and the London to Africa All Stars had a track called 'Djen Magni' remixed by Alex Reuben. The master mix is a classic tune, with a funky sensibility, it had such an off-kilter beat and bass line that it could not fail to move a dance floor. But it was on African record label Sterns, so not many other funk DJs knew about it. Fela tracks were popular too – either slightly remastered bootlegs or great homegages like those put together by Nuphonic's Soul Ascendants.

After a few months, Cubop was dropped to make way for a happy house night. I wanted to play more African and Latin music so I joined a small collective of people to establish a club with more of a world-music feel. Collectives often have difficult dynamics but we managed to get a night going, somewhat dubiously called Gondwana – a night that helped start One Tree Island. (The geologists among you might realize the reference to the sound of splitting continents: Gondwanaland was a 550-million-year-old super continent that mostly comprised what's now Africa and South America.) For a while, this was a respectable alternative (a complete opposite) to the mainstream in Manchester. As well as DJs, Gondwana also promoted live music, from roots and folk to African and Latin. We got off to a good start with bands like Suns of Arqa and, memorably, we also promoted the great African artist Remy Ongala.

Remy was from Tanzania, and overtly political. He was one of the first African artists to sing about AIDS. His sound has become a favourite of mine over the years. He had a heavy distorted guitar sound with much more of an East African feel, the opposite of the Zairian polished sound of soukous which used chorus and other super-sweet studio effects. Remy had grit. He joined a band called Orchestra Matamila, which eventually became his own band, Orchestra Super Matamila.

Virtually every time he came to the UK he'd play in a small bar in Oldham, where he had a good relationship with Kevin, the bar owner. The bar's regular drinkers were Oldham Athletic supporters who had formed a samba band to entertain the crowds at Boundary Park. They also became friends with Remy and set up the only UK African tribute band I have heard of, named Orchestra Super Smashing – very Jim Bowen!

At Gondwana you could drop a soukous track like ex-TPOK Jazz guitarist Shaba Kahambra's 'Litiot' into the mix, play some South African jive or North African Rai. This was post-Madchester time – Happy

Mondays. But Manchester was a house city, with The Haçienda still going strong and major nights like Bugged Out starting up. There was a sizeable crowd of people who had become alienated from mainstream club culture – those who, like me, had grown into African music, those who liked the Afro elements of house and wanted to find out more, and then also the new generation of politicos who were into Earth First and Green politics. There were also promoters who wanted to try something different, people such as Gary McClarnan and Eric Barker, who were also part of setting up One Tree Island.

Early DJs at One Tree Island along with me were Mr Scruff, Jake Strangebrew, Stephano and Jane Funk Boutique. The nights had a mad mix of headcases from Green students to Hulme heavies, acid casualties to people from the gay village, all rolled into one. Between popping pills, they were fed vegan food by Paula and Robin, the couple who ran a vegan café in Ashton-Under-Lyne. The night took up in strange locations, from the *Fitzcarraldo,* an old trawler turned theatre boat on the Manchester ship canal, to barns in the Peak District. At times that odd crowd went nutty to fast tracks such as Zitany Neil's 'Asec Mimosas' or even an early, post-Housemartin, pre-Fat Boy, Norman Cook remix like 'Kazeet' by Mahlathini and the Mahotella Queens.

Perhaps the humanism connection to the music was wearing thin, but I prefer to think that we got subsumed into the party. By now everyone was very pre-millennial – more end-of-the-world party and less dawning of the Age of Aquarius; a little bit of nihilistic hedonism.

Strange then that a continent so badly affected by tribal and civil wars, dictators, famine, the dumping of waste from the north, the unfair trade practices, multinationals, disease and the legacy of colonialism had such fantastic party music. Even with a big element of education and agitprop in African lyrics, the music is largely upbeat and happy. Music can help people forget a bit and party. I remember a Lingala-speaking African friend's answer when I asked what Wenga Musica were singing about; he said that the lyrics in the chorus went, 'You make my heart go…', then he made a sound like you'd make to a small child on a swing, 'Weeeee'.

In the sixties and seventies, when the yoke of colonialism was lifted from Africa, there was an evident feeling of optimism in the fledgling states. Empowerment had the potential to generate wealth and a quality of life similar to that enjoyed in the West; subsequently, the record business briefly flourished in Africa. Mobutu Sese Seko hosted the Rumble in the Jungle, the fight between Joe Frazier and Mohamed Ali, with an extravagant concert to show that Zaire was a dominant force in developing Africa. Mobutu became a dictator, and the term 'kleptocracy' accurately described his government. In 1972, he changed his name to Mobutu Sese Seko Kuku Ngbendu wa za Banga. Translated, this means the all-powerful warrior who, because of his endurance and inflexible will to win, will go from conquest to conquest leaving fire in his wake.

With this new optimism came the confidence to develop individual styles in contemporary popular music. In Zaire, one of Africa's truly great styles – soukous – developed around rumba. And one of the most influential giants of the scene was Franco. Franco had been brought up listening to missionary music and to the abundance of Cuban music on the Belgian Congo's radio. In his career he produced classic tracks such as 'Mamou', 'Na Lingaka Yoyo Te' and the TPOK jazz classic that has become an African standard, 'Shauri Yako'. I can't begin to tell you how beautiful these songs are: slow majestic grooves full of effortless energy, punching horn lines and the most fluid and beguiling guitar.

Franco was a big man – larger than life, a giant in every sense at over twenty stone. His songs often related to political issues and he fell foul of the authorities once or twice. Towards the end of his life, and having lost a lot of weight, he recorded a track, 'Attention Na SIDA' (Watch out for AIDS). It was a tragedy when a year or so later he died from an HIV-related illness.

In other parts of Africa, new styles emerged. In Ghana there was hi-life, which easily fused with jazz and funk. Cameroon had makossa. Nigeria developed Afrobeat. Into this music poured influences from abroad. It was as if the centuries of dislocation suffered through slavery and colonial domination were being cast aside. The combination of decolonialization, the development of youth culture, the widespread use of electric instruments, the means to record them and copy them, meant the biggest explosion in musical culture on earth. The new types of music were much more than the sum of the parts – they created whole new styles.

I was drawn to the absolute beauty of the music produced at this time. The bands had big horn sections, several guitarists and backing singers – they were orchestras. But as these new states lost out to corruption, exploitation by multinationals, poverty and disease, the big-band era sadly disappeared and with that the optimism evaporated.

For soukous, Paris became the dominant centre of production. At times this production became too slick, and some of the technology hasn't stood the test of time. A Yamaha DX7 playing the horn parts of a six- or seven-piece horn section will never replace the sound generated in a hot recording studio in seventies or eighties downtown Accra, Lagos or Kinshasa. The music became more pop. Soukous had lost some its rumba after Kanda Bongo man popularized a new and more upbeat version, and it moved towards the high-paced, dance-orientated sebene.

The older sound is the big influence for Rick and me in Yam Yam; we love some of the chaos in the production and arrangements. Huge horn sections often sounded out of tune or overenthusiastically played. Funk-guitar chops in ragged offbeat patterns. Guitar solos were often beautifully 'badly' played. Try Prince Nico Mbarga on 'Sweet Mother' or 'Happy Birthday' – if you know the cover to the *Africa 70* compilation albums, you'll recognize him as the dude with a great line in catsuits and platform shoes. Brilliant rhythms played on drum kits were often so badly mixed and equalized that the overall effect can only be described as lo-fi. Recording conditions were poor and lacking in finesse, but this was compensated for by sheer feeling and grace.

There are many other important Afro influences in dance and house music that were important to me. Now funky Afro-disco loops are put into dance records and producers such as Masters at Work have taken on Afrobeat. Labels like Afro Art, Codek and F Comm's Frederic Galliano are putting interesting Afrocentric dance music out and things are cooking.

At the same time it's hard to work out what's new and 'cutting edge' from Africa. The application of technology in Africa to record and produce music is potentially exciting, especially as recording studios are hard to come by. (This musical revolution happened in the West with the advent of Atari and the sequencing programme Cubase.) Both hip hop and house have African scenes. Kwaito in South Africa has some tunes that cross over well – Arthur's 'Oyi Oyi' or Phezulu's classic house, for example. The Senegalese hip-hop scene has some potentially big names, from Positive Black Soul to Daara J. Yves Wernert, who has produced some great music from his Studio Bogolan in Bamako, Mali. It's a hot spot a bit like the Shed in Zimbabwe, where most of the jit scene in the eighties was recorded, including the Bhundu Boys' early sessions. Yves produced Issa Bagayogo's album *Sya*. Issa is known as Techno Issa in Mali and his album is destined to become a crossing point in musical styles. In countries such as Guinea Bissau and Cape Verde the mix of Portuguese influence and older music is really apparent as artists are sampling and looping their influences; for example, rap artist Aze uses the Cesaria Evora track 'Sodade'.

The technology revolution has yet to comprehensively hit the African music scene. A lot depends on how African musicians reference their influences. Will they look to their roots and explore tradition, like the black American scene rediscovered funk in hip hop and rap, or will they use western pop as a yardstick? Wider access to computers, programmes and digital technology will help bring change. The musical revolution of the postcolonial seventies and eighties could be about to be re-emerge, round the corner right now…

recommended listening

Bhundu Boys – *Shed Sessions* (Sadza Records)
Franco et le TPOK Jazz – *En entre OK en sorte KO* (Visa)
Various – *Ghana Soundz* (Soundway)
Issa Bagayogo – *Sya* (Six Degrees/Cobalt)
Youlou Mabilala and Kamikaze Lonningisa – *Best of Vol 2* (Sono Disc)
Various – *D'Afro Disco* (Codek Records)
Sali Sidibe and the London Africa Allstars – 'Djen Magni' 12" (Sterns Records)
Tony Allen vs Bigga Bush – 'Drum Fire' 12" (Comet Records)
Various – *Nigeria 70* (Afro Strut)

Manu Dibango – *Afrovision* (Decca)
Fela Anikulapo Kuti – *Black President* (Arista)
Franklin Boukaka – *A Paris* (Sonafric)
Various – *Soweto* (Rough Trade)
Remmy Ongala and Orchestra Super Matimila – *Nalilia Mwana*
    (Womad)
Mualtu Astatke – *Ethiopiques Vol 4* (Buda Music)
Peter King – *Omu Lewa* (Orbitone)
Sunny Ade and his African Beats – *Synchro System Movement Vol 12*
    (African Songs)
Tala AM – *Super Tchamassi* (Feista)
Rochereau – *Le Seigneur Rochereau à l'Olympia* (African)
Nguashi N'timbo with l'Orchestre Festivale de Zaire – *Shauri Yako*
    (ASL)
Ndombe Opetum and Orchestre Afrizam – *20ème Siècle Ike Ike*
    (NGOYARTO)
T. P. Orchestre Poly-Rythmo – *De Cotonou* (African Music)
Waldamar Bastos – *Pretaluz* (Luaka Bop)
Lee Perry with Seke Molenga, etc. – *From the Heart of the Congo*
    (Runnetherlands)
Reggie's Soweto Magic Band – *Bump to Bump* (Gallo)

reggae: sweet memory sounds

DJ Derek

'one love' (bob marley): part one

It is a terrible old joke. It was told on *The Goon Show* when black musician Ray Ellington went to shake hands with one of the characters. He said, 'Oh no, you'll rub off on me!' And I've always said, the only thing that's ever rubbed off on me is the music and the love. And I feel as strongly about that now.

I mean, I'll do parties now for somebody's, say, diamond wedding anniversary or seventieth-birthday party, or 'going back to Jamaica' party, because they've retired. And when I do those functions, I go into a room and it's like meeting a huge extended family, many of whom I haven't seen for years. Unless you've done it and experienced it – you can't describe it. It's an almost overwhelming feeling of love!

Or take the other night – when I was playing for four hundred people in the little town of Totnes in Devon. There were a few black faces there, a few different nationalities; predominantly young people, I'd say most of them were less than thirty, some significantly younger. It's the sixth time I've played down there in two years and they were screaming and shouting for more when I had to end the night. I felt like a young pop star! All these pretty girls going 'We love you, Derek, we love you!' You know, it makes an old man happy!

I could never have guessed even twenty years ago that at the age of sixty-two I'd be coming up to play reggae music at some of London's fashionable clubs. It seems astounding. Sometimes I just think, how the hell did this happen? I was an accountant, for God's sake. I could have had a salary twenty times what I'm making doing this. And an ulcer. And I'd be the most miserable man on earth. As it is, I've got just enough to get by on. I wouldn't change places with anybody else on earth.

Then I think that in the late seventies I got through two marriages and lost both parents in a five-year period. I went through domestic hell and almost had a nervous breakdown. But if those certain things hadn't happened I wouldn't have ended up in a position where I felt I could jack in what I was doing and just say, What the hell am I going to do? And people came along and said, 'DJ for me.'

'all i have to do is dream' (everly brothers)

I was nine or ten, I suppose, when rock'n'roll happened. I started drumming by beating on an old cheesebox, one of the old round ones with some parachute material stretched over it. I made it myself. My dad was a carpenter so I must have found some way of using a hammer and nails. I probably drove my parents mad. Bill Haley would come on the radio and I'd be beating the hell out of this cheesebox!

I ended up joining this group because their washboard player dropped out. What on earth made me think I could play a washboard? It was a question of getting a thimble on each finger, a metal thimble, preferably padding the washboard to get a nice crisp sound out of it, and strumming a rhythm with two guitars and a string bass – what we called skiffle music.

There were hundreds and hundreds of bands all over the country. The Beatles were doing the same thing. They were originally called The Quarrymen, while we were called The Vampires. We came second in a contest at the Hippodrome in Bristol and we got taken up by a manager, a drummer called Dave who played for one of the well-known Bristol trad bands. He took us on so we could do a spot in the interval, in between them playing – a sort of novelty act.

He knew the manager of The Colston Hall in Bristol. And we used to get in there and practise for nothing on a Saturday lunchtime. One day he bought a hi-hat and a snare drum down, because skiffle was going out by those days and he wanted the sound of drums in it. So he put these things up on the stage and said play that! And I played it.

The next week he brought the whole drum kit down, set it up and said, see if you can play that. And I said, I can't play that. He said, you haven't tried. I said I know, but I'm left-handed, you're going to have to turn the whole kit round! So he did and I sat down and just played it. He was gobsmacked: 'I took lessons for three years, and I can't play like that!'

I've still got newspaper cuttings and people have told me I was number one in Bristol when it came to being a natural drummer. I was due to become professional. But I had a good job, I'd just had a promotion at work and I'd got married. I thought, well, it's a bit insecure, so I packed it in.

I've always been good at maths. As an ex-accountant I do my own books. I'm probably one of the only people who actually enjoys sitting down and working out their tax return! And I've also done the books for various clubs and charities along the way.

Surely there's a connection between being a drummer and a mathematician, whether you're conscious of it or not. It seems to me that a drummer is always solving in his mind fairly complicated mathematical patterns, fitting certain beat patterns into a set number of bars. You must always come back in the right place because if you don't the rest of the band are in a hell of a mess!

I certainly know that my sense of rhythm helps me as a DJ. I can beatmatch almost instinctively. Sometimes I surprise myself, especially with a minidisc where you can't actually see when the needle's going to start playing a record. It just happens. And because I know the music so well I can take those variations in time to create a pattern during the evening – taking the tempo up and then bringing it down, taking it up again and hopefully peaking just before the end when you really want to bring it down.

I'd have to practise like hell if I wanted to play drums again. But I don't need to now. I can express it when I'm DJing. I'm always tapping out the rhythm while I'm playing the music. Before I got married, I was with a girlfriend and we were in a clinch and there was some good music on. She suddenly said, 'Would you mind not treating my bottom like a drum?' Not very romantic, maybe, but it's in me and it's got to come out!

At the same time as I started playing the washboard in a skiffle group I was listening alongside my elder brother to Radio Luxembourg or AFN. Because there you'd hear proper black American R'n'B music. It was the thing that the kids listened to in those days. The BBC always played watered-down music. They didn't even really play the white American rock'n'roll. I think the first radio show that ever featured that sort of music was *The Goon Show* and they had the Ray Ellington Quartet, a black guy along with Edmondo Ros, who played Latin American stuff. That was the nearest thing you ever heard to what was authentically coming out of black America.

Of course, I didn't know at the time, but the Jamaican people were listening to that too – it was the source of their music. Their local bands were playing southern-states American rhythm and blues, New Orleans, Miami. They didn't have their own recording studios in those days, but all the local bands were playing that music.

Now these days kids call rhythm and blues what we'd call soul music. I loved this music. Having gone through a skiffle group where we had a main singer who looked like Elvis Presley and I played the washboard and cymbals, I always used to think the music of Chuck Berry, Fats Domino, had a genuine feel of…I couldn't define it…soul.

It wasn't a case of pretty boy stuck up there for the fourteen-year-old schoolgirls to swoon at either. These people didn't even have to look very good; their musical ability carried them through. Most people don't realize that Fats Domino outsold every other artist on earth in the fifties apart from Elvis Presley. He had twenty-two gold discs! And he was a big fat black guy; he looks exactly the same today, still plays wicked New Orleans-style piano and sings in a beautiful non-threatening way.

'you can't judge a book by the cover' (bo diddley)

The Jamaicans loved Fats Domino, I found out afterwards. And when the Jamaican people started coming over to Bristol, I started to hear some Jamaican music. It was blue beat – the early stuff was identical to American r'n'b. But as it developed and more bands started to try and play it, they had a problem – as there weren't many in-tune pianos in Jamaica! So they used to ska the upbeat of the boogie beat

on a banjo or a guitar! 'Oom cha oom cha oom cha oom cha – ska it, man, ska it!'

I got to know some of these guys. A club opened in the St Paul's area of Bristol in the sixties called The Bamboo Club. And it was really the best West Indian club outside of London. It was started by Tony Bullimore, who'd come from South Africa because he didn't like the politics going on there and had married a Jamaican woman over here. So many of the Jamaican people were saying, 'We tried to go into white nightclubs, but if we do get in we don't like the music because it's just watered-down pap. Or we're just not made welcome.' So Tony opened up his club.

I can remember the comments now: 'Oh don't go down there, it's a terrible place. A wicked place.' I was born in St Andrews, literally north of the tracks, just by the Montpelier Station line that goes through Bristol. The southern side of that line, by that time, had started to become an Irish and Jamaican ghetto. As the Jamaican people moved in, the white people tended to move out.

Luckily that didn't happen entirely, because the white people who remained alongside that first generation of West Indian people still remain to this day. Some of my closest friends still live there, although some have gone back to Jamaica or time's taken its course and they've died.

So I went to The Bamboo Club and ended up being invited to various types of illegal drinking houses, shebeens as they were called, or blues dances, or the upper-class house party. They were all illegal in that they sold liquor out of hours. But they differed in one very crucial way, and, if I hadn't got involved, I would have been like the average white English person who assumed that if you were black, you all tended to think the same way, like the same thing and behave the same way.

And it's utter rubbish, of course. I still bump into people now who assume you can walk into a black man's pub and roll up a spliff! If you tried to do that at some of these drinking houses you'd be thrown out on your ear even if you were black. If you wore dreadlocks you wouldn't get in. You couldn't play dub music, you couldn't play toasting music; that was considered downtown lower-class music. People don't realize that.

Also, a lot of the girls in those rougher places were prostitutes. I worked in a strip club for years. Some of them had horrible pimps who were beating them up. I'd always encourage them to get away if they could, but a lot of them had a load of kids and absentee fathers and it was literally the only way to make money to bring up these kids. And most of them have done a damn fine job of it.

You can't be hypocritical, there was a demand for it. I got no problem with that at all, never gave it a moment's consideration. I had a damn sight more time for these women than I did the average punters who came in, most of them either lager louts, 'Awwwrrr, get your stuff offfff!', or sad old men, you know.

And I went there with an open heart. I thought that anybody who could make such beautiful music can't be as bad as people are painting them. But I had to keep that very quiet. I didn't tell a lot of my white friends. It just wasn't worth the hassle. Because all you got was, 'Oh, it's rough down there, I wouldn't go down there.'

'boogie in my bones' (laurel aitken)

Everybody says music is an international language. But it's really the rhythms that are international in the end. Different cultures have developed different harmonic scales, and so on. There's nothing more alien to me than listening to Chinese music, for instance. But if you strip it back, it's still got a heartbeat rhythm, the same way as Indian music has. It's like a river that continuously flows. But then you go back to the African, that's where it all came from, it came from the DRUM! As Eddie Grant warned South Africa, 'Do you want to hear the sound of drum?'

Until the early to mid sixties there was no Jamaican music being cut in this country; it was all imported or brought over by the Jamaican people themselves, on the early Coxsone Dodd's Studio One label, and then Treasure Isle. And then Chris Blackwell decided to start issuing these things as they came over on Island Records. These early 7" Island records were red and white, very distinctive. In good condition they're worth an absolute fortune these days. I had a load of them! But I got rid of them and put them on minidisc.

I then heard this record, I think it was played once on the BBC and then it was banned. It was by Derrick Morgan. He used to come down to The Bamboo Club along with Prince Buster and Desmond Dekker – those reggae artists who, since having white chart success in this country have become household names, along with a load of other brilliant, talented artists. But even today, apart from somebody who really loves that music, if you mention them to any white British person they'll just say 'who?' And these guys are so talented it's unbelievable.

The record was called 'Blazing Fire', and was part of the so-called record feud between Prince Buster and Derrick Morgan. Derrick Morgan had left the Studio One label and gone to work under a Chinese producer who was really influential in early ska/blue-beat music, Leslie Kong. And Prince Buster called Morgan a 'blackhead chinee man, don't you know where you belong!' Morgan came back with this record and said, 'I'm a blazing fire, you said it, I'm a black with Chinee', and the BBC banned it because they thought he said, 'I'm black and shiny'!

I bought this, my first West Indian record, at Mr Pugh's. This guy opened a record shop in Picton Street and he could've sold anything. His method of stocktaking and stock-keeping was absolutely immaculate. You could go in there and ask him for anything you thought he might have and it was all written down and he knew exactly where to pick it up. I then found out he had all these Jamaican blue-beat records.

By the time I got married and stopped being in the band, I already had all the early rock'n'roll records, because that's what I had to learn to play when I played the drums, or if I was singing in the band and had to learn the words. Like most bands in the fifties and sixties we were copying the hit parade, really. And of course I had all this other stuff, which I never played out to anybody else apart from some of the guys in the band, like the early Ray Charles stuff from America. I had a little portable record player that you could play in the coach going to a gig!

My first wife loved stuff like The Seekers and typical white pop music of the sixties. But she was also into early rock'n'roll. In fact, she taught me to dance rock'n'roll! I'd been so wrapped up on stage playing the drums I'd never actually gone out and danced. And we could actually dance it to what somebody described as championship class. When I started jiving with the Jamaican women they thought I was great! All rock'n'roll was really 1940s black jive music! It was taken over like most things five years later by the white music industry and plastered about as the best thing since sliced bread!

And I always preferred that type of music. The Beatles wrote some nice tunes, but they were never my favourite band – I've never bought a Beatles record in my life. I'd go out and find original American R'n'B, as it was then, people like Ray Charles and Aretha Franklin and all that stuff. And when I was married I was still buying music to listen to, but I'd no intention to ever get back into playing it. I was heading to be an accountant.

'my new name' (toots)

When I started to play in a Jamaican pub and the old guys from the Jamaican bakery next door were coming in on a Saturday lunchtime, I played Fats Domino's 'Blueberry Hill' and, as I say, the Jamaicans love that man. This guy came up to me and said, 'Bwoy, you bring some sweet memory sounds back, man!' And I thought, that's it, I'm DJ Derek Sweet Memory Sounds.

I did a soul night on a Thursday night when disco music first came in. I was playing all this disco and a bit of sixties soul, and one night, just for the hell of it, I grabbed that Fats Domino tune and put it on and got a round of applause! Dug out a fifties tune for all these people dancing to sixties soul and funk and got a round of applause!

Another guy who turned me on to this music was Ray Charles. That guy had a voice second to none. He was the first to really mix gospel and blues together – a forerunner of soul. And then, later on, Aretha Franklin. There are some singers today I'll listen to and I'll think, she's good, she's close. And then I listen to Aretha in her heyday in the sixties and I'll think instead about the others, she's good, but not that good!

There was an artist called Johnny Nash, a close associate of Bob Marley, who made a record called 'Rock Me Baby' in the late seventies or early eighties. It shot to number thirty in the charts and was mashing up the Bristol reggae scene. And all of a sudden you couldn't buy it in the shops. I've never proved it, but I'm pretty certain that it was taken off the market, because it would have gone to number one and the record companies wanted one of their big white acts to get a number one instead.

Years later I started to find boxes of 'Rock Me Baby' for a quid each in these second-hand record shops. I reckon the major companies just put a block on it. Mind you, I made a killing when I could get hold of it because the Jamaican people still wanted it. I must have sold hundreds of copies in Bristol. But I'm afraid the music industry have always been scared to death of black talent in this country. A lot of this white pop music doesn't cut the mustard. And that's why black people are just not interested in it. It hasn't got any feeling, literally no feeling.

There's a soul song called 'Stealing Love On The Side' by Paul Kelly. He didn't do anything over here; in fact, I only managed to get it on a 7" import in the end. That record could get to number one now if anybody had the guts to put it on the radio and play it three or four times a day. If I went through my collection at home, there's several records like that – music and words so timeless and the production just brilliant, they'd always chart.

Listen to the words of most Bob Marley songs. There are always good melodies and fantastic rhythms, but when he's at his best, his words are absolutely true. Carleen Davis made a record just after the First Gulf War called 'Hey brother Bob, talk to me, words you said are true.'

'until the colour of a man's skin is of no more significance than the colour of his eyes – we say war,' (bob marley)

International peace will never be attained until that happens. And that's as true today as it was then. And you've got these people on both sides who are so convinced that what they're doing is right that they can't see the damage they're causing and the enemies they're making.

'living on the front line' (eddie grant)

In the seventies I met a Jamaican guy from Birmingham and got involved in promoting some reggae bands and sounds into Bristol. I also had a tie-up with a (white) club in Clifton while I was still an accountant. Some black guys used to come in there because it was one club they felt at home in. One of them had a big building business in this country – and he opened up his own club in 1978.

Having heard me introduce the white crowd to reggae at Clifton, he asked me, 'Derek, man, I'm opening this club. And you must come down and play for me. If you don't play for me, I'm going to have to go to Jamaica to get a DJ because the youths in this city, they only play for themselves and their friends. We know you have all the music for everybody!'

The first big black audience I ever played outside of Bristol was a dance at the Pavilion in Bath. It was a beautiful boiling hot sunny day and all these coaches had come down. There was supposed to be a steel band playing after me. And I'd been playing for a half-hour, not at full volume because they'd had a sit-down meal and you instinctively know when people are ready to dance. You can never force them to, especially if they've just eaten, when they're still chatting, having a smoke and a couple of drinks.

I thought, better put the volume up a bit now, and the Barbados people like their soca and calypso, along with reggae, so I got them dancing and somebody came up and said, the steel band's not turning up, they've broken down on the motorway. And there's me, 500 people, 450 of which had never seen me before, and they're all looking at me, thinking, why have we got a white DJ? And I thought, I've got to carry this lot on my own at the Pavilion, a huge place.

Anyway, you've just got to go for it. I stuck on what I would regard as a killer tune for that sort of crowd, one of the first soca records called 'Sugar Bum Bum', by Lord Kitchener. It's got a very distinctive intro and everybody knows it and it's not too fast and everybody's up there dancing, and I thought, got 'em. I followed it up with another popular one and then three or four more slightly faster and faster calypsos and then as the fourth one came to an end I could see people were flagging. I thought, I don't want them to walk off the floor before I decide what to put on next, and I thought, there's a reggae tune by a guy called Eddie Lovett called 'Gypsy Woman'.

It's quite an uptempo rhythm but not as frantic as the soca; it's also got a very distinctive intro. So as the one finished and everybody started to just move off the floor, I hit them with the intro and they all turned and came back again! I had them from that time on. It was one of those occasions where I had people coming up asking, have you got so and so, and it was the next record I'd set up on the turntable. I was getting the hairs standing up on the back of my neck when this was happening. I'd been almost panicky when I knew I had to play all night, but the night just flew by!

I didn't have to think about keeping people on the floor in the end, there was such a harmony between what I was playing and that crowd. It gave me so much confidence from that day to go out into different towns and play to black audiences because you'd always get the comment, 'Why've you brought a white DJ?' and the guy would say, 'You wait until you hear him play.' By the end of the night they'd all be coming up asking me where I got my music.

When Bristol elected its first black Lord Mayor they asked me to do the DJing. I'd established myself well enough by then in the black community. It was fantastic. When he came in I said, 'Please be upstanding for his worship, the Lord Mayor,' and Jim the mayor, who was a friend of mine anyway (he used to be a bus driver), he came in and proudly smiled. I said, 'This is a great honour for me. And what a role reversal, tonight we've got the black dignitary being entertained by the white entertainer, what a difference!' That went down very well. And there again, I knew what those people wanted, and it was just a lovely occasion, very special.

When I was playing regular slots in regular pubs, people would come up to me and say, 'Where did you get the record?' Well, as I said, there was one main supplier of reggae music in Bristol right back from the sixties, and that was Mr Pugh. At first I used to get my stuff from him. I'd get a 10 per cent discount because he knew I'd be selling it on. But he let slip one day that he thought reggae was the product of an inferior mind. And I never went back into his shop.

Instead I went to the warehouse where he bought his music and I found I could get it, obviously, a hell of a lot cheaper. I started buying in bulk and taking it round all the pubs and selling to all the DJs. I was making a couple of thousand pounds a year, just selling records, alongside the DJing.

And then CDs came in and then the minidiscs. So I sold all my vinyl. I'd had enough of all those years carrying vinyl and spending hours in second-hand record shops looking for stuff. I really can't be bothered any more, I've got everything, more than I could ever play. I've got 32,000 tracks at least!

I've stayed in Bristol because I had residencies there, twenty years in The Star And Garter and various Jamaican pubs. There's The Plough I've played in for ten years. And it's a nice central place to go anywhere from.

I sometimes wonder where that sombre feeling for the 'Bristol beat' came from. I'd heard of Massive Attack. And the next thing I hear they're citing me as one of their great influences! I knew Daddy G's father when Daddy G was knee-high to a grasshopper. And he's now a foot taller than me. I found that really amusing! But you know, I listen to their music but I can't say I can ever play their music in many of my sets because it's a bit sombre for me.

'stir it up' (bob marley)

Like Marley said, 'I feel like bombing a church now I found that the preacher is lying.' The Rasta man (all right, the foundations of his religion are just as shaky as any other, but at least he hasn't gone and built massive wealth and dragged people in), he's still teaching peace and love, fairness and justice among other human beings. That's why I love those people, even though in Jamaica at the time their own brothers and sisters were decrying them.

I remember, at the age of fourteen I was walking up Somerville Road to my house in Derby Road where I was born. I'd had a discussion with my religious instruction teacher, and it struck me that there's all these religions saying they're all 'right'. Well, they're either all right or all wrong! I brought this up with my teacher and said, 'I'm sorry I can't accept any of this any longer.' When I left school she actually came up and said, 'By your conduct, you're probably the nearest thing to a Christian I've ever met. And I hope one day you'll come round to my way of thinking!' And I replied, 'No, there's no way I could put my blind faith into something that's so obviously flawed by man's interpretation. I'd sooner live my life by my own rules and not by listening to some hypocritical priest.'

When we had the Bristol riots in the eighties I'd become part of the area, part of the integrated society we had there. The older Jamaican guys I knew said, 'Well, we don't like what's happening, but you can understand it. We came over here and saw notices saying "no Irish, no dogs" and then on the bottom, "no blacks". At the time we thought, well, we've come over here, we're going to have to put up with that and just make our way. But our kids were born here. And they grew up alongside their white peer group. They're not prepared, when they leave school, to start going back down to what we were treated like when we were that age.'

I walked down the City Road alongside an African called Manny, who was a youth-project worker, in the early hours of the morning after the riot. And the police parted like the Red Sea! We had people waving and shouting, 'Yo'right, Manny, Yo'right, Derek!' And we went into a pub called The Inkerman, which was right opposite the Black'n'White Cafe which had been raided. We walked in there, opened the door and it was literally like somebody had taken the top off a kettle which was about to burst.

Oh, some horrible things happened during those riots all over the country but the relief that it had happened and that people had expressed their outrage was quite amazing. Although I'd always felt that undertone, the older generation I grew up with now felt free to express to me just how deeply they resented how they'd been treated all those years.

Black people consider me a white black man and a black white man. They say I'm white outside and black inside. Now people say there's no difference between people. Well, there isn't, basically, but there's a difference in how people are with each other.

I mean, I observe people. When I went abroad to Singapore for the first time, invited by WOMAD, I didn't have any culture shock. And I don't anywhere I go. I just look on people as people, I see body language even when I can't understand the language. The way they react together and that's it, they're people, man! There's good, bad, indifferent, the greedy man, the lazy man. They're all there!

'bass culture' (lynton kwesi johnson)

When I started to put on sound systems, or 'sound clashes' as they were called, with a guy I knew from Birmingham, most of them in a place called The Ventures in Lawrence Hill, it was strictly illegal, really. But the police used to turn a blind eye because there was never any trouble there; people just used to drink Red Stripe and smoke ganja. And listen to the heaviest sounds – not the stuff you'd hear in The Bamboo Club or a nightclub, but on a much grander scale in a big hall, where you could whop up 2,000 watts of bass. That was the thing in those days – who had the heaviest bass line without distortion.

We had a sound system in Bristol called Enterprise, and would challenge all comers from London and Birmingham. There was Mafia Tone, Hi Fi and Quaker City from Birmingham, and Coxsone from London. They'd come down and we'd have these sound clashes. Sometimes they'd bring one of the latest reggae groups to do a live act. Remember Musical Youth? Their producer Tony Owen was also producing reggae groups that had sprung up in the Birmingham area. That's where Steel Pulse sprung from, and The Naturalites, and Rasta groups singing peace and love. People love this now, because it's got integrity – integrity and the rhythm shine through.

I used to sit down with these guys and we'd be discussing money terms – who was paying for the bar, who was getting what share. And they're talking nineteen to the dozen in Jamaican patois and I started getting lost. You always think, however well you know the guy you're working with, I could be getting stitched up here. And I knew the guy well enough to tell him how I felt. And he said, 'Look, man, you know the barber on the front lines, by the Black'n'White Cafe? I've talked to the guy already, I'm going to take you down there and you can sit there on Saturday mornings. Listen, keep your eyes open, your ears open and your mouth shut until you're ready to say something.' And I did that for about six months.

I got to the point where I could ring up a record producer in London who had a record that I wanted but couldn't get in the warehouse. I'd talk to him on the phone and then I'd go up there, knock on the door and he'd open it.

'Hi, I'm DJ Derek from Bristol.'

'Jeeeezus Christ, you're a WHITE man. I thought you were the tax inspector!'

Even now, when they hear me on the microphone when they're coming into a venue and they haven't seen me before, the look on their faces when they see this old white guy and they think it's going to be a seven-foot Rasta!

I didn't learn it with the intention to use it on stage. But when I'm among a lot of West Indian and Jamaican people I start to think in that language, and I start talking in it. Sometimes I end up in the ludicrous situation where I've come across a similarly minded white man and the two of us are sitting there talking patois to each other!

But I've developed a confidence so that now I can get up in front of a whole group of people irrespective of race and just talk. And if I'm with Jamaican people I'll talk in Jamaican. I've played wedding receptions and I've gone on the mike. And people have come up afterwards and said, 'That's beautiful, did you rehearse that?' 'No, that came from the heart.' I don't know how or why it happens.

'turning point' (slim smith)

If there was a turning point in my life, the BBC film *DJ Derek Sweet Memory Sounds*, transmitted in 1994, was it. If it hadn't been for that I certainly wouldn't be doing what I'm doing to the extent that I'm doing it now. It gave me nationwide exposure. And it also led to me getting the work with The Big Chill, WOMAD and the London clubs. Before that, I assumed I'd still be DJing – that's if there'd been enough money in it to just be going around all the little pubs and Domino dances and things.

The film started like this: we were having trouble, like most neighbourhoods, with unruly kids, and so we had a meeting in a local hall. There was a black guy in there, I'd seen him in the pub a few times, and afterwards he said, 'I've never seen a white man so completely at home within a black society. I'm connected with a BBC2 project, a series about normal people doing extraordinary things. Would you be interested?'

I'm very wary of the media. They can make you look like a patronizing idiot, depending on the slant they want to take. The project sounded like a series about eccentrics and I can't deny that I'm an eccentric. I'm off-centre, there's no doubt about that. I'm in the middle of what I do, but it's not the middle of everybody else of my colour or age. But I've built a reputation among the black society. I don't want to appear patronizing and I don't want them to start thinking that I'm using them in any way. I don't know whether you can get that across.

I said, 'I'm interested,' I said, 'Get somebody from the BBC to talk to me, to find out exactly what's involved, and I'll see if I want to take it any further.' I met one of the producers, who was half-Nigerian and half-British – Helena Appio, her name was. We hit it off within fifteen minutes of meeting each other. Along with the cameraman, she turned it into a work of art. It was highly commended in a documentary festival a year later.

I came down to London to watch it in her house in Greenwich. The following day I was on my way over to the warehouse in Harlesden and I bought the *Daily Mirror*. I flicked through and I came to the television page and I was the headline! It was an absolutely fantastically complimentary little review and then I found out it was mentioned in virtually every national newspaper. And I got on the tube with that under my arm, and I thought people were looking at me.

And suddenly a lady asked, were you the man on television last night? I said, yes. She said, 'Wonderful! Wonderful music! Shake my hand, you must have done so much for race relations!' And this kept happening to me until I got to the stop for the bus to the warehouse. Instead of getting on the bus I went to a pub and buried myself behind a newspaper. Then I got the next tube to Victoria and went straight back to Bristol. I couldn't cope with it! It happened so quickly and so suddenly I just couldn't cope with it. Back in Bristol, they took the mick more than anything else.

I had a load of letters from all over asking about the music, or just complimenting me on the show and what I was doing. It was very gratifying.

'one love' (bob marley): part two

When I meet people of my age who've never been in contact with music and have done the nine-to-five thing, they do seem to be twenty years older than I am. I sometimes meet forty-to-fifty-year-olds who seem to be twenty years older than I am. They've got no comprehension of what I do or why I do it. Or anything. They'll go home after work to their wife and they watch soap operas and football on television. The kids have grown up. And they might go down the pub once or twice a week and that's it.

But not everybody can be like me! I just thank God that I am like me!

I'll carry on DJing until people stop asking me. I've got no other great ambition and while I've got the mental and physical capabilities, why should I want to do anything else?

This might sound soppy but I do get an enormous amount of respect, love and affection from people. I might get up feeling a bit depressed sometimes. I'll have read a newspaper and gone downtown. And by the time I've come back the car horns have been tooting, people of all ages and colours have shouted, 'Y'all right Derek!', 'Hello DJ!', 'All right, Mister Music!' And you get home and think, yeah, life ain't so bad!

I use that word a lot, 'love'. It's got so many connotations, but I can only put it in those terms – however corny it may sound – because people keep using that word back to me. It's because of the love. It's a two-way thing: if I'm giving it to a receptive audience, I can feel it come back. I think any genuine artist will tell you that. It's a very emotional thing.

I've had a few relationships since my last marriage. None of them have lasted very long. I found that the music did become a more important part of my life and yes, to be completely honest, I didn't want the hurt. I love women. I love looking at women. And I'm not averse to having the occasional relationship. But I don't want anything cloying or long-term. As soon as it looks like it's going to go that way, I think, hang on, I ain't losing this for the sake of that.

Because this – the music – is going to last me and, in my experience, my relationships with women haven't. You can call me selfish. But I mean, at my age now, I really can't be bothered. I'm very very content. When I shut my front door that's my bolt hole. If once in a while there's somebody there to share that space with me, that's cool, no pressure.

This is my life. I've always said if I ever thought that the only reason I was getting booked was because of the novelty of my age, I'd give up. But people would only book me once, if that was the case. I just play what I love and people come up to me and say we booked you because the love comes through.

recommended listening

Julia Lee – 'Last Call For Alcohol' (Bear)

Fats Domino – 'Blueberry Hill' (Prism)

Ray Charles – 'What I'd Say' (Rhino)

Ray Charles – 'Tell The Truth' (Rhino)

Owen Gray – 'On the Beach' (Dice)

Lord Kitchener – 'Sugar Bum Bum' (Trinidad)

Arrow – 'Hot Hot Hot' (Mango)

Aretha Franklin – 'Respect' (Atlantic)

Rico Rodrigues – 'Take Five' (Island)

Maceo Parker – 'Blues For Shorty Bill' (BMG)

Bob Marley – 'Waiting In Vain' (Island)

Bob Marley – 'Stir It Up' (Live) (Island)

Toots and the Maytals – 'Reggae Got Soul' (Mango)

Toots Hibbert – 'Spiritual Healing' (Island)

Carlene Davis – 'Stealing Love' (Creole)

Arthur Conley – 'Sweet Soul Music' (Capricorn)

Nina Simone – 'Baby Just Cares' (Charley)

Ernest Ranglin – 'Honky Tonk' (Island)

Chaka Demus and Pliers – 'Murder She Wrote' (VP Records)

Marvin Gaye – 'Let's Get It On' (Tamla Motown)

Eastwood and Saint – 'Stop That Train' (Greensleeves)

Morgan Heritage – 'Don't Haf Fi Dread' (VP Records)

Luciano – 'Amen' (Jetstar)

Bob Marley – 'War (No More Trouble)' (Island)

Stevie Wonder – 'Superstition' (Tamla Motown)

biographies

Susanna Glaser

Susanna Glaser was born in a small fishing village on the west coast of Norway. After the family relocated to Britain, Susanna attended the Italia Conti Stage School before focusing her academic bent at Cambridge University and as a postgraduate journalism student in Cardiff.

She relocated to London, where freelance journalism followed, including writing regularly for *i-D Magazine*, *Dazed & Confused*, *D-Side*, *DJ*, *Muzik*, *Mixmag* and *Ministry*. She also entered the world of state51 – a pioneering new media company.

Susanna DJs as The Legendary Jesse Belle. She took over as The Big Chill's Web and programmes editor in 2003. She's also moving into radio on Big Chill FM. Susanna is also working on the biography of her violinist father.

Ally Fogg

Ally grew up in Perth, Scotland, and graduated in psychology at Dundee University. He is now a Manchester-based writer and journalist, and is currently arts and music editor of the *Big Issue in the North* magazine. His alter ego, Enchanted Gordon, is a regular contributor to www.bigchill.net and is the host of his own radio show, the Café del M12 on ALLFM community radio in South Manchester and over the ether at www.allfm.org.

When not DJing or writing, Ally spends most of his time at his home in Longsight, Manchester, which he shares with his partner, the novelist Clare Sudbery, and their son Felix.

Tony Marcus

Tony Marcus is a former contributing editor to *i-D* and *Mixmag* magazines. He currently writes for *Zembla*, *FACT* and the *Sunday*

Times. He has been a journalist for over ten years – a lot of his work is about the mythologies of pop culture. He also teaches journalism and creative writing. Years ago, when he used to work in theatre, he once made a cup of tea for Leslie Phillips.

Mixmaster Morris

Mixmaster Morris started his DJ career in 1985 with his 'Mongolian Hip Hop Show' on pirate radio in London. He began releasing material as Irresistible Force in 1987 and in 1990 he made what is widely regarded as the first chill-out compilation, *Give Peace a Dance 3*, followed by the series *Chill Out or Die* for Rising High. He has performed many remixes since 1985, perhaps the most celebrated being Coldcut's 'Autumn Leaves'.

Throughout the 1990s he wrote extensively for *New Musical Express*, *Mixmag*, and *i-D Magazine*. He has played in over fifty countries and in 1998 he joined the UK's Ninja Tune record label and multi-media collective. 1999 saw him win 'Best Ambient DJ' at the Ibiza DJ Awards, and play at most of Ibiza's famous chill-out bars.

Hillegonda Rietveld

Dr Hillegonda C. Rietveld is Senior Lecturer in Arts and Media at South Bank University, London, where she is also Subject Leader for Sonic Media. Her research work is focused on cultural aspects of dance-club culture and she has published a range of work in this field, including her 1998 book *This Is Our House: House Music, Cultural Spaces and Technologies* (Ashgate).

In 1982 she moved from Rotterdam to Manchester as electronic musician with Quando Quango (Factory Records), where she became closely involved with the development of The Haçienda nightclub. In 1992, she recorded in Chicago with Vince Lawrence for Rob's Records. Inspired by the DJ practices of Chicago and New York's deep house club DJs, her dance sets put love back into the beats. Currently she DJs at occasional dance events, such as The Big Chill.

Alan James

Alan James is currently Head Of Contemporary Music at Arts Council England. He started his working life as one of the UK's first full-time entertainment secretaries at the University of London Union (ULU), then co-programmed the ground-breaking ICA, Clevedon and Mersea Island WOMAD Festivals as well as touring with The Smiths.

At the close of the decade he became Executive Producer on the State of Bengal/Ananda Shankar tour and recording project, and managed the debut of Indian vichitra-veena player, Gopal Shankar Misra, for Real World Records.

In his spare time Alan is a stage compère for WOMAD and The Big Chill festivals as well as doing regular DJ slots in Europe.

Stuart Borthwick

Stuart Borthwick was born in 1970, and brought up in the seaside town of Hastings, East Sussex, before moving to Liverpool in 1989, where he still lives with his partner, Rachel.

As Principal Lecturer at Liverpool John Moores University, Stuart now runs an undergraduate programme in Popular Music Studies, whilst commenting on media and music for various broadcast and publishing outlets. Stuart has DJed (specialist subject: reggae) at a range of different events including The Big Chill festival, and its predecessor The Enchanted Garden, as well as in places as far-flung as Manchester, Malawi and Brick Lane, London. Stuart is co-author of a set of eleven pop-music histories entitled *Popular Music Genres: An Introduction* (2004, Edinburgh University Press).

Guy Morley

Guy is Head of Programming at the Brighton Dome, the south coast's largest arts centre, and also programmes the music in the annual Brighton Festival. On top of this, Guy is one half of Yam Yam, who will be releasing their new album through The Big Chill's label in 2004.

After leaving college Guy worked with George House Trust, a leading HIV and AIDS organization in Manchester, and as a DJ in his spare time. Guy was also a founder of One Tree Island and the promoter at Band on the Wall – one of Manchester's legendary nightclubs. Guy still DJs and had a regular night called Afrobase plus a weekly Sunday radio show of the same name on Brighton's Juice FM.

DJ Derek

Born and bred in Bristol, Derek was a washboard player in a skiffle band in the 1950s before he took up the drums. Derek seemed initially destined for a career in live music but instead got married and became an accountant.

In the 1970s, Derek abandoned accountancy after his second marriage broke down and his parents both died within a year of one another. He was asked to play at The Star and Garter, where he remains a white, middle-class legend on the reggae scene. He now DJs to huge crowds worldwide, including at The Big Chill, to punters at backstreet Bristol pubs and for his 'huge extended family' at weddings and anniversaries.